OXFORD LEGAL PHILOSOPHY

Series Editors: Timothy Endicott, John G.   *Green*

Why Law Matters

OXFORD LEGAL PHILOSOPHY

Series Editors: Timothy Endicott, John Gardner, and Leslie Green

Oxford Legal Philosophy publishes the best new work in philosophically-oriented legal theory. It commissions and solicits monographs in all branches of the subject, including works on philosophical issues in all areas of public and private law, and in the national, transnational, and international realms; studies of the nature of law, legal institutions, and legal reasoning; treatments of problems in political morality as they bear on law; and explorations in the nature and development of legal philosophy itself. The series represents diverse traditions of thought but always with an emphasis on rigour and originality. It sets the standard in contemporary jurisprudence.

Why Law Matters

Alon Harel

OXFORD
UNIVERSITY PRESS

OXFORD
UNIVERSITY PRESS

Great Clarendon Street, Oxford, OX2 6DP,
United Kingdom

Oxford University Press is a department of the University of Oxford.
It furthers the University's objective of excellence in research, scholarship,
and education by publishing worldwide. Oxford is a registered trade mark of
Oxford University Press in the UK and in certain other countries

First published 2014
First published in paperback 2015

Published in the United States of America by Oxford University Press
198 Madison Avenue, New York, NY 10016, United States of America

British Library Cataloguing in Publication Data
Data available

Library of Congress Cataloging in Publication Data
Data available

ISBN 978-0-19-964327-1 (Hbk.)
ISBN 978-0-19-876621-6 (Pbk.)

'If we knew what it is that we were doing, it would not be called research, would it?'
Albert Einstein

To the memory of my mother Aliza Harel (Guttman) who would have questioned why one would write so much about rights and justice rather than bring them about and to the memory of my father Yeshaayahu Harel (Herold)

Series Editors' Preface

'Law is a means... not an end,' said Hans Kelsen. That view was shared by Aquinas and by Bentham, by rights theorists and by economists. According to it, law is an instrument and is to be evaluated according to how well it serves its proper ends. Anyone who thinks that is obvious will need to confront the arguments of this powerful new book by Alon Harel. Instrumental explanations of, and justifications for, legal institutions here come under exacting scrutiny, and rarely emerge intact. Harel argues that law matters for non-instrumental reasons, neglect of which produces theoretical error and, sometimes, moral disaster.

On Harel's view, public institutions are not merely means to secure independently specifiable ends. They are constituent aspects of a just society, and the contribution they make to it is not contingent but necessary. He defends that thesis through an innovative treatment of linked issues in political and constitutional theory. Harel denies that rights are grounded in values like equality or dignity; in fact, such values are themselves partly constituted by rights and stand in a reciprocal relation to them. He claims that public officials—whether legislators or bureaucrats—are not merely charged with tasks that might in principle be assigned to others; they are members of public institutions who are to perform tasks that must be undertaken *by them*. Finally, he explains how entrenched constitutional rights and the practice of judicial review may be justified: not by the prospect of thereby securing just or correct outcomes, nor or even by procedural fairness, but by the way they express an urgent moral duty that binds legislators, and by constituting a right to a hearing and a forum in which that hearing can play out.

This fascinating volume offers arguments that are both significant and surprising, on matters ranging from the nature of value and agency to practical problems about judicial deference and the privatization of state services. A major work from a leading writer, it will force many to re-think why and how law matters.

TAOE
JG
LG

Acknowledgements

As this book includes portions of essays that have been previously published I will not be able to acknowledge all the people that contributed to it. I wish however to thank first the co-authors of the essays which formed the basis for some of the chapters. I also wish to thank the immense help of my editor Kim Treiger, who struggled with my feeble language skills and also provided helpful substantive comments. My research assistants, in particular Liran Ben-Ami, Jacob Becker, Erez Nitzan, Haggai Porat, Evyatar Sadeh, and Yishai Rivlin read and reread chapters of this book and provided invaluable comments. Scott Altman, Lior Barshack, Eyal Benvenisti, Brian Bix, Therese Bjorkholm, Rowan Cruft, Hanoch Dagan, Anthony Duff, David Enoch, Yuval Eylon, George Fletcher, Chaim Gans, Miri Gur-Arye, David Heyd, Avner Inbar, Mattias Kumm, Andrei Marmor, Barak Medina, Kai Moeller, Michael Otsuka, Shai Perry, Ariel Porat, Danny Priel, Ram Rivlin, Arthur Ripstein, Assaf Sharon, Francois Tanguay-Renaud, Phillip Schink, Re'em Segev, Andrew Simester, Ken Simons, Laura Underkuffler read different portions of the book (even before I thought it would become a book) and contributed greatly to it. I also want to thank Alex Flach from OUP and Leslie Green the editor of the OUP series both for their substantive comments and for their patience and willingness to tolerate the unexpected delays in submitting the manuscript.

The following articles are reproduced with the kind permission of the publishers:

Parts of chapter 2 are based on Alon Harel, 'What Demands are Rights? An Investigation on the Relations between Rights and Reasons' 17 Oxford Journal of Legal Studies 101–14 (1997).

Chapter 3 is based on Alon Harel, 'Why Only the State May Inflict Criminal Sanctions: The Case Against Privately Inflicted Sanctions' 14 Legal Theory 113–33 (2008). and on Alon Harel & Avihay Dorfman, 'The Case Against Privatization' 41 Philosophy and Public Affairs 67–102 (2013).

Chapter 4 is based on Alon Harel & Assaf Sharon, 'Necessity Knows No Law' 61 Toronto University Law Journal 845–65 (2011).

Chapter 6 is based on Alon Harel & Tsvi Kahana, 'The Easy Core Case for Judicial Review 2 Journal of Legal Analysis' 227–56 (2010) and on Alon Harel & Adam Shinar 'Between Judicial Review and Legislative Supremacy: A Cautious Defense of Constrained Judicial Review' 10 International Journal of Constitutional Law 950–75 (2012).

Contents

1

Introduction

Fortunately this book was completed much later than I expected (although perhaps it is still too early to complete it even at this stage). Had it been written when I first planned to write it, it would have been a very different book. I started writing this book (or perhaps another book) believing that law matters only because (under certain circumstances) it is likely (as a contingent matter) to protect rights and bring about justice. More specifically when I started writing a book I believed that: (1) rights are instruments to realize values that exist independently of these rights, and (2) public institutions such as the state, courts etc. are mere contingent instruments to facilitate the making of decisions and performing actions whose desirability, correctness, or appropriateness is independent of the identity of the agent performing them. There is nothing distinctively valuable in public institutions other than their (contingent) greater capacity to achieve worthwhile goals. I also began the project believing that (3) the modes and forms of deliberation are dictated exclusively by the concern to reach the right answer, to act in accordance with reason etc., (4) the desirability of constitutional directives hinges on the question of whether such directives are likely to guide the state or individual agents to act as they ought to, and (5) the desirability of judicial review (and its optimal scope) hinges exclusively on the question of whether judicial review is conducive to the reaching of the right decision/acting in accordance with reason. Had this book been written when I first planned and hoped to write it, I would have defended all these themes as passionately as I defend in this book their negation. I feel lucky that this book was not written when it was first planned.

This book examines various legal and political institutions and procedures and argues that the desirability of these institutions and procedures is not contingent and does not hinge on the prospects that these institutions are conducive to the realization of valuable ends. Instead, various legal institutions and legal procedures that are often perceived as contingent means to facilitate the realization of valuable ends matter *as such*.

It is fashionable among legal theorists to maintain that what makes a legal or political institution valuable is its ability to decide correctly or justly, and equally, what makes a procedure valuable is its propensity to generate just decisions. To justify an institution or a procedure one needs therefore to identify what the right or correct decision is and then to identify the institution or procedure which is most likely to get it right. Instead, this book sides with those who believe that sometimes the justness or correctness of a decision depends on the institution making the decision and/or on the procedure by which the decision came about. Justice is not always independent of the institutions and procedures which bring it about. At times those institutions are not mere contingent means to the realization of valuable ends; instead such institutions are necessary prerequisites for the realization of certain values. Let me illustrate.

In some situations, in the case of judicial review for instance (discussed in Chapter 6), the institution (or procedure) is desirable because it protects a right (the right to a hearing). The justification for judicial review is grounded therefore not in the superior quality of the decisions resulting from judicial review but in the willingness to hear individual grievances, consider their soundness, address these grievances in good faith, and act in accordance with the outcomes of the deliberation. Further I argue (in Chapter 3) that some goods—inherently public goods—can only be provided by public institutions. The value of such goods hinges on the agent providing the good. Thus, the desirability of public provision of some goods does not depend merely on contingent features of public institutions, such as their accountability; instead, the value (and even the nature) of the good provided depends upon its *public* provision. For instance, I argue that criminal punishment is a communicative practice involving a judgment concerning the wrongfulness of an act, and, consequently, it cannot but be provided by agents that are capable of making authoritative judgments concerning wrongfulness—agents who can speak in the name of the state. The public provision of punishment is not a contingent feature of punishment; the public provision is what makes it a valuable practice—a practice of condemning wrongful actions. These are mere illustrations of the approach defended in this book, namely, that legal institutions and procedures are often not mere *contingent* instruments to realize valuable ends; they are often necessary components of a just society.

As these concerns will be discussed at length in the following chapters, let me turn now to examine some of the difficulties of, what I believe, is the alternative position in political theory, namely the view that legal institutions and procedures are mere contingent means designed to identify what justice requires and to act in accordance with it.

Under such arguments, political and legal institutions are justified by pointing out that they bring about *contingently* desirable outcomes. For instance it is often claimed that legal or political rights are designed to realize pre-existing values underlying these rights; the state is designed to provide in the most efficient way public goods such as security; constitutional directives are designed to guide state officials to act in accordance with reason, and judicial review is justified only to the extent that it protects rights, amplifies minorities' voices, or protects the principles and values established by the founding fathers. The justifiability of a political institution or procedure is equated with its usefulness and conduciveness to the prospects of realization of desirable or just decisions and actions. Further, the desirability or justifiability of the decision is deemed independent of the institution making it or the procedure by which it was brought about.[1] Without denying that such explanations are often sound, I wish to explore here the reasons why some of these explanations can fail and why explanations of the type I develop in this book may at times (although by no means always) be superior.

First, the task of establishing that an institution or a procedure is conducive to a worthy goal often requires social science skills. Can social science establish that courts are typically more attentive to minority concerns than legislatures? Are public prisons more accountable

---

[1] There is one main exception to this generalization, namely democratic or majoritarian institutions which are often considered desirable irrespective of the outcome. It has been famously claimed by prominent political theorists that the democratic process is desirable for 'process-related reasons'. Jeremy Waldron, 'The Core of the Case against Judicial Review', 115 *Yale LJ* 1346 (2006). Democracy however is not among the institutions or processes I discuss here.

to the public than private ones? Are soldiers more likely to comply with humanitarian law than mercenaries? Are constitutional norms which bind the legislature more, or less, conducive to justice than legislative supremacy? Is judicial supremacy more, or less, conducive to justice than legislative supremacy? Given the breadth and generality of such sweeping questions even social science is sometimes impotent in substantiating such claims. The question of whether judicial review is conducive to justice or to the protection of rights depends upon the quality of the judges, the methods of nominating them, and other contextual parameters. The soundness of such claims differs from one society to another and one generation to another, while the claims of political theorists often transcend both place and time. To the extent that the political theorist wants to provide an argument that extends beyond a specific place at a specific time, she needs to provide a more solid foundation for its conclusions.

Second, the traditional structure of justifications suffers sometimes from insincerity and inauthenticity; it fails at times to identify (or capture) the real sentiments underlying the urge to sustain or design political institutions or procedures. The sentiments underlying and sustaining the passions of legislators, the public, and even the theorists themselves are grounded in different normative considerations from those officially used to defend the relevant institutions or procedures. There is a sense of incongruity between the official (allegedly rational) justifications of political institutions or procedures (in terms of the quality of the resulting decisions) and the underlying sentiments triggering the interest and passions of those who sustain these institutions, establish them, design them, or simply cherish them. To use an analogy, a theorist may provide a perfectly sound utilitarian justification for a categorical prohibition of slavery, or for an absolute prohibition on torture and other inhumane practices. But such justifications seem to miss the point and fail to explain why torture is wrong, as the revulsion triggered by such practices is not attributable to utilitarian considerations. Similarly, I believe that even perfectly sound contingent arguments for or against certain entrenched political institutions or procedures may miss the point as they purport to rationalize political institutions and procedures in terms that do not capture what make such institutions or procedures politically and morally attractive. A significant part of this book is designed to identify justifications which meet the test of sincerity, namely that address the genuine sentiments underlying the popular support of political institutions and procedures, rather than to rationalize these institutions and procedures in terms that are alien to those who establish the institutions and sustain them.

Note that I do not wish to argue that instrumental justifications (of the type I criticized above) necessarily fail or that the type of justification provided in this book (namely justifications that reject the view that law is a contingent means to valuable ends) is necessarily superior. I raise these two concerns only to illustrate that instrumental justifications which rest exclusively on contingencies are not free of difficulties. The book does not provide a general argument against a certain type of justification in legal or political theory (e.g., against justifications which rest on contingent sociological or psychological conjectures). It also does not provide an argument in favour of an alternative justificatory methodology (which does not rest on such contingencies). Instead this book seeks to provide sound arguments favouring or opposing the use of certain political and legal institutions and procedures. Hence its success does not hinge on establishing that a certain type of justification is superior to another but merely on the soundness of the particular justifications provided in the following chapters. What the following chapters seek to establish is that there is a close (or strong) affinity between legal and political institutions and procedures on the one hand and the desirable goals or values on the other, such that the latter can, even in principle, be realized only by establishing the former.

Let me provide a very brief exposition of the chapters of this book.

Part I (consisting of Chapter 2) discusses the nature of (some) prominent rights and identifies the reasons for protecting such rights. Rights, it is often argued, are valuable because of the values underlying them. Under this standard view rights are designed to realize (or facilitate the realization of) values whose content is independent of these rights. For instance it is claimed that the right to free speech is designed to promote autonomy; the right to freedom of religion facilitates self-realization, etc. But if this is so, I argue, it follows that rights are at least in principle redundant; values can function as well as rights. For instance, instead of protecting narrowly tailored rights designed to promote autonomy, autonomy as such ought to be protected and replace the specific rights designed to protect it.[2]

---

[2] This conclusion is not a mere hypothetical fantasy. As a matter of fact the advocates of the so-called 'rationalist paradigm' wish to distance legal and constitutional discourse from

Chapter 2 disputes this view and argues that certain rights are not mere norms designed to promote the realization of pre-existing values underlying these rights. The values underlying (some) rights are partially constructed by entrenching the rights designed to protect these values, so that the relation between these rights and the values underlying them is reciprocal: rights are grounded in values, such as autonomy and dignity, and justified in terms of these values. At the same time, the values underlying the (legally or politically) entrenched rights are also partly constructed by the rights, such that the (legal or political) entrenchment of the rights ultimately contributes to the construction of the values.

Part II (consisting of Chapters 3 and 4) is devoted to the investigation of dignity, and in particular its ramifications for political theory. Dignity, it is shown, demands that our decisions be based on respectful deliberation. More specifically, dignity imposes constraints on the deliberation of the agents. It dictates not only what agents ought to decide or how they ought to act but also how they ought to reason or deliberate. Further, I argue, the capacity to deliberate in certain ways is often agent-dependent, such that only certain agents are capable of engaging in certain forms of deliberation. The primary dichotomy drawn in Chapter 3 is between agents who operate on the basis of fidelity of reason (private agents) and agents who operate on the basis of fidelity of deference (public officials).

The difference between fidelity of reason and fidelity of deference is crucial. There are some goods that can only be provided by agents who operate on the basis of fidelity of reason and other goods that can only be provided by agents who operate on the basis of fidelity of deference. At times it is only public officials (agents who defer to the state) that can provide certain goods; and, at other times it is only private individuals (operating on the basis of fidelity of reason) that can do so. In such cases it is not that the agent (public official or private individual) is chosen on the basis of his or her (contingent) expected success in providing the good but the value of the good (or even the very possibility of providing the good) depends upon its being provided by the designated agent.

Part III defends 'robust constitutionalism'. Robust constitutionalism contains two components: (i) binding (but not necessarily enforceable)

---

what they regard as the fetishistic, rigid obsession with narrowly tailored rights and use, instead, broad and diffuse values. See the discussion in Chapter 2 C2.

constitutional directives (Chapter 5), and (ii) the judicial power to enforce such directives (judicial review) (Chapter 6).

Chapter 5 argues that the constitutional entrenchment of pre-existing moral or political rights is valuable, independently of whether such an entrenchment is conducive to the protection of these rights. More specifically, the chapter defends what I label 'binding constitutional-ism', namely a scheme of constitutional directives binding the legisla-ture. The value of binding constitutionalism is grounded not in its likely contingent effects or consequences, e.g., better protection of rights; but rather in the fact that constitutional entrenchment of rights constitutes public recognition that the protection of rights is the state's *duty* rather than a mere discretionary gesture on its part. Decisions that are made in accordance with constitutionally entrenched duties are thus not at the 'mercy' of the legislature; instead, the legislature is bound to act in accordance with such decisions. In the absence of binding constitutional directives, a state which protects a right can be analogized to a debtor who gives what he owes to his lender but insists that his act is a charitable donation rather than a repayment of a debt.

Failing to constitutionally entrench rights is not merely inconsider-ate in the manner that the act of the debtor is. In addition the failure to entrench rights constitutionally is detrimental to freedom, as freedom requires not merely the de facto protection of speech, religion, and other basic rights but protection that is not contingent on the good will of the legislature. Free citizens ought not to live 'at the mercy of' their legislatures even if such legislatures are good-hearted and are likely to protect their rights. Constitutional entrenchment of rights is therefore a necessary precondition for freedom rather than merely a contingent instrument for protecting freedom. To put it bluntly, democratic deliberation is (at times) necessarily detrimental to freedom. It is not only detrimental to freedom for contingent reasons (namely, for the reason that democratic deliberation may result in oppressive decisions), but even when democratic deliberation results in decisions or choices that are protective of rights, it sometimes fails to acknowledge the *duty* to protect rights—a duty which is independent of judgments or pre-ferences of the legislature or the people.

Chapter 6 completes the defence of robust constitutionalism by justifying judicial review on non-instrumentalist grounds. This chapter argues that the state has a duty to provide a hearing to its citizens, and that this duty requires the state (a) to provide individuals with the opportunity to challenge decisions that they believe (rightly or wrongly) violate their rights; (b) to justify its decisions to those who raise such grievances; and (c) to reconsider its decisions on the basis of the deliberation. Judicial review is valuable not because it is likely to result in 'better' decisions, or to better promote worthy goals or values, but because judicial review is (nothing but) a hearing to which individuals have a right. I also explore the relevance of this observation to what I label 'constrained judicial review', namely systems which grant courts a privileged, but not a supreme, role in shaping constitutional rights. Both Chapter 5 (defending the entrenchment of binding constitutional directives) and Chapter 6 (defending judicial review) challenge the standard dominant justificatory framework used in constitutional theory: constitutional instrumentalism. Under this view the value of constitutions or the value of judicial review depends exclusively upon contingencies such as the likelihood that constitutions, or judicial review, contribute to the quality or the justness of the resulting decisions.

Identifying the non-contingent value of legal institutions and procedures often helps not only to identify why these institutions or procedures are desirable, but also to better understand the nature of the institutions in ways that deviate from conventional understandings. For instance, Chapter 3 identifies who public officials are and what differentiates public officials from other individuals. Public officials are those agents who can speak in the name of the state, and they can do so because they participate in 'integrative practices'—practices characterized by their openness and willingness to absorb ongoing political guidance and intervention. Similarly, Chapter 6 argues that judicial review is not a practice which must be conducted by courts or judges. The rationale underlying judicial review implies that what is important about judicial review is the adjudicative process which is equated with a process of an individualized hearing. It is the process of adjudication that renders the practice valuable, rather than the fact that it is conducted by courts or judges.

My conclusion is that political and legal institutions and procedures matter but they matter not for the reasons many legal and political theorists believe they matter. Legal (and political) institutions matter as such, not merely as contingent instruments to bring about desirable outcomes. In establishing these claims in different areas of law and politics I wish to be attentive to the sentiments of politicians, citizens, and activists and to theorize their concerns in a way that is as authentic as an academic enterprise can be to these sentiments. It is my wish to capture as much as possible the concerns that are cherished by these groups and that have been the trigger for writing this book.

PART I

Why Rights Matter

2

Why Rights Matter: The Interdependence of Rights and Values

A. Introduction

Rights, it is often argued, are valuable because of the reasons and/or values underlying those rights. Joseph Raz famously stated: 'Assertions of rights are typically intermediate conclusions in arguments from ultimate values to duties.'[1] Raz holds what I label here *the primacy of values over rights hypothesis*, namely the view that the values underlying rights are normatively prior to rights, and that values dictate (subject to institutional and pragmatic concerns) the scope and strength of rights. This view has even led some contemporary constitutional theorists—advocates of what is labelled 'the rationalist paradigm'—to question the need for having a list of distinct narrowly tailored rights such as a right to free expression, religion, or privacy and to suggest instead the entrenchment of a general right to liberty or autonomy.[2] This chapter challenges that hypothesis and offers an alternative that I label *the reciprocity hypothesis*. It argues that at the very least some rights are not mere norms designed to promote the realization of pre-existing values underlying these rights. Rather, the realization of the values underlying some rights is made possible by entrenching the narrowly defined rights designed to protect these values, so that the relation between these rights and the values underlying them

---

[1] Joseph Raz, *The Morality of Freedom* (Oxford: Clarendon Press, 1986), 181.
[2] See the discussion in section C2.

is reciprocal. The rights—for example the right to free speech or to freedom of religion—are grounded and justified in terms of values such as autonomy and dignity. At the same time, the values underlying the (legally or politically) entrenched rights depend upon the rights, such that the (legal or political) entrenchment of the rights ultimately facilitates and contributes to the realization of the values. One of the implications of this view is that the formalistic legal definitions of narrowly defined rights are not an accidental (or pragmatic) feature of rights; they are essential for facilitating their exercise. I shall focus my attention in this chapter on autonomy, although I believe this observation can be extended to other values.

Note an important qualification: I do not argue that the reciprocity hypothesis is a necessary feature of rights, or even that it applies to all rights. In later chapters I identify some rights to which it clearly does not apply. Nor does it provide a key to the understanding of what rights are. Yet I maintain that the analysis in this chapter applies to some of the most important rights, and provides the key to the understanding of central features of those rights.

To establish the reciprocity hypothesis I start by identifying a neglected feature of rights, namely the dependence of rights on reasons. More particularly, I establish that rights are 'reason-dependent demands'.[3] The identification of a demand as a right turns on the fact that the demand is grounded in certain reasons. Most typically these reasons are values such as autonomy, dignity, or equality. I also argue that a satisfactory account of rights should distinguish between (1) reasons that are intrinsic to a right, namely, reasons by virtue of which particular demands are classified as rights, and (2) reasons that are extrinsic to a right, namely those reasons that may affect the strength with which a demand should be protected but do not justify the classification of the demand as a right. To illustrate, autonomy seems to be a reason which is intrinsic to the right to freedom of speech. It is not merely a reason to protect speech, but also a reason *by virtue of which* the protection of speech is classified as a right. In contrast, the potential contribution of free speech to economic prosperity may be a reason to protect freedom of speech, but it is not a reason to protect *a right* to free speech.

---

[3] This is based on my article 'What Demands are Rights? An Investigation into the Relation between Rights and Reasons', 17 *Oxford J. of Legal Studies* 101 (1997).

Although, as I show in section B, this distinction is deeply entrenched in the discourse of rights, it is also puzzling for two reasons. First, in evaluating the desirability of protecting speech, arguably *all* reasons should be considered in accordance with their strength. Why should some reasons (e.g., autonomy, dignity) be 'privileged' as the ones by virtue of which a demand is classified as a right, while other reasons (e.g., economic prosperity) are treated as merely extrinsic to the right? I label this phenomenon '*the differential treatment of reasons*'. Second, if what justifies the protection of a particular right such as free speech are (only) the reasons or values underlying the relevant activity, why should some activities be privileged relative to other autonomy-enhancing activities? For example why are the autonomy-enhancing activities of speech and religion privileged relative to other autonomy-enhancing activities? Why not simply evaluate all the relevant reasons and values in accordance with their weight, and identify which demands ought to be honoured on the basis of a comprehensive evaluation of the reasons justifying protecting the activity? The second puzzle is what I label '*the differential treatment of activities*'.

There is however a tension between the differential treatment of values or reasons and the differential treatment of activities on the one hand and the primacy of values hypothesis on the other. In the absence of a special justification, the primacy of values over rights implies the rejection of both the differential treatment of values or reasons and the differential treatment of activities. If rights are merely designed to promote the realization of values, then all values (or reasons) should be treated in accordance with their strength and all activities should be measured in accordance with their contribution to the realization of values. Further, the primacy of values hypothesis implies that one need not have rights at all; it is (at least in principle, absent any pragmatic or institutional concerns) sufficient simply to be guided by the values underlying the rights.[4] Rights are, at most, pragmatically or institutionally useful features of legal and political discourse, but no principled theoretical considerations justify their centrality to the governing of liberal societies. Why care about speech or religion, if what is really important and valuable is autonomy or dignity?

Despite its intuitive appeal, this chapter maintains that (at least with respect to some rights) the primacy of values hypothesis needs to be

---

[4] This seems to me to be the underlying motivation for the 'rationalist paradigm'. See the discussion in section C2.

re-evaluated and eventually rejected. The hidden premise underlying the primacy of values hypothesis is that the activities which enhance (or facilitate the realization of) the relevant values can be identified and realized independently of the legally or politically protected rights designed to enhance those values. Freedom of speech and religion are important and conducive to autonomy, irrespective of whether they are *legally* protected or not. The task of the polity is to identify the activities that are autonomy-enhancing or dignity-enhancing, and to protect those activities either legally or in some other way.

I do not challenge the importance and significance of this description. There are activities and interests whose protection is conducive to the realization of autonomy or dignity or whatever other values are worth promoting. Values dictate the protection of vital activities and interests and, at times, those activities and interests can be identified and secured either by entrenching legal or political rights designed to realize those values or in other ways. However this chapter complements that observation with an equally important observation, by challenging the assumption that the values underlying rights (and, in particular, the ability to benefit from the realization of those values) are independent of the legally entrenched rights designed to protect those values. It is argued here that legal, constitutional, or political rights are part of a set of social, political, and legal practices which facilitate and contribute to the realization of the values. Let me briefly illustrate this claim by using the example of autonomy.

The value of autonomy is realized when individuals exercise their autonomy; potential to exercise autonomy is not sufficient.[5] To the extent that the actual exercise of autonomy is valuable, the value depends (at least partly) on the willingness and readiness of individuals to exercise their autonomy in appropriate ways, namely to have the capacity to make choices that constitute an exercise of their autonomy, to make such choices in their lives and, further, to make them in a way that makes the exercise of choice valuable. Such willingness and readiness requires sustaining and reinforcing certain societal practices and beliefs. The legal entrenchment of rights is an important component for the sustaining and reinforcing of social and cultural practices

---

[5] I do not deny that the potential or the capacity to exercise autonomy is also important. For my purposes here it is sufficient to assume that the actual exercise of autonomy has greater value than the mere potential to exercise it. For a discussion of the value of exercising autonomy, see Raz, *The Morality of Freedom*, 372 (n 1).

designed to facilitate the exercise of autonomy, as they signal which choices are important and significant and what the appropriate reasons for making such choices are.

To use an example, take the case of choosing one's spouse. In some societies the choice of one's marital partner may serve primarily economic or status-related purposes and, consequently, 'choosing' one's partner is a matter of judgment not as to whether the partners' personality and inclinations suit each other, but whether the marriage is suitable in terms of the economic or status-oriented interests of the partners. Failing to exercise a choice (and merely yielding to judgments made by parents) is not therefore detrimental to autonomy in such a society. As had such a choice been made it would have been based on status or economic considerations. It follows that the legal or political entrenchment of a right to make such a choice is not conducive (or at least not conducive in the same way) to autonomy as it is in our society.

Entrenching a political or legal right to choose one's partner and the type of public controversies and litigation following such an entrenchment may serve to transform the significance of marriage from an institution which serves economic interests to one which is designed to facilitate and express intimacy and friendship. Such a transformation implies that the success of the marital relationship turns on preferences, tastes, and judgments of the partners to the relationship and, hence, that the success of the relationship requires the exercise of autonomous choices on the part of the partners.[6] Choosing one's partner *becomes* a significant choice partly as a result of entrenching a legal right to protect these choices. It follows that the legal or political decision to entrench a right to choose one's partner bolsters the significance of the choice concerning personal matters, and *transforms* this choice into a significant exercise of autonomy.

---

[6] Some sociologists made an even more radical claim under which the relations between love and choice are not natural but are characteristic of contemporary societies. In her intriguing discussion of the transformation of love, Eva Illouz describes the relations of love to autonomy as follows:

[o]ne of the most fruitful ways to understand the transformation of love in modernity is through the category of choice. This is not only because to love is to single out one person among other possibilities and thus to constitute one's individuality in the very act of choosing a love object, but also because to love someone is to be confronted with questions of choice: 'Is s/he the right one?' 'How do I know this person is right for me?' 'Won't there be a better person along the way?'

See Eva Illouz, *Why Love Hurts* (Cambridge: Polity Press, 2012), 18–19. Illouz also establishes that choice is characteristic of the modern understanding of love. In her view it is part of 'the great transformation of love'. See Illouz, *Why Love Hurts*, 18.

This chapter defends the conjecture that rights and values are inter-dependent. Rights are not a mere replica of the underlying pre-existing values; they change and transform the autonomous choices that can, in reality, be made by individuals, and what the grounds for these choices are. What characterizes rights is precisely a persistent tension (rather than harmony) between the protected activities such as speech, religion, or privacy and the values underlying these activities. I suggest that this tension is necessary for the values to be realized effectively. To sustain such a tension rights must be 'formalistic'; they must to some extent protect certain activities and interests without measuring in each and every case the degree to which such protection promotes values and serves the reasons that underlie those rights.

This observation has an additional implication which is central to my analysis, and which seems to fit with the significance attributed to rights in liberal societies. If protection of a right such as the right to free speech is important simply because it is conducive to autonomy, the polity need not *protect* a right to freedom of speech; it is sufficient that it protects or, more accurately, does not regulate speech (without legally or constitutionally entrenching a right to free speech). As a matter of fact, the protection of speech need not even be deliberate or inten-tional. It could be a by-product of indifference towards the speech—indifference which results in non-interference. In contrast, if the entrenchment of rights facilitates the realization of the values under-lying the rights, the entrenchment of legal rights is essential. It is only by deliberately entrenching a right to free political speech that political opinions gain personal and societal significance. Incidental protection of speech is not sufficient to serve the purpose that the protection of a right to free speech is designed to serve.

B. Rights as Reason-dependent Demands

It is common to classify some demands as rights and justify their protection (or at least prima facie protection) on the grounds of that classification. Thus, when a person demands that the government allows her to publish a book or to demonstrate she is often described as demanding respect for her 'right to free expression'. On the other hand, if a person demands that the government pursue certain eco-nomic policies or that the municipality provides more or less police protection, she is often described as making a demand which may be important, valuable, and justified but which is not rights based.[7]

It seems as if the reasons for the classification of my demand to publish this book, or to demonstrate, as an example of the right to free expression (or, in the terminology coined by Raz, as a right derivative of the core right to free expression) are self-evident. Publishing a book or demonstrating counts as 'an expression' and prohibiting the publication of the book or punishing me for protesting count therefore as an infringement of the right to free expression.[8] Naturally there could be disputes as to whether a certain activity counts as 'expression' in the first place. But, ultimately what dictates an answer to the question of whether an activity counts as an expression is related to the nature of the activity. Does the activity really constitute speech or expression? More generally, what identifies the freedom to do X as a right to do X is that X falls within the scope of activities or benefits that are properly covered by the relevant right.

There is however something that is missing in this description. Of course, to be protected by the right to free expression an activity ought to be properly described or labelled as expression. Yet, this is often not sufficient. For example, think of a case in which I make a demand to protect my right to publish this book *on the grounds* that the book would greatly contribute to economic prosperity. I demand therefore that the government be compelled to allow me to publish this book on

---

[7] Some people may justify the demand for certain economic policies or the demand for more police protection on the grounds that a person has a right to certain economic policies or to a certain degree of police protection. Irrespective however of what the rights are, there is a broad consensus that rights protect only a subset of justified demands, and that that subset differs from (justified) demands that rest on considerations of policy or public interest.

As I stated in the introduction to this chapter, some theorists have challenged this view and argue for a 'rationalist human rights paradigm'. Under this paradigm, rights are designed to protect all justified demands by creating a culture which is conducive to critical thinking based on reason. Hence, under this paradigm, the traditional protection of well-defined activities such as speech, religion, or sexual practices is obsolete. According to Kumm: 'Interests protected as rights are not restricted to the classical catalogue of rights such as freedom of speech, association, religion and privacy, narrowly conceived. Instead . . . there is a tendency to include all kinds of liberty interests within the domain of interests that enjoy prima facie protection as a right.' See, e.g., M. Kumm, 'Political Liberalism and the Structure of Rights: On the Place and Limits of the Proportionality Requirement', in S. Paulson and George Pavlakos (eds.), *Law, Rights and Discourse: The Legal Philosophy of Robert Alexy* (Oxford: Hart, 2007), 131, 140. I shall critically examine this view in section C2.

[8] Some interpretative practices advocated by constitutional theorists of the American Constitution clearly follow this approach. See the judgment of Justice Black in *Bridges v California* 314 US 252, 262 (1941).

the grounds that the book industry enhances prosperity and that censoring my book is inimical to economic growth.

My demand in this case is of course a demand to engage in a type of activity that is protected by the right to free expression, and yet it does not seem to be a demand to protect a *right* to free expression. Economic prosperity may indeed be a good reason to protect expression (to the extent that protection of expression is conducive to economic prosperity), but it is simply not the right type of reason to justify a *right* to free expression. Such a justification seems to be alien to the discourse of the right to free expression; it deviates too radically from the discursive practices characteristic of this right. But, it is not obvious why such reasons ought to be precluded from the discourse of rights. After all, economic prosperity is an important concern that ought to be promoted by the government. Why not promote economic prosperity by protecting a right to free speech?

Before seeking an explanation, let us first identify the feature of the discourse of rights that explains why justifying the protection of my right to free expression on the grounds that it promotes prosperity sounds so alien to the discourse of rights. To demand *a right* to free expression, the demand must be presumed to be grounded in certain privileged reasons, e.g., autonomy or dignity; no sound reason to protect expression automatically gives rise to a *right* to free expression. Without identifying explicitly or implicitly the reasons for the demand not to be subject to censorship, its classification as a right cannot be established. To fall within the scope of the (prima facie) activities protected by the right to free expression, it is not sufficient that the regulated activity counts as expression; in addition its regulation ought to be presumed to be inimical to certain reasons—reasons that give rise to rights. Most of the more influential reasons used in justifying rights are values, e.g., autonomy, dignity, etc.

This example may be too remote from the actual discourse of rights. Arguably what makes this case peculiar is the fact that protecting freedom of expression is at least in general not particularly conducive to economic prosperity.[9] Let me therefore defend this claim by investigating not an imaginary situation (opposing censorship on the grounds that such censorship is inimical to economic prosperity), but

---

[9] Although some economists have argued otherwise. See R. H. Coase, 'The Market for Goods and the Market for Ideas', 64 *American Economic Review* 384 (1974); 'Advertising and Free Speech', 6 *Journal of Legal Studies* 1 (1977).

by investigating examples taken from the discourse of rights as it is conducted in legal and political reality. I shall focus my attention on the arguments used in the debate over the regulation of expression and propose that these arguments are premised on the presupposition that the characterization of a demand to protect speech as a right to free expression is based on the reasons underlying the demand.

Some advocates of regulating pornography argue that while the right to free expression provides prima facie reasons to protect pornography there are powerful reasons which justify its regulation.[10] The regulation of pornography should therefore be regarded as a justified infringement of the right. In contrast other advocates of regulating pornography argue that the production and distribution of pornography is not protected even by a prima facie right, i.e., its regulation is not an infringement of the right to free speech.[11]

But why would the regulation of pornography or other forms of speech not be an infringement (even if justified) of the prima facie right to free expression? In justifying the view that the regulation of pornography is not an infringement of a prima facie right to free expression, the advocates of regulation use one of two arguments. Some base their view on the premise that pornography is not expression at all.[12] Others prefer to argue that while pornography is an expression, its regulation does not constitute an infringement of the right to free expression because, arguably, the right to free expression extends only to certain (valuable, or at least non-harmful) forms of expression.[13]

A close investigation reveals that the difference between these views is not as dramatic, as in both cases the issue is whether the reasons underlying the protection of expression also justify the protection of pornography. The denial that certain forms of speech, e.g., pornography, hate speech, or commercial speech, constitute 'expression' is typically based on illustrating that the values that justify the protection of expression are not ones which can justify the protection of these kinds of expression. Consequently, identifying the values underlying

---

[10] Catherine MacKinnon, *Only Words* (Cambridge, Mass.: Harvard University Press, 1993), 71–110. For a survey and a critique of the feminist views on pornography, see Alon Harel, 'Freedom of Speech', in Andrei Marmor (ed.), *The Routledge Companion to Philosophy of Law* (London: Routledge, 2012), 610–14.

[11] See, e.g., Harel, 'Freedom of Speech', 610–13 (n 10).

[12] For a survey of these views, see Harel, 'Freedom of Speech', 613–14 (n 10).

[13] For a survey of these views, see Harel, 'Freedom of Speech' (n 10).

the protection of the right to free expression also influences which activities count as 'expression'. Thus in legal discourse, the question of what counts as expression and what counts as valuable expression are often interrelated; 'expression' is equated with valuable (or non-harmful) expression, namely expression that promotes (or is conducive to the realization of) certain values. Further, even when pornography or hate speech is classified as 'expression' it is sometimes excluded from the scope of the protection of the right to free expression on the grounds that the reasons justifying the protection of speech as a right are not ones which can justify the protection of these forms of speech. This is not (necessarily) a claim that one ought not to protect pornography, hate speech, or commercial speech. An advocate of excluding commercial speech from the scope of speech protected by the right may believe that there are forceful reasons justifying the protection of commercial speech. Such an advocate merely denies that the protection of commercial speech is grounded in the type of values which justify the protection of a right to free expression and, consequently, she denies that the protection of commercial speech should be classified as an instance of the right to free expression.

An influential justification for excluding commercial speech from the scope of expression protected by the right to free expression can illustrate this argument. Some opponents of the view that the First Amendment of the United States Constitution protects commercial speech argue that while protection of the right to free expression is justified on the grounds that it promotes autonomy, the protection of commercial speech does not serve this purpose.[14] Under this view, the 'speakers' of commercial speech do not exercise autonomy but operate under constraints dictated by monetary or commercial incentives, and operating under such constraints implies that their speech is not autonomous. Hence, the protection of commercial speech is not required by the right to free expression because the value underlying the protection of a right to free expression (i.e., autonomy) cannot justify the protection of commercial speech.

This reasoning however does not entail that commercial speech does not deserve to be protected, or that it ought to be censored. The protection of commercial speech can be justified on the grounds that it promotes economic prosperity or happiness. This justification may

[14] Edwin Baker, *Human Liberty and Freedom of Speech* (New York: Oxford University Press, 1989), 194–244.

support a very stringent protection of commercial speech. But the implicit premise of this argument is that while the contribution of commercial speech to economic prosperity may be a valid reason justifying the protection of commercial speech, it cannot provide a reason to classify the protection of commercial speech *as an instance of the right to free expression*. It is only when a demand not to be subject to censorship is justified on certain grounds, e.g., autonomy, that the demand is properly classified as an instance of the right to free expression.

The view which classifies the demand to protect speech as a right only when the demand is grounded in certain values is not endorsed merely by the advocates of regulation of speech. Some advocates of protection of controversial forms of expression (on the grounds that these forms of expression are protected by the right to free expression) share a similar view. The argument for the protection of controversial forms of speech by the right to free expression does not rest simply on the ground that there are good reasons to protect these forms of expression. In addition, it is often argued that the protection of these forms of expression is grounded in certain privileged reasons: reasons which give rise to the right. To illustrate, advocates of protecting pornography often describe its protection as required by the right to free expression on the ground that the reasons underlying the protection of political speech, e.g., its contribution to the marketplace of ideas, also justify the protection of pornography. More particularly it is argued that the protection of pornography conveys a hedonistic vision of life; a vision which cherishes rebellion against conventional morality and promotes uninhibited sex or sex for pleasure rather than sex as part of a long-term intimate relationship or companionship.[15]

[15] Steven Gey believes that: 'It cannot be said that porn does not represent "a different vision of humanity or the world". The rejection of the very concept of social worth is a fundamental characteristic of the vision pornography expresses.' See 'The Apologetic of Suppression: The Regulation of Pornography as Act and Idea', 1628 *Michigan L. Rev.* 86 (1988). Deana Pollard defends the protection of pornography on similar grounds by arguing that: 'Ultimately, pornography even violent pornography, does express certain ideas that deserve first amendment scrutiny . . . Pornography generally endorses the concept of sex that is uninhibited and without commitment, of sex just for pleasure.' 'Regulating Violent Pornography', 43 *Vanderbilt L. Rev.* 125, 137 (1990). Further, Steven Shiffrin believes that '[P]ornography can be characterised as a form of dissent. It rebels against the puritanical outlook of an uptight society': Steven Shiffrin, *The First Amendment, Democracy and Romance* (Cambridge, Mass.: Harvard University Press, 1990), 104. These are all premised on the view that pornography contributes to the 'marketplace of ideas', which is one of the most influential justifications for protecting a right to free speech.

Both the denial that commercial speech should be protected (on the ground that it is not an expression of autonomous choice) and the view that pornography should be protected (on the ground that it promotes the marketplace of ideas) presuppose that the classification of the demand not to be subject to censorship as an instance of the right to free expression depends upon the reasons justifying the demand. Hence, claiming that one has a (prima facie) right to free expression entails more than claiming that the right-holder's demand not to be subject to censorship or her demand to express herself are justified. It requires the right-holder to establish also that her expression should not be subject to censorship *by virtue of certain reasons*. The classification of the demand as a right presupposes that its protection serves (directly or indirectly) the values underlying the right to free expression and that not all reasons to protect free expression count as reasons to entrench a right to free expression.

This observation can be described by drawing a distinction between two types of reasons which justify one's demand not to be subject to censorship: *intrinsic reasons*—reasons by virtue of which one's demand is classified as an instance of the right to free speech, and *extrinsic reasons*—reasons which may constitute sound grounds to protect expression but are not the reasons by virtue of which it is protected as a right to free expression.[16] Intrinsic reasons include (in the context of the right to free expression) reasons such as autonomy, dignity, the marketplace of ideas, and/or self-realization.[17] Extrinsic reasons include reasons such as the financial costs of regulating speech, or the contribution of speech to economic growth, etc.

Not all rights are necessarily grounded in the same intrinsic reasons. According to some, the marketplace of ideas is an intrinsic reason with respect to the right to free expression. Advocates of free expression maintain that this is the reason by virtue of which the legal system protects a right to free expression. The implication is that this reason does not merely justify the protection of expression. Rather it justifies the protection of expression as a right. But the very same reason could be an extrinsic reason relative to another right. To identify what the intrinsic reasons for a certain right are one ought to examine the way the right is justified by examining political and legal discourse pertaining to the right.

The discourse of rights is governed by two distinct types of intrinsic reasons: primary and secondary intrinsic reasons. Primary intrinsic

---

[16] This is the claim I defended in Harel, 'What Demands are Rights?' (n 3).
[17] For a survey, see Harel, 'Freedom of Speech', 600–8 (n 10).

reasons are reasons by virtue of which one protects the right in the first place. Thus, if one believes that autonomy is the reason by virtue of which the right to free speech is protected in the first place, autonomy is a primary intrinsic reason. But, certain demands not to be subject to censorship may be classified as rights even if the protection of these demands is, in itself, not conducive to autonomy. Some intrinsic reasons are used in order to justify the expansion (and at times the contraction) of the scope of the right beyond the boundaries determined by the primary, intrinsic reasons. Typical reasons of this type include institutional reasons, procedural reasons, slippery slope arguments, and so on. These reasons can serve to expand the scope of a right such that it will cover demands which cannot be justified on the basis of the primary intrinsic reasons, or to contract the scope of a right such that it does not cover demands that are justified on the basis of the primary intrinsic reasons.[18]

To sum up, rights are (at least sometimes) *reason* or *value-dependent demands.* Classifying a particular demand as a right requires establishing that the reasons underlying the demand are intrinsic to the right, i.e., that they are the reasons by virtue of which the right was protected in the first place. Section C shows that this characteristic of rights raises doubts concerning the soundness of the primacy of values hypothesis and, consequently, an alternative account of rights and their relations with values needs to be developed.

C. The Failure of the Primacy of Values Hypothesis: The Dependence of Values on Rights

1. Introduction

This section starts by establishing two puzzles of the discourse of rights: the differential treatment of values and the differential treatment of activities. More specifically I show in section C2 that the primacy of

---

[18] An example of the latter case is the treatment of conscientious objection under Israeli law. It has been argued that while 'selective refusal', e.g., refusal to serve in the occupied territories may be justified and, ideally, ought to be protected, it cannot be protected in reality given the difficulties in differentiating between cases of conscientious objection and civil disobedience. Hence the scope of the right ought to be contracted in a way that deprives some individuals of a moral right of refusal because of institutional limitations.

values hypothesis cannot account for these two puzzles. I also examine various traditional ways to address these puzzles. Section C3 proposes the abandonment of the primacy of values hypothesis and defends the reciprocity hypothesis, namely the view that the values underlying rights are partially shaped and constructed by entrenching the rights designed to protect them, so that the relation between rights and values is reciprocal: rights are grounded in values, such as autonomy and dignity and are justified in terms of these values. Section C3 also shows that rejecting the primacy of values hypothesis has important consequences: the protection of rights needs to be deliberate or intentional; it cannot be incidental. It is of course important not to restrict speech unjustifiably and to provide the opportunity for individuals to engage in speech; but it is also important to actively entrench its protection legally or constitutionally and to do it for the right reasons. Unlike other goods, such as a clean environment, the value of some rights can be fully realized only by deliberate and reflective protection of these rights, because such deliberate and reflective protection facilitates the realization of the values underlying the rights.

2. The Hypothesis of the Primacy of Values over Rights

Advocates of the primacy of values over rights adhere to the view that the values underlying rights determine the scope and weight of the rights we have. To identify what rights we have, one needs to explore the values underlying them and to specify what demands are conducive to the realization of these values. I show here that this view cannot explain the discourse of rights as it is currently practised. More particularly, I point out that it cannot explain two features that characterize the discourse of rights: the differential treatment of activities and the differential treatment of values.

The primacy of values hypothesis seems to reflect the way the discourse of rights is practised. After all it seems that the right to free expression deserves protection *because* it contributes to autonomy, self-realization, the marketplace of ideas, or the pursuit of truth. It is natural to conclude from this that to justify the claim that X infringes my right I ought to establish that X is detrimental to the realization of the (intrinsic) values underlying the right or to establish that protecting X serves in the long run to detract from the realization of these values. It is not surprising therefore that the primacy of values hypothesis has become influential among political theorists. Most famously it underlies Raz's influential characterization of rights according to which: 'Assertions of rights are typically intermediate conclusions in arguments from ultimate values to duties.'[19] Values (or, more generally, reasons) stand at the top of the justificatory hierarchy: rights follow and finally, duties which derive from these rights.

Before developing an alternative view in section C3, let me identify here two primary puzzles which arise from the primacy of values hypothesis. First, the advocate of the primacy of values hypothesis has to explain the *differential treatment of reasons*, namely why some reasons for protecting rights, such as the values of autonomy and dignity are classified as intrinsic reasons—reasons which justify the *right* to free speech, while others are merely used to justify the protection of speech. Arguably, in evaluating the desirability of censoring speech, it seems arbitrary to distinguish between autonomy, or the marketplace of ideas (classified as intrinsic) and other reasons, such as economic prosperity (classified as extrinsic).

Secondly, the advocate of the primacy of values hypothesis has to explain the reasons for the *differential treatment of activities*, namely why only some activities are protected (e.g., speech or religion) rather than all autonomy-enhancing activities. If expression, for instance, is protected only because its protection is conducive to autonomy, then arguably protection should be granted to any activity which is as autonomy-enhancing as expression (provided that protecting these activities does not conflict with other valuable objectives). If the reason for protecting rights is indeed grounded exclusively in the values underlying these rights, one would expect that the scope of these rights and their strength would fully converge with the strength and the scope of the values underlying them. If what really counts is autonomy per se (or any other intrinsic reasons underlying the protection of the right), then the very classification of rights in accordance with the protected activities seems capricious. Instead of classifying rights as rights to certain well-specified narrowly defined protected activities, such as speech or religion, rights should be protected in accordance with the degree to which their protection is conducive to the realization of the values underlying the rights, e.g., autonomy, self-realization, or dignity. By protecting speech or religion rather than all autonomy-enhancing activities, one fetishizes the protected activities

---

[19] Raz, *The Morality of Freedom*, 181 (n 1).

and thereby erodes the significance of the underlying values. Speech or religion are perceived to be important instead of what really matters, namely autonomy or dignity. The culture of rights is nothing but a form of fetishism, coming at the expense of identifying what is really important, namely the underlying values and protecting (all and only) the activities that are conducive to the realization of those values.

Let me examine now three main strategies to address this objection, without abandoning the primacy of values hypothesis. The first strategy concedes that there is not a complete overlap between rights and values, but maintains that such divergence serves pragmatic/institutional concerns. The other two strategies claim that despite the apparent divergence there is a full convergence of rights and the values underlying them and the values fully dictate the scope and the weight of the rights. The second strategy requires the expansion of the scope of the protected activities such that they will fully converge with the values underlying them. It rejects therefore the allegedly formalistic characterization of narrowly defined protected rights-based activities, e.g., the right to free expression or the right to freedom of religion. The third strategy also claims that the underlying values fully dictate the scope and the weight of the rights. Yet, instead of rejecting the formalistic characterization of narrowly defined activities it requires the contraction of the values underlying the rights to converge with the scope of the narrowly defined rights-based protected activities.

Under the first strategy—*the pragmatic strategy*—advocated by Joseph Raz, the ultimate justification for the use of rights protecting narrowly defined activities (rather than protecting all value-enhancing activities indiscriminately) is pragmatic. Ideally we would want to protect the values by protecting all activities and interests that are conducive to the values, but disagreement about what the values dictate requires the use of rights as an intermediate, 'so that not every time a practical question arises does one refer to ultimate values'.[20] This is so 'not only because it saves time and tediousness, but primarily because it enables a common culture to be formed around shared intermediate conclusions in spite of a great degree of haziness and disagreement concerning ultimate values'.[21]

Obviously there are institutional advantages in protecting well-defined activities such as speech and religion, rather than in identifying

---

[20] Raz, *The Morality of Freedom*, 181 (n 1).
[21] Raz, *The Morality of Freedom*, 181 (n 1).

the activities that are value enhancing. Yet, contrary to Raz, it seems that the disputes concerning the values often spill over to disputes concerning the rights themselves. The debates concerning the scope of the right to free speech illustrate the degree to which disputes concerning the values inevitably are translated to disputes about the scope of rights.

Further, the protected activities are often cherished in a way that does not facilitate challenging the protection, on the grounds that protecting the practice is not conducive to the relevant values. It is often (although not always) sufficient to identify the activity as speech (and in particular, political speech) in order to trigger the conclusion that it is value enhancing. Challenging the contribution of political speech to the value of autonomy or self-realization would not typically lead one to abandon the protection of speech, but merely to look for a different rationale or to interpret the value of autonomy or self-realization more broadly. The protected activities form fixed points of reference for the discourse of rights; they are not regarded as mere means to realize the values underlying them—means which can be dispensed with once it is shown that the value does not support the protection of the activity. Of course a theory of rights can dismiss this sentiment. But to the extent that a theory of rights wishes to be faithful to the sensibilities characterizing the discourse of rights, it needs to account for this sentiment.

The pragmatic view does not fully explain the great appeal of the protected activities, and the importance attributed to them in the discourse of rights. It suffers from what I labelled in the introduction insincerity or inauthenticity; it fails to identify the real underlying motivations and rationales for cherishing the protected activities. I would argue that the great importance attributed to the rights-based protected activities is the by-product of the role these activities have in facilitating the realization of the values underlying them. In the absence of protected practices that facilitate the realization of auton-omy, autonomy would remain abstract, and could not be realized in the lives of individuals.

The second strategy—*the rationalist human rights paradigm*—defends the primacy of values hypothesis and endorses its consequences, includ-ing the rejection of what I have labelled the differential treatment of activities. As this paradigm has become influential, and as it is often presented as an alternative to the traditional protection of narrowly tailored rights, let me present this paradigm in some detail.

Under the 'rationalist human rights paradigm', the discourse of rights and, in particular, the legal or constitutional discourse ought to distance itself from its fetishistic obsession with the well-defined 'classical catalogue of rights', and require instead a justification for any act of public authorities in terms of public reason.[22] Under this view, rights ought to be understood in broad terms, and the discourse of rights ought to reject the arbitrary, rigid, traditional focus on distinct narrowly defined interests and activities such as speech, religion, or privacy (as, indeed, it does in practice, in certain jurisdictions). It is argued that instead, rights ought to protect a broad, comprehensive set of liberty-based or autonomy-based interests. As a matter of fact, instead of identifying rights on the basis of the type of activities or interests they uphold, rights ought to be identified on the basis of the values they promote or help to realize.

There are many variations of this theme, for example those advocated by, among others Robert Alexy,[23] Aharon Barak,[24] Mattias Kumm,[25] Moshe Cohen-Eliya and Iddo Porat,[26] Kai Moller,[27] and many others. This view has become highly influential among constitutional theorists, in particular those who are influenced by the German Constitutional Court, the European Court of Human Rights, the Canadian Supreme Court, and the Israeli Supreme Court. Most importantly, the rationalist human rights paradigm challenges the view that rights protect narrowly defined activities that do not fully converge with the underlying values. Speech, religion, and privacy are all instantiations of the values underlying their protection, e.g., autonomy. Let me present some of the more influential versions of this paradigm, and challenge them.

Robert Alexy believes that constitutional rights operate as principles, and principles are demands for optimization that are subjected to a

---

[22] Mattias Kumm, 'The Idea of Socratic Contestation and the Right to Justification: The Point of Rights-Based Proportionality Review', 4 *Law and Ethics of Human Rights* 142, 143 (2010).

[23] Robert Alexy, *A Theory of Constitutional Rights*, trans. Julian Rivers (Oxford: Oxford University Press, 2002).

[24] Aharon Barak, 'Foreword: A Judge on Judging. The Role of a Supreme Court in a Democracy', 116 *Harv. L. Rev.* 19 (2002–3).

[25] Kumm, 'The Idea of Socratic Contestation' (n 22).

[26] Moshe Cohen-Eliya and Iddo Porat, 'Proportionality and the Culture of Justification', 59 *American Journal of Comparative Law* 463 (2011).

[27] Kai Moller, *The Global Model of Constitutional Rights* (Oxford: Oxford University Press, 2012).

proportionality analysis.[28] Under his view, statements concerning principles are structurally equivalent to statements of value.[29] Alexy rejects the narrowly defined lists of rights in favour of general rights to liberty and equality. He further argues that this is a faithful description of the rights jurisprudence of the German Constitutional Court.

Aharon Barak maintains that 'the role of the judge [is] to give effect to democracy by ruling in accordance with democratic values and foundational principles. In my view, fundamental principles (or values) fill the normative universe of a democracy. They justify legal rules. They are the reason for changing them. They are the spirit (*voluntas*) that encompasses the substance (*verba*). Every norm that is created in a democracy is created against the background of these values.'[30] Barak continues and sides with Justice Dickson's statement saying that: 'The underlying values and principles of a free and democratic society are the genesis of the rights and freedoms guaranteed by the Charter and the ultimate standard against which a limit on a right or freedom must be shown, despite its effect, to be reasonable and demonstrably justified.'[31]

Mattias Kumm argues that the interests protected as rights are not restricted to the 'classical catalogue of rights such as freedom of speech, association, religion and privacy narrowly conceived'.[32] Instead, the discourse of rights is primarily about the process of public justification as such. Kumm identifies the values of the discourse as grounded in the virtues of 'Socratic contestation'.[33] In describing the emerging practice of rights protection in Europe, Kumm argues:

Human and constitutional rights practice in Europe is, to a significant extent, not legalist but rationalist. It is generally focused not on the interpretation of legal authority, but on the justification of acts of public authorities in terms of public reason...Both the German Constitutional Court and ECJ, for example, recognise a general right to liberty and a general right to equality. That means that just any act infringing on interests of individuals trigger are

---

[28] Alexy, *A Theory of Constitutional Rights*, 47–8 (n 23).

[29] Alexy, *A Theory of Constitutional Rights*, 92–3 (n 23).

[30] Barak, 'Foreword', 41 (n 24).

[31] Barak, 'Foreword', 44 (n 24).

[32] Kumm, 'Political Liberalism' (n 7).

[33] Mattias Kumm, 'Institutionalizing Socratic Contestation: The Rationalist Human Rights Paradigm, Legitimate Authority and the Point of Judicial Review', 1 *European Journal of Legal Studies* 1 (2007).

open up for a constitutional or human rights challenge and requires to be justified in terms of public reason.[34]

Cohen-Eliya and Porat pursue this line of thought and identify a transition from a 'culture of authority' to a 'culture of justification'. In their view: 'At its core, a culture of justification requires that governments should provide substantive justification for all their actions, by which we mean justification in terms of the rationality and reasonableness of every action and the trade-offs that every action necessarily involves, i.e., in terms of proportionality.'[35] A culture of authority is founded on the premiss that the 'legitimacy and legality of governmental action is derived from the fact that the actor is authorized to act'. In contrast, in a culture of justification, the 'crucial component in the legitimacy and legality of governmental action is that it is justified in terms of its "cogency" and its capacity for "persuasion," that is, in terms of its rationality and reasonableness'.[36]

Lastly, in a recent book on global constitutionalism Kai Moller defended a similar view and questioned the need for a set of distinct constitutional rights on the grounds that 'nothing would be lost in theory by simply acknowledging a comprehensive right to personal autonomy'.[37] Moller also added:

This section proposes and defends the idea of a general right to personal autonomy. In a nutshell, it relies on two arguments to reach this conclusion. First, any attempt to limit the scope of rights to certain especially important autonomy interests will come at the price of incoherence of the underlying conception of autonomy; thus, the only way to avoid this incoherence is to include all autonomy interests in the scope of rights. Second, in order to defend the claim of a right to autonomy, one must abandon the idea that rights hold a special normative force (for example, that they act as trumps or side constraints); rather their point and purpose is to give the right-holder an entitlement to have his autonomy interests adequately protected at all times. . . . Hence, one ought to reject the independent existence of separate and distinct rights and turns instead to the values underlying the right.[38]

---

[34] Kumm, 'Institutionalizing Socratic Contestation', 5 (n 33).
[35] Eliya-Cohen and Porat, 'Proportionality and the Culture of Justification', 466–7 (n 26).
[36] Eliya-Cohen and Porat, 'Proportionality and the Culture of Justification', 475 (n 26).
[37] Moller, *The Global Model of Constitutional Rights*, 88 (n 27).
[38] Moller, *The Global Model of Constitutional Rights*, 73 (n 27).

Moller continues and suggests that:

For framers of new constitutions, the idea of a comprehensive right to personal autonomy calls into question the necessity of a set of distinct constitutional rights. Nothing would be lost in theory by simply acknowledging one comprehensive prima facie right to personal autonomy instead.[39]

Even under the rationalist human rights paradigm, the protection of narrowly defined rights could serve important institutional and pragmatic concerns, and could therefore be justified as a judicial strategy. Perhaps protecting a general right to autonomy (rather than particular rights to freedom of speech, religion, and privacy) may in the long run be destructive of personal autonomy.[40] Specifying well-defined spheres of protected rights may focus public attention on those spheres in which autonomy is particularly vulnerable and fragile. Yet, in principle, on this view the only constitutional right worth protecting is a general right to autonomy, liberty, or equality.

There are important differences between these theories which I am not going to explore here. For my purposes what is crucial is that the rationalist human rights paradigm rejects the view that rights protect narrowly defined activities such as speech or religion. Rights-based reasoning is ultimately value-based reasoning. To determine whether a person has a right one ought to explore whether the grand values of autonomy, equality, and dignity require the protection of an activity or an interest. The special protection of well-defined activities such as speech, religion, and privacy may at best be justified on institutional or pragmatic grounds, but they are not features which a normative theory of rights ought to explain or address on principled grounds.

The advocates of the rationalist human rights paradigm defend it both as a descriptive view (describing the way the German Constitutional Court, the European Court of Human Rights, and other constitutional courts operate) and as a normative view (concerning the way constitutional courts ought to operate). Most typically they contrast the paradigm with the way the American courts operate. In their view, US courts differ from European jurisdictions precisely on the grounds that they are disposed to protect well-defined activities rather than ground

[39] Moller, *The Global Model of Constitutional Rights*, 88 (n 27).
[40] Moller, *The Global Model of Constitutional Rights*, 89–90 (n 27).

their decisions in the underlying values and protect all the value-enhancing activities and interests.[41]

I disagree with the claims made by the rationalist paradigm; claims which, if taken to their logical extreme, obliterate the distinction between rights and policy or rights and rational governance. First, despite the evidence provided by the advocates of the rationalist human rights paradigm, the rationalist paradigm deviates too radically from the way rights are discussed, understood, and, most importantly, practiced even in the German and European jurisdictions. Even if courts are less strict in adhering to the traditional catalogues of rights, these catalogues are still relevant, and form a significant part of the discourse of rights. In addition to the broad provisions in the German Basic Law protecting dignity and free development of the personality, the German Basic Law entrenches many specific rights, and such an entrenchment cannot be dismissed as a relic of the past. Given the long tradition of constitutionally entrenched specific 'catalogues of rights', a theory of rights ought, at least, to account for these catalogues on principled grounds.

Further, Kumm and other advocates of the rationalist paradigm emphasize the broadness and diffuse nature of rights. Rights in their view are identified with the virtues of critical thinking, reasons-based deliberation, 'Socratic contestation', and 'a culture of justification'. Nobody would dispute that Socratic contestation and a culture of justification are desirable features of public life. Yet, they are as desirable in determining the rates of interests of central banks and the size of the budget as they are in determining whether hate speech ought to be criminalized and/or whether homosexuals can be excluded from the army. Despite the willingness of advocates of the rationalist human rights tradition to extend the scope of rights much beyond traditional boundaries, there are significant spheres of public life that are not governed by rights. Rights cannot be simply equated with the duty of public authorities to use reason in making decisions, because such a requirement is called for not only in the context of rights.

In defending the rationalist human rights paradigm, Alexy, Kumm, and other advocates of the rationalist paradigm point out that the European and the German courts are willing to protect relatively trivial liberty-based interests such as a right to ride horses through public

---

[41] Kumm, 'The Idea of Socratic Contestation', 151 (n 22).

woods, feed pigeons in public squares, smoke marijuana, and bring a particular breed of dog into the country.[42] Hence they conclude that what courts protect are not the traditional well-defined rights but a general right to liberty and/or equality.

This conclusion is too hasty. Even if there is a general constitutionally protected right to liberty and equality as Alexy and Kumm maintain, this does not imply that there is no distinctive value in the well-defined rights protecting narrowly defined activities including those protected by the 'catalogues of rights'. The mere fact that courts recognize a general right to liberty does not imply that the classical rights are redundant and/or that these rights can simply be derived by the general right to liberty. Alexy and Kumm are right in that the reliance on abstract values may often open the possibility for expanding (or contracting) the scope of protected activities, either by creating new protected activities or by expanding (or contracting) the scope of existing protected activities. This expansion may be desirable, and indeed the argument developed in section C3 supports the desirability of such an expansion. Yet, I will argue that this does not undermine the need for distinct narrowly tailored rights. In fact my argument in section C3 will be designed to show that the rights enumerated in the 'catalogues of rights' are at least sometimes necessary to facilitate the realization of the underlying values.

Lastly, even if the rationalist paradigm successfully addresses the differential treatment of activities, it fails to address the first puzzle I identified, namely the differential treatment of reasons. Autonomy, liberty, and equality are central concerns of a liberal society, but they are not the only concerns worth pursuing. There are other competing goods that society should strive to achieve. Why should autonomy-based concerns be classified as 'rights' while other concerns are relegated to the non-rights category? What is it that makes autonomy-based concerns or equality-based concerns so different from other utilitarian concerns? These are questions that are not satisfactorily addressed by the rationalist paradigm.

In his discussion of freedom of speech, Joshua Cohen resorts to a third strategy—*the narrowly tailored values hypothesis*. In Cohen's view, an adequate understanding of the rationales for protecting expression requires delineating a narrower category of grounds or reasons than

---

[42] Kumm, 'Political Liberalism and the Structure of Rights', 141 (n 7).

the more traditional value of autonomy. This is precisely because autonomy protects many more activities than expression or religion. Therefore, to defend the practice of protecting expression (and, perhaps, other narrowly defined rights), it is necessary to identify values that are narrower in scope and which can justify the protection of expression and not other activities. In other words, Cohen believes that there are 'free expression values'—values which are specifically designed to justify the protection of free expression.[43]

In defending the right to free expression, Cohen identifies three types of underlying interests 'that are protected by stringent assurances of expressive liberty and whose importance makes the demand for substantial protection reasonable'.[44] The three interests identified as the grounds of the right to free speech include the expressive, deliberative, and informational interests. Those interests underlie the protection of speech. Like the advocates of the rationalist paradigm, Cohen believes that there is (at least in theory) a complete convergence between the values justifying the right to free expression and the scope of the protected right. Yet he reaches this conclusion using precisely the opposite strategy from that used by advocates of the rationalist paradigm. Unlike the advocates of the rationalist paradigm, the convergence is not the by-product of broadening the scope of the protected activities and granting an indiscriminate protection of all autonomy-enhancing activities, namely by eliminating the allegedly arbitrary specification of distinct autonomy-enhancing activities such as speech or religion. Instead, the convergence between the right to free expression and the values underlying it is the by-product of constructing well-defined narrow values that are designed to justify only the protection of the narrowly defined activity, e.g., expression.

Even if Cohen can explain the protection of a right to freedom of expression on the basis of these three interests, it is almost inconceivable that all rights can be explained on similar grounds, and indeed Cohen does not aim to extend his analysis to other rights. Further, while Cohen can account for the differential treatment of activities, he cannot explain on principled grounds the differential treatment of reasons and values, namely why expressive interests give rise to rights and justify classifying the activities designed to enhance these values as rights while other interests and values do not give rise to rights.

---

[43] Joshua Cohen, 'Freedom of Expression', 22 *Philosophy and Public Affairs* 207 (1993).
[44] Cohen, 'Freedom of Expression', 223 (n 43).

More generally, I believe that the differential treatment of reasons and activities are fundamental features characterizing the discourse of some rights—features which, if only possible, must be explained (rather than explained away). The tension between the conviction that the intrinsic reasons or values (e.g., autonomy) is what is ultimately important (and, consequently, what justifies the protection of rights) and the fact that the legal or political protection is granted to narrowly defined activities (and not indiscriminately to all value-enhancing activities) is a central characteristic of the discourse of rights and, I shall argue, the key to understanding the distinctive function of at least some rights.

To provide an adequate explanation for this tension, I argue in section C3 that the effective protection of some values requires the construction and protection through rights of conventionally recognized activities and practices designed to sustain and facilitate the realization of the values. By protecting speech for the sake of autonomy, the polity does not simply protect an activity which is autonomy enhancing. As a matter of fact, by protecting a right to free expression the polity contributes to the construction of a practice within which the exercise of autonomy becomes possible.

3. The Dependence of Values on Rights: Defending the Reciprocity Hypothesis

This subsection adds an additional layer to the traditional primacy of values hypothesis. While the primacy of values hypothesis points out that rights derive their normative force from the intrinsic reasons/ values underlying the rights, I show below that legal or political rights help to facilitate the realization of these values. Political and legal rights, as well as the litigation and political discourse triggered by these rights, are components of a variety of societal practices which must be sustained to facilitate the realization of (certain) values. More particularly, I defend the view that autonomy can be effectively exercised only when a set of activities is legally, politically, and socially identified as an arena suitable for the exercise of autonomy. In the absence of identifying such practices and sustaining them autonomy cannot be successfully exercised. The legal or political entrenchment of rights contributes to the forming of such social practices, and is thus essential for the realization of the values underlying the rights. I shall focus my discussion on autonomy, although I believe that a similar analysis could apply to other values that are perceived as intrinsic to rights, such as dignity.

In his attempt to explain the concept of 'socially constituted goods', Joseph Raz argues that some goods are 'socially created goods'. Socially created goods owe their goodness to the social practices that bring them into existence. Raz argues that there are two ways in which social practices can give rise to value:

On the one hand, it is possible that values and goods are created or maintained in existence by social practices, and the shared beliefs and understandings which are part of them. I will call practices which bring into existence goods or values, or sustain them in existence sustaining practices. On the other hand, it is possible that shared understandings affect not the existence of values and goods, but our ability to learn of them, and perhaps to benefit from them. Such practices control access to the values and the goods concerned.[45]

Raz points out that social practices have two important roles in facilitating the realization of values. First, some values are created and sustained by social practices. Raz believes that social practices 'thicken the texture' of societal goods and 'allow them to develop greater subtlety and nuance'.[46] New socially created goods develop only once the practices sustaining them are created. These goods are not merely new manifestations of existing values; they are indeed new values, which emerge with the practices sustaining them. Second, access to certain values depends on the societal understanding of these values and the transmission of this knowledge. Such transmission depends on the possession of concepts which are sustained and created by social practices.[47] To live an autonomous life, certain choices need to be made 'autonomously'; yet facilitating the realization of autonomy requires sustaining institutions such as marriage and practices that facilitate choosing one's partner such as dating.

This section uses Raz's observations concerning 'socially created goods' to clarify the relations between some rights and the values underlying these rights. More particularly it argues that the entrenchment

---

[45] Joseph Raz, *Engaging Reason: On the Theory of Value and Action* (Oxford: Oxford University Press, 1999), 147.

[46] Raz, *Engaging Reason*, 205 (n 45).   [47] Raz, *Engaging Reason*, 204–5 (n 45).

of legal or political rights is in itself a value-sustaining practice; in particular it is a practice that facilitates access to values.

There are two important observations that I ought to make at the outset. First, I focus in this part on Raz's second theme, namely on the claim that social practices are necessary to facilitate access to the values, rather than on the first theme, namely that the existence of the values depends on social practices. This focus is not accidental; the thesis concerning access to values is much less controversial and I do not wish for my analysis to depend upon the highly controversial first claim. To the extent that the first theme is also defensible, it may even strengthen the argument I develop here.

Second, as mentioned above, I do not explore all the values that are considered to be intrinsic; instead, I focus on autonomy. Autonomy is particularly useful for my purposes, as it is considered to be among the most cherished values that justify the protection of many rights. Some theorists of rights even believe that autonomy is the sole value which underlies all rights.[48] But, even if this is not so, it is clearly among the most paradigmatic values that justifies the protection of rights. I shall argue that to exercise autonomy certain social practices need to be established, and that entrenching legal or political rights protecting certain designated activities is a practice that contributes to and facilitates the exercise of autonomy.

Let me start with the observation that the value of autonomy (like many other values) may remain unfulfilled or unrealized if individuals do not exercise their autonomy. This implies that it is essential not only to protect autonomy but also to facilitate its realization.

This is part of a more general theme. Values in general, as Raz maintains, depend on 'valuers for their realization, for the value of objects with value is fulfilled only through being appreciated'.[49] More specifically, Raz argues:

That the value of objects remains unfulfilled, if not valued, is explained and further supported by a familiar fact. That an object has value can have an impact on how things are in the world only through being recognized. The normal and appropriate way in which the value of things influences matters

---

[48] Moller, *The Global Model of Constitutional Rights* (n 27).

[49] Joseph Raz, *The Practice of Value* (Tanner Lectures on Human Values, delivered at Berkeley, 2001), 124.

in the world is by being appreciated—that is respected and engaged with because they are realized to be of value."[50]

Let me apply this general observation to the case of autonomy. Autonomy makes people's life better if, and to the extent that, they exercise it in their lives. The exercise of autonomy can take different forms. For instance, one can exercise autonomy by actively participating in political activity or by choosing to abstain from participation. Yet the choice to be autonomous ought to be informed by appropriate reasoning. A person who 'chooses' his political views on the basis of the physical attributes of the candidates fails to exercise autonomy (or at least fails to exercise autonomy in a valuable way).

Acquiring the skills to exercise autonomy in a particular arena requires a certain environment that is conducive to autonomy. To see why, think first of how to instruct or guide a person to exercise his or her autonomy. What does it take for autonomy to be exercised? It is sufficient to raise such questions in order to see that the task of instructing or guiding people to exercise their autonomy seems impossible in the absence of a rich cultural and contextual background as to the type of choices that ought to be made and the type of considerations that ought to be taken into account in making such choices.

A useful starting point is to instruct the agent to exercise choice in a particular context and/or with respect to a certain activity. Thus a person can be instructed to make a choice with respect to a favourite political party, to choose a spouse, to select a favourite course at university, or to choose a profession. Not any choice made in these spheres would count as an autonomous choice or, even if it did count as an autonomous choice, it would not count as a valuable autonomous choice, namely as a choice that explains why autonomy is protected in the first place. To exercise autonomous choices in a valuable way, one needs to know what the criteria upon which the selection of spouses, professions, or political platforms ought to be based. Could I autonomously follow blindly (without further reflection) the spouse that is favoured by my parents or by religious authorities? Could I autonomously vote for the political party that is recommended to me by my religious instructor, my psychologist, or my spouse? Do such choices constitute autonomous choices? Could I autonomously choose my spouse by conducting a lottery among all potential partners who

---

[50] Raz, *The Practice of Value*, 28 (n 49).

consent to participate in such a lottery? Would such a method of 'choice' be a futile or an inappropriate exercise of autonomy, or perhaps, not an exercise of autonomy at all?

These are difficult questions and, presumably some of the methods proposed above and the resulting decisions should be considered a genuine exercise of autonomy while others probably should not. Sometimes it is difficult to draw the line between an autonomous choice that is wrong (choosing the wrong spouse or an inappropriate profession) and a decision that is not autonomous at all as it fails to identify the relevant reasons on the basis of which such choices ought to be made. Blindly following the advice of my parents would presumably (at least in most cases) not be a genuine exercise of autonomy. A lottery is a creative and an ingenious idea for choosing spouses. It may even relieve one of the agonies and uncertainties that are involved in making such a choice. But even if the decision to marry the winner of such a lottery should count as an autonomous choice, it is hardly the method for the sake of which autonomy is being legally protected.

Note the difference between a lottery and selecting one's partner on the basis of his wealth, or purely on the basis of sexual attraction. The latter choices may be ones that one ought not to make and perhaps the chooser may be criticized for having made them. But I believe that they are ones that still can plausibly be perceived as autonomous choices and, further, they still constitute methods for the sake of which autonomy is being legally protected. Selection of a spouse on the basis of wealth is not a choice that merits praise but it is one that merits a degree of deference on the part of the state. In contrast, selecting one's partner on the basis of a lottery cannot even count as a type of choice for the sake of which autonomy is being protected.

These examples illustrate the significance of creating a culture that facilitates the exercise of autonomous choices. To facilitate autonomous choices, a common culture has to be formed—a culture which establishes conventional rationales underlying autonomous choices, identifies the paradigmatic cases of autonomous choices, and determines the appropriate deliberation preceding the choice. Choices such as the choice to establish a political party or to support a particular political agenda are important because they reflect judgments concerning what is just or unjust, and those judgments merit respect because and to the extent that they are likely to be correct judgments. In such cases the autonomous choice merits respect to the extent that it has been reached by rational deliberation, weighing the pros and cons of each decision. In contrast in choosing a spouse or a profession, autonomous choices reflect tastes and preferences that presumably make the life of the person who made the choice better off. In such cases instincts and intuitions should govern the choice. In contracts, autonomy implies the ability to bind oneself in the future in order to facilitate the realization of life plans. With wills and sexual relationships, autonomy implies the power to change one's mind whenever one is inclined to do so. The variety and complexity of what autonomous choices are in different contexts requires sustaining practices, institutions, and a common culture that will guide, instruct, and give effect to choices that meet the designated criteria.

Political and legal entrenchment of rights helps to construct such a common culture and therefore to facilitate the exercise of autonomy. By protecting paradigmatic cases of valuable autonomous choices, denying protection in cases in which the decision was not reached in the designated ways and elaborating the rationales underlying such decisions, the legal system contributes to the formation of autonomy-enhancing practices. Further, constructing such a culture often requires not merely the protection of a right but also establishing and sustaining other institutional practices that reflect the respect owed to autonomously made choices.

Examine the justificatory relationship between political speech and autonomy. The advocate of the primacy of values hypothesis contends that political speech is an autonomy-enhancing activity and therefore it ought to be protected. Under this view the autonomy-enhancing potential of speech does not depend upon the question of whether speech is protected or not. In contrast, I suggest that political speech becomes an autonomy-enhancing activity *as a result* of being protected, being recognized as an autonomy-enhancing activity, becoming the subject-matter of litigation, etc. In societies in which the right to free political speech is protected for the sake of autonomy, people exercise their autonomy via speech. The recognition that autonomy can be exercised via speech is internalized and perfected; the appropriate forms of deliberation develop and, as a result, individuals can be said to 'exercise their autonomy'. Autonomy after all is an abstract concept; exercising autonomy requires the making of choices in particularly designated spheres that are publicly acknowledged to be autonomy-enhancing spheres because only such public acknowledgment facilitates the exercise of autonomy.

The meaningfulness of the autonomous choices hinges on broad and subtle societal understandings, as well as institutional facts and practices. To make free choices in the realm of politics such choices must have political effects. A monarchy can presumably protect (or at least not curtail) one's rights to promulgate political opinions, to protest against political decisions, and to oppose government policies. But given that in a monarchy (at least the monarchy I construct here) those political opinions have no real impact, the choice to form such opinions and to promulgate them does not have the same significance that such a choice has in a democratic society—a society in which public opinion matters. This does not imply of course that people cannot form autonomous political opinions in a monarchy; only that democracy is superior in facilitating the formation of such opinions because such opinions have real effects.

Autonomous choices may merit respect for different reasons. Some choices, such as the choice to promulgate political opinions merit respect because they are publicly acknowledged to be founded on valuable individual judgments. The autonomy-enhancing value of such choices hinges on the fact that they are deliberative and rational. In other cases (such as in the case of marriage) choices matter because they are perceived to reflect individual tastes and preferences. Choosing whom to marry or what profession to acquire matter because such choices are 'authentic'; they are grounded in one's identity, tastes, or preferences and thus merit respect. But to guide individuals as to which forms of deliberation are genuinely autonomous, practices need to be formed and sustained. Presumably the legal doctrines that govern different spheres of choice (e.g., the political sphere, or the sphere of intimacy) are designed to promote and facilitate choices that are appropriate for the relevant sphere.

If these observations are correct, the autonomy-enhancing potential of speech or any other choice hinges on sustaining practices in which such choices matter and, often, such practices include the legal entrenchment of rights protecting certain activities such as speech or religion. The heightened protection of political speech serves to bolster the significance of political activity and its potential contribution to the self-definition and self-realization of citizens. The successful exercise of autonomy in forming a family, or choosing a vocation, depend upon public acknowledgement of the value of these choices as reflecting one's identity, tastes, and preferences. Lastly, under this hypothesis the protection of freedom of religion contributes to the fact that religions have remained arenas in which individuals find their spiritual destiny. The special constitutional protection of religion indicates that choices to be or not to be religious are important and significant above and beyond the question of which, if any, religious conviction is 'correct' or justified.

Further, it is not merely that constitutional protection of designated activities matters; what also matters is the resulting litigation concerning the scope of rights and their strength. Litigation serves to identify the forms of deliberation which merit protection in each and every sphere, and to identify the appropriate scope of protection, and to reveal the underlying rationales for protecting autonomous choices. Litigation helps to disseminate information, identify the complexities of exercising choice, expose dilemmas, and enrich the practice of exercising autonomy. Litigation also draws public interest, and recruits individuals who take sides and support or oppose the cause. Because litigation also prompts different ideological groups to join the controversy and to explore how their political and ideological commitments bear on the controversy it contributes to the establishment and the perfection of the social practices that facilitate the realization of autonomy.

It follows that to facilitate access to autonomy it is necessary to establish certain conventions as to the type of activities that need to be protected, the boundaries of the protection, and the rationales underlying the protection. Legally entrenched rights give rise to such conventions and practices. Yes, as advocates of the primacy of values point out, rights are indeed grounded in values but, to facilitate the realization of these values it is necessary to entrench certain conventions and the political or legal protection of narrowly tailored rights contributes to the emergence of such conventions. Hence, the protection of specific activities such as speech, religion, or the integrity of the family are not merely pragmatic institutional devices designed to overcome institutional deficiencies. The protection of such spheres of activity is necessary for the emergence of a public culture that facilitates in turn the exercise of autonomous choices. The value of both autonomy and specific rights protecting distinct spheres of activity is indispensable for sustaining a liberal autonomy-enhancing society; the values are indispensable for identifying which activities merit protection and the narrowly defined rights are indispensable for guiding, instructing, and ultimately facilitating autonomous choices. Rights are not therefore dispensable, and values cannot, even in principle, replace them effectively.

But do not people have a right to make choices autonomously, even when no such culture exists? Assume that you are living in a society which does not recognize the right of individuals to make choices concerning their marital partner. Most people in that society lack 'access to the value of autonomy' or, at least, lack the necessary understanding of what it means to choose one's partner and why it is important. Yet suddenly and unexpectedly Juliet falls in love with Romeo and she 'chooses' autonomously to pursue a relationship with him. Should she not have such a right even when she is the only one that is capable of exercising such a choice? And, if so, it seems that even in a society in which most or even all people are incapable of exercising choice, a right to make such a choice ought to be recognized if only for the exceptional Juliet!

It seems right to protect Juliet's choice in such a case. Perhaps an exception could be made in such a society to enable Juliet to exercise her choice. This may be valuable for Juliet, but this is not the only reason why rights are necessary. Rights under the view I propose have an additional important value: they facilitate the creation of a culture in which the exercise of autonomy can be made possible. To facilitate the exercise of rights, it is necessary to establish well-defined activities in which autonomous choices could be made on the basis of the right reasons. Those should be applied to normal cases rather than to the exceptional, and the contribution of legal rights to the establishment of practices that facilitate the exercise of autonomy is an important function of rights.

Let me end by making two observations supporting my proposal. First let me show that my proposal can account for the two puzzles identified in section C2: the differential treatment of reasons or values and the differential treatment of activities. Second, I wish to establish that my proposal explains why rights must in principle be salient features of public life. It is not enough that rights are maintained or preserved and/or not violated; they must be publicly acknowledged and protected for the right reasons.

As I have argued, under my view the coexistence of rights and values is essential to the viability of value-enhancing culture. The differential treatment of reasons or values, and the differential treatment of activities, are both necessary as some values, e.g., autonomy, need to be grounded in certain protected activities to maintain their vitality. To facilitate the exercise of autonomy, a common culture needs to be formed around certain identifiable activities. Such a culture needs to identify which choices ought to be protected; to guide individuals as to what counts as an autonomous choice; to facilitate the emergence of other practices which strengthen and enhance the significance of autonomous choices; etc. It is the dual nature that characterizes the discourse of rights—the values underlying rights on the one hand and the careful designation of certain well-defined protected activities such as speech and religion on the other hand—that can facilitate the valuable exercise of autonomy. Neither component is redundant; nor is either component reducible to the other.

The coexistence of values and protected activities which do not fully converge is not always a happy coexistence. At times it seems that the constraints imposed by rigid provisions protecting only certain activities are unintelligible or, more likely, too formalistic. In such cases one may be disposed to adopt the rationalist paradigm disposition and to be guided by the values rather than by the provisions defining the protected activities. But even in such cases the protected activities provide one with a guide as to how to extend and complement the rights in order to better reflect the values underlying them. Even if at times the protected activities seem arbitrary, they are important in facilitating the exercise of autonomy. At the same time, the delicate balance between the narrowly defined rights and the values underlying them is a dynamic one; it provides opportunities for expanding or contracting the protected activities, but it does not imply that the protection of rights (rather than values) is redundant.

Finally, the reciprocal relations between values and rights can explain the salience that rights have and indeed must have in a liberal society. In liberal societies rights are sometimes enshrined in constitutional documents, they are litigated in courts, and they are discussed in legislative and executive bodies. Many of the demands made by various groups are phrased in terms of rights, and controversies concerning rights are an integral part of political discourse.

These institutional mechanisms and processes are traditionally perceived to be instrumental; under this view, the institutions are designed to help and identify the proper scope of rights. Constitutional documents entrenching rights are means to guarantee that rights are not violated; courts are a means to protect rights against the potential encroachment by the executive or the legislature; etc. Arguably, in principle these institutions and mechanisms are dispensable; if a society is not inclined to violate rights, it is not necessary to entrench these rights in legal or constitutional documents, to debate about their boundaries, or to guarantee their salience in the public sphere.

If I am right, the traditional way of looking at the legal or political rights is flawed. The salience of rights is not merely a reflection of their pre-existing importance; it is what partially facilitates the realization of the values. In the absence of legal entrenchment of rights and their salience in the public sphere, the values underlying the rights could not even in principle be realized as individuals would be deprived of access to these values.

This analysis bears on the plausibility of the rationalist human rights paradigm, and in particular on Moller's proposal to defend a general constitutional right to 'autonomy-enhancing activities' without specifying the spheres in which autonomous choices count. My view implies that this proposal is simply self-defeating. A person cannot be asked to exercise her autonomy without specifying designated activities in which choices matter, without developing coherent rationales for the protection of such choices, and without a public culture which grants respect to choices made within these designated spheres. Such a public culture hinges on the existence of legally or politically entrenched rights. It also follows from this description that rights cannot be incidentally protected; they must instead be intentionally protected, and they must be protected for the right reasons. While some goods such as a clean environment do not require transparent rationales, i.e. rationales that are understood by those who promote such goods, the protection of rights requires attentiveness to the values underlying the rights.

For example, compare two states: state A and state B. State A does not protect the right to free speech; yet, incidentally, it does not violate the right. We may presume that it does not violate the right to free speech out of indifference to the speech. The politicians simply do not care what is being said. In contrast in state B speech is protected, and the boundaries of its protection are passionately litigated. The entrenchment of rights in society B is crucial for the emergence of a common culture of the type that facilitates access to autonomy. Under this view, it is not merely important to protect or not to infringe certain freedoms; it is important to protect them *for the sake of promoting autonomy*. Incidental protection or blind protection that is not attentive to the underlying values would inevitably fail to contribute to establishing a public culture that can facilitate the exercise of autonomy. It is this feature which I believe to be crucial for the understanding of some of the traditional rights, and which explains why some rights need to be differentiated from other important norms that promote other social concerns.

D. Summary

Advocates of the primacy of values hypothesis rightly argue that rights are grounded in values. But some values require the emergence of a common culture. In this chapter I have argued that the uneasy coexistence of narrowly tailored rights protecting specific activities and broad values underlying the rights is an essential feature of the discourse of rights. The legal and political entrenchment of rights contributes to the formation of a common culture which is necessary to facilitate the realization of autonomy. This observation implies that anti-formalist efforts to substitute rights with values (as recommended by the rationalist paradigm) are self-defeating. To promote autonomy, certain protected spheres of activity have to be designated. Such a designation is not merely useful for pragmatic or institutional reasons; it is an essential component which is necessary for sustaining an autonomy-enhancing culture.

PART II

Why the State Matters: Dignity, Agency, and the State

Introduction to Part II

Chapters 3 and 4 analyse, identify, and defend a view concerning the distinctive role of the state. In particular I claim that certain tasks must be performed by the state while others should be performed by private individuals. Chapter 3 identifies a type of decision which must be made (and executed) by the state (i.e., by public officials). It is argued that there are certain goods that are 'intrinsically public'; they cannot be provided by private individuals. Chapter 4 identifies a type of decision that must be made by private individuals. Both claims are grounded in dignity-based concerns.

Dignity, I argue, demands that decisions and actions be based on certain reasons. Dignity imposes constraints on the deliberation of the agents; it dictates not *what* agents ought to decide or do but primarily *how* they ought to reason. Further, I argue, deliberation is often agent dependent, such that only certain agents are capable of engaging in respectful deliberation. Thus an agent making a particular decision (or performing a certain act) ought to address not only the question of *why* she decides (or acts) in the way she did, but also to ask the question *who is she* to decide (or act) in the first place? More specifically, the chapters differentiate between public officials on the one hand and private individuals on the other hand, and maintain that there are decisions that must be made by public officials (Chapter 3) and other decisions that must be made by private individuals (Chapter 4). Authorizing the right agents to make these decisions or to perform these actions and precluding such authorization from other agents does not rest on contingent factors concerning the superiority of the former agents in deciding or acting justly or correctly. Instead, at times it is grounded in the identity of the agent or her status.

Dignity, under the view developed in this part, depends (at least sometimes) upon the identity of the deliberating agent: some agents are capable of deciding or acting in a respectful manner, while others are incapable of doing so. The latter's failure to deliberate in a respectful manner is not a result of any contingent flaws in their character; it is a matter of the political status of such agents, and their relations with the individuals whose dignity is at stake. Hence some agents ought to be barred from rendering certain decisions not because their decisions or their actions are likely to be wrong, flawed, or unjust, but because their decisions or actions cannot result from the required respectful deliberation. To illustrate by using an analogy: one may maintain that parents can make decisions with respect to their children *simply because of their status as parents* (and not necessarily because they have superior expertise in raising children in general or superior expertise in raising their own children, or because their educational strategies are likely to be correct);[1] and individuals can make decisions that impact the lives of their friends in certain ways (for example, interfering in their lives in ways that non-friends cannot) *simply because of their status as friends* (and not because they have superior knowledge or capacity).

This part explores the differences between public and private deliberation, i.e., deliberation conducted by public officials and deliberation conducted by private individuals. It develops the theme that dignity-based considerations dictate that certain decisions be relegated to public officials (as only their action constitutes an action of the state, and only an action of the state can successfully provide 'intrinsically public goods'), while other decisions must be made by private individuals. The difference between public and private agents does not follow from the superior or inferior capacity of the former or the latter to decide (or act) justly or rightly. It does not even rely on the alleged lack of accountability on the part of individual agents.[2] It follows, instead, directly from the type of deliberation that such agents are capable of

---

[1] This privilege of parents has been recognized in the common law. According to the common law the only agent for whom it is permissible to exercise the privilege of moderate chastisement would be a parent or, in special cases, somebody to whom the parent delegated the power, e.g., teachers. William Blackstone, *Commentaries on the Laws of England* (1769) (Chicago: University of Chicago, 1979), Book I, Chap. 16. Note of course that I am not committed to defend this view and do not want to argue here in favour of this privilege.

[2] This is the standard claim made by opponents of privatization. See, e.g., Martha Minow, 'Public and Private Partnerships: Accounting for the New Religion', 116 *Harvard Law Review* 1229 (2003).

engaging in (simply by virtue of their different status). Chapter 3 identifies decisions that must be made by the state (i.e., by public officials) while Chapter 4 identifies decisions that must be made by private individuals.

Chapter 3 draws a distinction between public officials and private individuals, and it establishes that only public officials may engage in the infliction of punishment and in the conduct of wars. Such activities ought not to be privatized not because public officials are more likely to make better or more just decisions or even decisions that are more faithful to the public interest, or to conduct these activities in a more humane way. Instead, only the deliberation of officials can be attributed to the state, and such an attribution is necessary for successfully making these decisions and acting on their basis. Punishment for instance conveys a judgment concerning the wrongfulness of one's behaviour. But not every agent is capable of making such a judgment; it is only those agents whose judgments can count legitimately as superior to the judgments of the person who is subjected to the punishment.[3]

Chapter 4 establishes that only private individuals may be engaged in certain activities in cases of emergency, such as torture or the shooting of a plane under 9/11 circumstances.[4] It is only the decision of private individuals (and never that of public officials) that can count as a truly exceptional rule-free decision that is not guided by general norms. Further, under exceptional circumstances, only truly rule-free decisions are ones that do not violate the dignity of the victims of the decision.

The use of rules or principles in exceptional cases presupposes the commensurability of human lives: some human lives may have to be sacrificed for the sake of protecting others. But, as human life has value

---

[3] 'Superiority' here does not necessarily imply epistemic superiority. It has to do with the legitimacy of the decision made by the relevant agent. Under this view, to justify the infliction of punishment it is not sufficient that the punishment is justified (or even likely to be justified given the epistemic qualities of the agent); it is also necessary that the agent inflicting it has power to do so. See, e.g., John Simmons, 'Locke and the Right to Punish', 20 *Philosophy and Public Affairs* 311, 312 (1991). Simmons argues: 'neither one's general level of virtue nor one's particular talents in the area of punishing . . . are normally taken to establish any special claim to be the one who should punish others.'

[4] This is based on the famous German plane case decided by the German Constitutional Court. In this case the German court decided that a statute authorizing the Defence Minister to order the shooting down of a plane in 9/11 situations is unconstitutional. See BVerfGE 2006 115.

but no price, no such exchange value can be fixed and, consequently, the use of rule-based reasoning is impermissible. As the acts of the state, namely acts performed by public officials, are governed by rule-based practices, it follows that the state cannot act on the basis of these judgments. Dignity requires that in cases of emergency, sacrificing the lives of one person for the sake of others is permissible only when it is perceived to be an exceptional, unprincipled act, i.e., when it does not indicate a commitment to comparative evaluation of the lives of one person against another.

The analysis in this part challenges the instrumentalism that infects much of contemporary political and legal debates. It challenges the conviction that what is right and wrong can be determined independently of the agent who makes the decision and, consequently, that selecting the right agent to perform an enterprise is simply and invariably a matter of selecting the agent that is more likely to identify what the just decision is and act accordingly. It shifts the type of considerations bearing on the question of 'who the appropriate agent is' from considerations concerning the likely correctness or justness of the resulting decision or action, to considerations concerning the legitimacy of the agent to make the decision. It also shows that the persistent hostility to phenomena as diverse as private prisons and the use of mercenaries in security operations and wars is rooted in an unarticulated conviction—the conviction that, at least in some cases, an act (such as punishment) cannot acquire its public nature (i.e., judgment made by the polity concerning the wrongfulness of an act) independently of the identity of the actor. Consequently, the person subject to punishment may justifiably challenge the decision or the act not by asking *why* you made such a decision or performed such an act, but by asking *who you are* to make such a decision. Respectful deliberation performed by the appropriate agent has its own demands—demands that are independent of and, at times, may even conflict with the urge to authorize agents who are the most capable of rendering the right decisions, or identifying correctly what is just or prudent or desirable.[5]

---

[5] Further, at least in Chapter 3 I argue that (within certain limits) the traditional view is not merely incomplete (in that if fails to acknowledge the significance of choosing the right agent), but it ought to be inverted on its head. Under the traditional view one ought to judge who is the best agent to perform a task on the basis of who is most likely to identify what the right or just decision is. For instance, a judge is assigned with the task of inflicting a criminal sanction because she is capable of and willing to inflict the proportionate sanction. Instead, I argue that (within certain limits) one ought to judge whether a decision is right or just on the basis of who made the decision.

The duty resulting from dignity that is in focus in these chapters is the duty to deliberate in respectful ways—ways that convey the appropriate attitude towards others. The deliberation required of the agent depends upon their status; in particular, it is contingent upon the question of whether she is an agent of the state (a public official) or a private individual. One may raise the question of what makes dignity the most appropriate value underlying these normative conclusions. As I say relatively little on the concept of dignity in the following two chapters, the rest of this introductory part briefly addresses the issue of dignity and, in particular, asks why dignity is the most appropriate value underlying the choice of an agent to make a decision or perform an act.[6]

As many writers on dignity concede, dignity is an elusive concept.[7] It is often difficult, if not impossible, to identify dignity as the value underlying a right. While both autonomy and equality are highly contested values, dignity seems to be even more vague than autonomy or equality.[8] Further, violations of dignity-based concerns often involve other values such as equality and autonomy and it is sometimes difficult to see what the distinctive contribution of dignity is to judgments that can be grounded in values such as equality or autonomy.[9] In some contexts the concept of dignity is equated with human rights as such, and such an equation is perceived by political theorists to be founded on confusion.[10] The vagueness of the concept of dignity also explains why opposing sides in contemporary disputes often resort to dignity to justify conflicting rights claims.[11] Arguably the inherent

---

[6] At the same time, I believe that my conclusions in this chapter can be grounded in values other than dignity. Dignity is a natural but not the only way to reach the conclusions I reach in this chapter.

[7] Tarunabh Khaitan, 'Dignity as an Expressive Norm: Neither Vacuous Nor a Panacea', 1 *Oxford Journal of Legal Studies* (2011); Neomi Rao, 'On the Use and Abuse of Dignity in Constitutional Law', 14 *Columbia Journal of European Law* 201, 211, 218 (2008). These concerns have also been echoed in the courts. See, e.g., *R v Kapp* 2008 SCC 41. The Canadian Supreme Court raised the concern that dignity is 'an abstract and subjective notion' that 'can become confusing and difficult to apply'.

[8] Khaitan, 'Dignity as an Expressive Norm', 3 (n 7).

[9] Khaitan, 'Dignity as an Expressive Norm', 3 (n 7).

[10] Jack Donnelly, 'Human Rights and Human Dignity: An Analytic Critique of Non-Western Conceptions of Human Rights', 76 *American Political Science Review* 303 (1982); Rhoda E. Howard and Jack Donnelly, 'Human Dignity, Human Rights and Political Regimes', 80 *American Political Science Review* 801 (1986).

[11] Christopher McCrudden, 'Human Dignity and Judicial Interpretation of Human Rights', 19 *European Journal of International Law* 655, 702 (2008); Mirko Baragic and James Allan, 'The Vacuous Concept of Dignity', 5 *Journal of Human Rights* 257, 266–8 (2006).

fuzziness of the concept of 'dignity' and its imprecision provides reasons to resist the use of dignity in moral reasoning and political theory and to resort instead to other values—values that can dictate determinate normative implications.

These concerns have led some theorists to conclude that dignity ought to be eradicated from the dictionary of clear-headed minds.[12] Yet despite this opposition dignity has a compelling, almost magical appeal. Both philosophers and legal theorists are drawn again and again to apply it and, as is acknowledged even by its opponents, judges, as well as legislators, make extensive use of it.[13] This appeal in itself provides some reasons to attempt to make sense of this concept, despite its elusive nature, or alternatively, at least to explain its persistent appeal.

I examine here four strategies designed to explicate the concept of dignity: the catalogue strategy, the last-resort strategy, the historical strategy, and the mode of operation strategy. While I defend the mode of operation strategy, I also maintain that other strategies are valuable and can help in understanding the distinctive role that dignity plays in political morality.

The *catalogue strategy* is based on identifying a list of concerns, values, or rights that are currently identified or categorized as dignity based. Dignity, as Christopher McCrudden points out, is increasingly present in the interpretation of particular substantive areas of the law. These areas include for instance prohibition of inhumane treatment, assurance of individual choice, protection of group identity, and cultural and socio-economic rights. It seems natural to rely on the current usage of dignity to analyse what dignity means.[14]

---

[12] See Baragic and Allan, 'The Vacuous Concept of Dignity' (n 11). For a description of the 'skeptics', see Khaitan, 'Dignity as an Expressive Norm', 3 (n 7). For a recent attack on the concept of dignity on various grounds, see also Steven Pinker, 'The Stupidity of Dignity', *The New Republic* (28 May 2008). Other writers dispute this view and believe that although abstract definition of dignity may be too vague the term can be characterized by identifying the prominent uses of the term in adjudication. See, e.g., Oscar Schachter, 'Human Dignity as a Normative Concept', 77 *American Journal of International Law* 848, 851–2 (1983).

[13] See, e.g., Baragic and Allan, 'The Vacuous Concept of Dignity' (n 11).

[14] McCrudden, 'Human Dignity', 685 (n 11). For another attempt to construct such a catalogue, see Neomi Rao, 'Three Concepts of Dignity in Constitutional Law', 86 *Notre Dame L. Rev.* 183 (2011). Note that I do not claim that McCrudden or Remi adhere to the catalogue strategy. In fact I know of nobody who believes that the catalogue strategy is conclusive in identifying dignity-based rights or in clarifying what dignity means.

While lists of dignity-based rights may be valuable for both lawyers and theorists, they are unsatisfactory for my purposes as they take contemporary practices as given and endorse them uncritically. The philosophical challenge is to explicate, justify, or challenge the use of dignity in moral and legal reasoning, rather than to identify when it is being used. Catalogues may be used as a first step in the process of identifying how dignity operates in existing legal and social practices, but an account of dignity must also be able to justify (or challenge) such a use.

The *last-resort strategy* is based on identifying important normative concerns that are inexplicable on other grounds, and using dignity to fill the justificatory gap. In an influential article Meir Dan-Cohen purports to establish that some of the most entrenched legal norms are (exclusively) dignity based, as they cannot be justified on any other grounds (such as welfare or autonomy-based concerns).[15] Dan-Cohen uses slavery as one example of a practice that can justifiably be prohibited only on dignity-based grounds. After all, Dan Cohen argues, we abhor slavery even when it is voluntary and even under circumstances in which slavery is conducive to the welfare or to the autonomy of the slaves. Under extreme circumstances one may have chosen autonomously (and also rationally) to sell oneself to slavery. Furthermore, de facto, such a person may have more autonomy as a slave than as a free person, as the master may be an enlightened one—a master who respects the autonomy of his slaves and provides them a broad array of choices that they may be deprived of otherwise. Yet slavery is wrong even if it promotes both the welfare and the autonomy of the slave. It follows therefore that neither welfare considerations nor autonomy-based considerations can justify the prohibition of slavery. Dignity is needed to fill the gap and account for the prohibition of slavery (as well as other norms discussed by Dan-Cohen).

As Dan-Cohen himself concedes at the outset, his methodology is limited in its ambitions. He primarily establishes his position on the grounds that it 'helps account for our considered judgments in a number of test cases in which the idea of harm fails'.[16] Dan-Cohen has no ambition to provide a positive account of dignity. His account suffers from several additional weaknesses. First, to successfully establish

---

[15] Meir Dan Cohen, *Defending Dignity in Harmful Thoughts: Essays on Law, Self and Morality* (Princeton: Princeton University Press, 2002), 150.

[16] Dan-Cohen, *Harmful Thoughts*, 151 (n 15).

that autonomy cannot account for slavery, Dan-Cohen has to provide a much richer account of autonomy (or liberty). The literature on liberty often maintains that limitations on liberty exist not only when a person is not free to perform an act but also when another agent has the power to prohibit or prevent her from performing this act. The concept of liberty as 'non-domination', namely the view that liberty ought to be equated with the privilege of being protected from interference by others has a long history and is characteristic of republican thought.[17] If indeed this is the case, Dan-Cohen's 'voluntary slave' is an antonym; the slave's liberty is curtailed even when he voluntarily chose to sell himself into slavery and even when his master provides him with a broad array of choices, as the master has the power (even if he does not exercise it) to limit the liberty of the slave. Such power seems to be a defining feature of slavery. Note that I am not defending the republican view under which the autonomy or liberty of agent A is inconsistent with the existence of an agent B who has the power to order A to act in certain ways (even when the power is not exercised). I merely argue that, to establish that autonomy or welfare cannot condemn the 'voluntary and autonomous slave' requires a richer account of welfare, autonomy, and liberty, and such an account is not provided by Dan-Cohen.

Yet the 'last-resort' approach proposed by Dan-Cohen suffers from an additional fatal flaw. Dan-Cohen believes that we can characterize a concern as a dignity-based concern by identifying norms that are inexplicable on other grounds (welfare or autonomy). This claim ignores the possibility that values such as autonomy or welfare or equality and dignity are interrelated, such that the same limitation on a person's autonomy or welfare or equality is an infringement both of one's autonomy, welfare, or equality and dignity. The last-resort approach would fail to identify infringements of dignity whenever such infringements are also accompanied by infringements of autonomy or encroachment on equality and welfare.

The *historical approach* is founded on identifying the historical evolution of the concept of dignity, and extracting its meaning from the way the term has been used in the past. The most influential writer who investigated the history of the concept among legal theorists is James Whitman, who has shown in a series of essays that the legal concept of

---

[17] Phillip Pettit, *Republicanism: A Theory of Freedom and Government* (New York: Oxford University Press, 1997).

dignity (as it is currently practised) should be constructed as an evolution of rank- or honour-based legal norms. Whitman describes a 'leveling up process' in which gradually the respect and solicitude previously confined to certain subgroups such as nobles and knights has been extended to all human beings, or to humanity as such.[18] Other theorists, most notably Stephanie Hennette-Vauchez and Jeremy Waldron, later developed this approach and used it to establish their own conception of dignity.[19] Hennete-Vauchez argues that:

the very purpose of rank-based dignity was also to ground obligations and prohibitions: obligations to respect, to treat in certain ways, to yield to, to comply with orders given by, and the like. Anyone who infringed such obligations was to be sanctioned (the *dignitas* bearer as well as any third party). Offenses to a *dignitas* bearer were sanctioned by whatever punishments were associated with insult or affront.[20]

These ancient views are very different from those that are often associated with dignity, in particular the influential claim that dignity is at the foundation of human rights. Yet Hennete-Vauchez argues that the ancient values associated with dignity are echoed in many of the contemporary uses seen in legal and political discourse. To fully understand how dignity functions one ought to be aware of the ancient uses of the term. Yet, as is acknowledged both by Hennette-Vauchez and by Jeremy Waldron, history alone cannot provide the key to the understanding and accounting for the concept of dignity. We can use historical sources to better our understanding of the ways people use or understand the term 'dignity', but to justify them we need to identify

[18] James Q. Whitman, 'Enforcing Civility and Respect: Three Societies', 109 *Yale LJ* 1279 (1999–2000); James Q. Whitman, 'The Two Western Conceptions of Privacy: Dignity versus Liberty', 113 *Yale LJ* 1151 (2003–4); James Q. Whitman, *Harsh Justice: Criminal Punishment and the Widening Divide between America and Europe* (New York: Oxford University Press, 2003).

[19] Stephanie Hennette-Vauchez, 'A Human Dignitas? Remnants of the Ancient Legal Concept in Contemporary Dignity Jurisprudence', 9 *International Journal of Constitutional Law* 32 (2011); Stephanie Hennette-Vauchez, 'A Human Dignitas? The Contemporary Principle of Human Dignity as a Mere Appraisal of an Ancient Legal Concept', 18 *European University Institute Law* (2008). Using historical sources, Jeremy Waldron defends the view that: 'the distinctive contribution that "dignity" makes to human rights discourse is associated paradoxically with *rank*: once associated with hierarchical differentiations of rank and status, "dignity" now conveys the idea that all human persons belong to the same rank and that that rank is a very high one indeed, in many ways as high as those that were formerly regarded as ranks of nobility.' See Jeremy Waldron, 'Dignity and Rank', 48 *European Journal of Sociology* 201 (2013).

[20] Hennette-Vauchez, 'A Human Dignitas?', 44–5 (n 19) (notes omitted).

the distinctive features of dignity and to examine the way it operates in moral reasoning.

The *mode of operation approach* maintains that dignity is a norm or a value that is distinctive not because of the particular concerns or values it protects or promotes, but because of the ways in which it justifies such concerns and values. What characterizes dignity is not *what* it protects or requires but *how and why* it protects and requires certain decisions or actions. Thus, for instance, Khaitan maintains that dignity ought to be understood as an 'expressive norm': 'whether an act disrespects somebody's dignity depends on the meaning that such act expresses'.[21] Such an approach identifies a distinctive mode of operation of dignity. It does not identify any particular norm or decision as a dignity-based one; instead it aims at capturing the distinctive ways in which dignity operates to justify certain decisions or actions.

This seems to me to be a superior approach, and I shall develop it in Chapters 3 and 4. Yet, such an approach can become more successful and appealing if its resulting findings are supported by evidence based on the other strategies mentioned here. It is useful to show that the dignity-based concerns identified by a justificatory mode of operation can account for existing rights which are perceived to be dignity-based (the catalogue strategy), and also to show that there are some concerns that cannot be accounted for without using dignity (the last-resort strategy). Further, historical and evolutionary accounts can also contribute to the success of such a theory as they uncover latent intuitions associated with the concept of dignity, and they can alert us to layers of meanings and associations of the concept of dignity that are not explicitly articulated or understood.

What is the mode of operation distinctive to dignity? One answer is that (unlike other values and/or rights) dignity does not directly govern how we ought to act or what we ought to decide, but rather how we ought to deliberate. In other words in asking whether a decision conforms to the dignity-based requirements, one ought to ask whether the deliberation resulting in that decision conformed to the require-ments of dignity. When dignity is at stake one may scrutinize not only what the agent did or decided, but also how the agent deliberated: did she take into consideration the interests and the welfare of others, did she deliberate in a way that recognizes the interests of others, etc.

---

[21] Khaitan, 'Dignity as an Expressive Norm', 4 (n 7).

Further, the analysis in the next two chapters does not merely rely on the mode of deliberation of the agent; it also identifies cases in which the mode of deliberation depends upon the political status of the agent. Deliberation made by public officials differs in important respects from deliberation made by private individuals. To convey an authoritative judgment concerning the wrongfulness of my act an agent must be in a superior position to me; such an authoritative judgment cannot emanate from other individuals who are one's equals. It must emanate from the state because no other entity can claim the privilege of making an authoritative judgment of this type. It is precisely the equality among citizens that bars the infliction of private sanctions, as those convey a judgment of superiority of one person (the punisher) over another (the punished). In contrast, certain judgments concerning life and death in emergency situations cannot be performed by the state because they would be conveying a judgment concerning the comparative value of lives of different people. Thus the deliberation of the agent and the status of the deliberating agent are at times interrelated. It is only certain agents that can deliberate in certain ways. Dignity sometimes involves hierarchy, and at other times non-hierarchical relationships among individuals.

The relevance of comparative status or hierarchy and its intimate relationship with dignity is familiar to anthropologists. Most prominently, Frank Stewart distinguishes between horizontal honour and vertical honour. Horizontal honour is honour that is due to a person as an equal to others. Horizontal honour can be contrasted with vertical honour, namely the right to special respect enjoyed by some who are superior.[22] Chapter 3 discusses vertical honour. Our dignity dictates that only an agent that is superior to us can make authoritative normative judgments concerning the wrongfulness of our behavior and inflict criminal sanctions. Given that only the state can justifiably claim such superiority, it is therefore only agents whose acts are attributable to the state, namely public officials that can inflict criminal sanctions. In contrast Chapter 4 focuses on horizontal honour, as it maintains that certain decisions must not be made by the state as making them by the state implies an authoritative judgment concerning the comparative worth of human lives—a judgment that the state ought not to make. Hence Chapters 3 and 4 illustrate the importance of both horizontal

---

[22] Frank Henderson Stewart, *Honor* (Chicago: University of Chicago Press, 1994), 54–63.

and vertical honour and the fact that both coexist in different ways in the legal system.[23]

Before I explore the implications of this observation in Chapters 3 and 4, let me explain the different ways in which dignity and rights can be related to each other, and clarify the way I use dignity. Sometimes dignity is understood as a right; at other times it is understood as a value underlying the protection of rights.[24] When dignity is understood as a right it is sometimes understood to be a specific right in par with the right to free speech, the right to equality etc.[25] The right to dignity can also be understood as a core comprehensive right such that all rights are derived from the right to dignity.[26] When dignity is used as a value underlying rights it is sometimes used as a value underlying a subset of rights,[27] and, at other times, as a value underlying all rights or, at times, as a precondition for having rights in the first place.[28] My account in

---

[23] See Stewart, *Honor*, 63 (n 22).

[24] For an analysis of the two uses, see Jeremy Waldron, 'Dignity and Rank', 203–4 (n 19). The two uses also can be found in legal documents in particular in constitutions. See Evadne Grant, 'Dignity and Equality', 7 *Human Rights L. Rev.* 299, 306 (2007).

[25] Section 4 of the Israeli Basic Law: Human Dignity and Liberty states that: 'All persons are entitled to protection of their life, liberty and dignity.' Under one influential view, dignity under Israeli law is a right to which persons are entitled along with other rights such as liberty, life, etc. This is one of the two interpretations of the Basic Law proposed by David Kretzmer. See David Kretzmer, 'Human Dignity in Israeli Jurisprudence', in David Kretzmer and Eckart Klein (eds.), *The Concept of Human Dignity in Human Rights Discourse* (Dordrecht: Kluwer Law International, 2002), 161, 169–72. Dignity is also understood sometimes as a separate right in Germany. See Eckart Klein, 'Human Dignity in German law', in Kretzmer and Klein (eds.), *The Concept of Human Dignity*, 145, 147. For a discussion of the use of dignity as a specific right, see Rex D. Glensy, 'The Right to Dignity', 43 *Columbia Human Rights L. Rev.* 65, 111–20 (2011).

[26] See, e.g., Arthur Chaskalson, 'Human Dignity as a Constitutional Value', in Kretzmer and Klein (eds.), *The Concept of Human Dignity*, 133, 136–7 (n 25). There was an attempt on the part of some Israeli legal theorists to argue for what was labeled as 'the expansive view' of the right to dignity, namely the view that the right to dignity entrenched in the Israeli law is a foundational right or (in the terminology coined by David Kretzmer) a 'super-right,' and therefore that all rights (or at least very many rights) can be derived from it. For a discussion, see Kretzmer, 'Human Dignity', 172–4 (n 25); Ariel L. Bendor and Michael Sachs, 'The Constitutional Status of Dignity in Germany and Israel', 44 *Israel L. Rev.* 25, 46–7 (2011). The Israeli Court rejected this view. See HCJ 453/94 *Israel Women's Network v Government of Israel* 48(5) PD 501, 536 [1994].

[27] For a discussion of this possibility under the label of 'foundational pluralism,' see Jeremy Waldron, 'Is Dignity the Foundation of Human Rights' 4–6 <http://papers.ssrn.com/sol3/papers.cfm?abstract_id=2196074&download=yes>. In support of this view, Waldron cites the fact that in legal texts dignity is used extensively in justifying certain rights and is rarely used in justifying other rights.

[28] This view is very influential among legal scholars. The most famous articulation of this view is in the International Covenant of Civil and Political Rights, which asserts that rights

Chapters 3 and 4 uses dignity as a value underlying some but not necessarily all rights. I identify some rights that are grounded in dignity, but I remain agnostic with respect to the question of whether other rights are also grounded in dignity.

To sum up, Chapters 3 and 4 explore two dignity-based rights. Dignity is understood to be a value underlying rights. More specifically, I argue that dignity imposes certain constraints on the deliberation of agents. Further, the deliberation of the agents is sometimes conditional upon whom the agents are: public officials or private individuals. Individuals have a dignity-based right that certain decisions regarding their fundamental interests be made by public officials as only such decisions are made in the name of the state. Individuals also have a right that other decisions regarding their fundamental interests be made only by private individuals. In both cases what matters is the particular significance of the agent who makes the decision and in particular whether this agent is the state, i.e., public agent or not.

'derive from the inherent dignity of the human person'. For a discussion, see Klaus Dicke, 'The Founding Function of Human Dignity in the Universal Declaration of Human Rights', in David Kretzmer and Eckart Klein (eds.), *The Concept of Human Dignity in Human Rights Discourse* (Leiden: Martinus Nijhoff Publishers, 2002), 111, 118. Under certain interpretations the German Constitution also regards dignity as a value that 'has a mutually nourishing effect' on human rights. See Edward J. Eberle, *Dignity and Liberty: Constitutional Visions in Germany and the United States* (New York: Praeger Publishers 2002), 41. See also Christoph Enders, 'A Right to have Rights—the German Constitutional Concept of Human Dignity', 3 *NUJS L. Rev.* 253 (2010).

3

The Case against Privatization

A. Introduction

The state provides some goods, such as security, educational services, and health. Some of these goods can also be provided or produced by private individuals. This chapter argues that certain goods must be provided by the state, namely goods whose value depends upon their public provision. I argue, further, that public provision requires provision by public officials. An attempt to privatize 'intrinsically public goods' is therefore self-defeating, as the value of the goods is conditioned upon the identity of the agent producing it.

To illustrate this, let us examine the debate concerning privatization. The privatization of government functions involving violence, such as waging a war or running a prison, has for the most part given rise to instrumental questions concerning the desirable ways of providing these services. In particular, current discussions typically cast the matter in terms of the trade-off between two forms of executing certain functions or services: public bureaucracy and private entrepreneurship.[1] Proponents of privatization emphasize the benefits of deploying the latter form in the service of executing more efficiently whatever objectives are set by the government. Opponents of privatization, by contrast, insist that the private form of executing government functions is a liability, rather than an asset, due to the loose fidelity on the part of

---

[1] See, e.g., Paul R. Verkuil, *Outsourcing Sovereignty: Why Privatization of Government Functions Threatens Democracy and What Can Be Done about It* (Cambridge: Cambridge University Press, 2007). My argument against privatization applies to for-profit as well as non-profit private organizations.

private entities to the promotion of the public good (in particular because of the lack of accountability on the part of private agents). The shared assumption of both advocates and opponents of privatization is that the service or the function in question can, in principle, be performed by either private or public bodies and that the choice of an agent to perform the function must be based on addressing the question of who is more likely to perform this function better.[2] Further, the question of who should be in charge is considered an empirical question that ought to be resolved on the basis of empirical investigation: the professional judgment of the agent, their ability to calculate and reason, the interests guiding the private or the public agent (and, in particular the degree to which the interests converge with those of the public), the likelihood of an impartial judgment on the part of public and private agents, interests or cognitive failures that may distort their judgments, etc.

This chapter challenges the terms of this debate, as it defends the following two claims: first, some governmental decisions simply cannot be successfully made or executed by private entities, as the goods resulting from these decisions can be realized only if the state performs these tasks; and, second, performance by the state requires the direct involvement of public officials.[3] The conjunction of these two claims implies that some decisions must be made and some actions must be executed by public officials and ought not to be privatized. Their privatization undermines the very possibility of providing the goods as their goodness depends upon public provision.

Section B defends the view that there are agent-dependent goods, namely goods that can only be provided by certain agents. I establish this claim by using examples in which the identity of the agent or its status are crucial for the provision of the good. I also show that the concern for the public provision of goods is deeply entrenched in legal doctrine. The concept of 'inherently governmental functions', and the intricate legal doctrines surrounding this concept, are used to illustrate the prominent significance attributed to the public agents performing

---

[2] Indeed, as was pointed out by Alexander Volokh, even when participants in the debate purport to make non-instrumental arguments a closer scrutiny reveals that, as a matter of fact, such arguments rest on instrumental considerations. See, e.g., Alexander Volokh, 'Prisons, Privatization and the Elusive Employee-Contractor Distinction', 46 *University of California Davis Law Rev.* 133, 148 (2012).

[3] This presupposes identifying who the public officials are and what distinguishes them from private individuals. This is the task of section D.

certain tasks. Section B identifies three types of justification for the public provision of goods. Under the first type, *instrumental justifications*, the state is simply more likely to execute the task efficiently and justly but, at least in principle, other agents can also perform the task. Under the second type, *normative constraints justifications*, while private agents can execute the task (and perhaps can do it better than the state), there are normative constraints that preclude the performance of the enterprise by agents other than the state. Under the last type of justification, *state-centred justifications*, only the state can provide certain goods—intrinsically public goods.[4]

But perhaps the concern that certain tasks be performed only by some agents (and not by others) and, in particular, the concern that they be provided only by public officials, is misguided. To establish the rationale underlying this concern I argue (in sections C and D) that public officials (and only public officials) can engage in certain forms of deliberation that are not available to other agents; more specifically, only public officials' deliberations are characterized by 'fidelity of deference'. It is this deference on their part that justifies the attribution of an act of a public official to the state.

Fidelity of deference to the state is founded on the presence of 'integrative practices', namely practices that integrate the political and the bureaucratic in the execution of the relevant functions. An integrative practice (as defined in section D) is characterized by its principled openness and willingness to absorb ongoing political guidance and intervention. Political offices are able in principle not only to set the practice into motion but also to determine its content, guide its development, and steer its course. Public officials are (by definition) those who engage in an integrative practice, namely those who deliberate in a way that is attentive and even deferential to political leaders and representatives, and consequently, their acts are performed in the name of the state and are attributed to it.[5]

These observations still leave the question of when and whether deference is desirable. Section E addresses this question and claims that fidelity of deference is required to facilitate the provision of certain

---

[4] The discussion here rests on Alon Harel, 'Why Only the State May Inflict Criminal Sanctions: The Case Against Privately Inflicted Sanctions', 14 *Legal Theory* 113 (2008) and Alon Harel and Ariel Porat, 'Commensurability and Agency: Two Yet to Be Met Challenges for Law and Economics', 96 *Cornell L. Rev.* 749 (2011).

[5] This argument is based on Avihay Dorfman and Alon Harel, 'The Case against Privatization', 41 *Philosophy & Public Affairs* 67 (2013).

public goods: the infliction of criminal sanctions and conducting of wars.[6] Finally, Section F identifies the boundaries of justifiable deference. It shows, as all observers of the horrors of the twentieth century know, that public officials ought not to defer in certain circumstances, and it identifies the circumstances under which they ought not to do so.[7]

My argument in this chapter seeks to strike an intuitive chord, one which instrumental arguments against (and for) privatization cannot but fail to explain. More specifically, it allows us to see that the intuitive dislike of privatization (an intuitive dislike which is also echoed in the legal doctrine classifying certain functions as 'inherently governmental functions'[8]) is not explained in terms of instrumental concerns about the efficacy of the provision of the goods;[9] nor is it a feature of the law's (arguably) inadequate regulation or supervision of the conduct of private entities in charge of executing government functions. The instrumental approach suffers from what I labelled in Chapter 1 the insincerity or the inauthenticity objection; it fails to identify the real underlying rationale for the opposition to privatization. The sentiments underlying and sustaining this opposition are grounded in different normative considerations than those officially used to justify the opposition to privatization. The persistent hostility to phenomena as diverse as private prisons, the use of mercenaries in security operations, and wars is rooted in an unarticulated conviction—the conviction that the identity of the agent is crucial in providing the good and in providing it in ways that do not offend the dignity of others.[10] The traditional justifications (based on efficiency and accountability) are merely

---

[6] This section is also based on Dorfman and Harel, 'The Case Against Privatization' (n 5).

[7] This section is based on Alon Harel, 'Outsourcing Violence?', 5 *Law & Ethics of Human Rights* 396 (2011).

[8] See, e.g., Federal Activities Inventory Reform Act of 1998 31 USC section 501 note (2006).

[9] In her comprehensive historical survey, Sarah Percy illustrates that there is a persistent opposition to mercenaries in European history. Yet, the reasons provided for this opposition shift and change in time. Percy's survey indicates that while most reasons provided for this opposition are instrumental the sense of discomfort is deeply entrenched and cannot easily be explained in instrumental terms. This provides support for the conjecture that the instrumental reasons are mere rationalizations of a much deeper resistance to privatization which this chapter aims to explicate. See Sarah Percy, *Mercenaries: The History of a Norm in International Relations* (Oxford: Oxford University Press, 2007).

[10] Of course, the identity of the actor need not be sufficient for success. The point, however, is that this element is a necessary one.

rationalizations of very different sentiments which I hope to identify and defend in this chapter.

B. Why We Care about Who the Agents Are: Agent-dependent Enterprise and the Significance of Public Agents

This section examines cases in which the identity or the status of an agent making a decision, performing an action, or engaging in an enterprise is a precondition for the permissibility of one's decision or the success of one's action or enterprise.[11] I start by examining cases where the value of the decision or action turns upon the identity of the agent making the decision or performing the action. I later focus my attention on the special significance of public agents—agents of the polity. Last I sketch three possible types of justifications for the significance of the public agent. Under the first (instrumental) justification, public agents are more likely to provide the good (as they are more deliberative, well-motivated, or 'accountable'); under the second there are normative constraints requiring that only public agents provide the good; while under the third, the good can only be produced (or provided) by public agents. The good in this final case is intrinsically public; its value depends upon its public provision. It is the third justification which this chapter defends.

Some agents are chosen to execute an enterprise because of their expected excellence in doing so, when excellence in executing an enterprise is understood and evaluated independently of the agent's identity or status.[12] At other times excellence (or even competence) in executing an enterprise is inseparable from the identity or status of the agent. In the latter cases, the quality of the execution of the enterprise cannot be measured independently of the agent's identity. Let me provide some illustrations for what can be labelled 'agent-dependent enterprises or practices', namely enterprises or practices whose success depends on the agent performing them.

---

[11] This section is based on the analysis I developed in Harel, *The Case Against Privately Inflicted Sanctions* (n 4); Harel and Porat, 'Commensurability and Agency' (n 4).

[12] See, e.g., Eyal Benvenisti and Ariel Porat, 'Implementing the Law by Impartial Agents: An Exercise in Tort Law and International Law', 6 *Theoretical Inq. L.* 1, 4–8 (2005).

The first example rests on a famous historical practice: blood feuds.[13] Blood feuds are ritualized ways of seeking vengeance for a wrong by killing or punishing a person belonging to a tribe or clan of the original perpetrator who committed the wrong. Although the reader most probably shares my dislike of this practice, it is an important social practice that deserves attention, and the institutional norms governing it provide us with a paradigmatic case of an agent-dependent practice. Most significantly, anthropologists say it is only a male relative of the deceased that is capable of performing a blood feud, while a person who is not a male relative of the deceased cannot perform a blood feud. A killing by the 'wrong agent' is not merely an inappropriate or an impermissible blood feud; it does not even count as a blood feud, and it cannot redress the injustice.[14]

The disciplining of a child is another example where it seems that the identity of the agent matters. To illustrate, think of the rule in the common law, which dictates that parents are legally justified in spanking their children.[15] It is not at all evident that the parents could be assisted by third parties in fulfilling their educational tasks. Even if one disagrees with this view and believes that third parties could assist parents in disciplining their children, it does not seem right that parents could delegate the powers to spank their children to others.[16] This view is also deeply entrenched in some legal systems.[17]

Another influential example of an agent-dependent analysis may be found in the very famous discussion of punishment in the *Metaphysics of Morals*. In this passage Immanuel Kant writes:

---

[13] The example is borrowed from Harel, *The Case Against Privately Inflicted Sanctions*, 121 (n 4).

[14] See Pamela Barmash, *Homicide in the Biblical World* (Cambridge: Cambridge University Press, 2005), 24.

[15] This privilege of 'moderate chastisement' is mentioned in by William Blackstone in his *Commentaries on the Laws of England* William Blackstone, *Commentaries on the Laws of England* (1769) (Chicago: University of Chicago, 1979). Anne McGillivray, '"He'll learn it on his body": Disciplining Childhood in Canadian Law', 5 *Int'l J. of Child. Rts* 193, 202 (1997) (citing Blackstone, *Commentaries on the Laws of England*, paras. 452–3). For a short description of the common law rules concerning physical disciplining of children, see McGillivray at 201–6.

[16] See *Johnson v Dep't of Soc. Services*, 177 Cal. Rptr. 49, 53 (Cal. Ct. App. 1981).

[17] Common law also allowed delegates of parents to punish children. It was said that moderate chastisement is a 'power' belonging to the father *or his delegate* to 'lawfully correct his child being under age, in a reasonable manner for this is for the benefit of his education' (emphasis mine). See Blackstone, *Commentaries* (n 15).

Even if a civil society were to be dissolved by the consent of all its members (e.g., if a people inhabiting an island decided to separate and disperse throughout the world), the last murderer remaining in prison would first have to be executed, so that each has done to him what his deeds deserve and blood guilt does not cling to the people for not having insisted upon this punishment; for otherwise the people can be regarded as collaborators in this public violation of justice.[18]

Under the standard interpretation of this passage Kant conveys in this passage his retributivist theory, namely his conviction that criminals ought to be executed because they deserve it. Yet one could challenge this interpretation and question why 'the last murderer ... would *first* have to be executed' (rather than later), namely why the execution ought to take place *before* the dispersion of the society.

To understand this passage one must explain why the great injustice of not executing the murderer *before* the dispersion of the society should not (or could not) be remedied by killing him *after* the dispersion of the society. The answer I propose is that such a killing (namely, killing after the dispersion of the society) would constitute a private act of killing rather than a public act of execution, and unlike a public execution, a private killing could not be done in the name of the people as a collective. The (political) practice of state-inflicted execution of murderers is thus fundamentally different from a practice in which murderers 'who deserve to be punished' are killed by non-state agents. It is the difference in who the agents are that explains why the former act is required by justice (and constitutes a legally required execution) while the latter is prohibited (and is classified as mere murder). The agent performing the execution before the dispersion of the society is the polity, while the agent performing the execution after the dispersion of the society—when the polity is no more in existence—is a private individual.[19]

---

[18] Immanuel Kant, *The Metaphysics of Morals*, trans. and ed. Mary Gregor (Cambridge: Cambridge University Press, 1996), 106.

[19] This conclusion also follows from the interpretation given to Kant's theory of punishment by Thomas Hill. Hill believes that Kant's theory of punishment is a mixed theory. Establishing the practice of punishing wrongdoers in the first place is designed to protect freedom, rather than to inflict sanctions. Once this scheme is established, state officials are required to impose sanctions as prescribed by law without deviating for pragmatic reasons. The paragraph cited in the text is understood by Hill to highlight the officials' duty to apply the law, in order to 'reaffirm the idea that those responsible for enforcing the law must apply the legally prescribed sanctions without concern for whether punishment has any deterrent

Kant need not of course deny that some of the desirable by-products of criminal punishments (e.g., deterring crimes or inflicting deserved sufferings on the guilty) can be achieved by sanctions inflicted by private agents. Yet, under this interpretation, he also believes that there are compelling reasons that the agent performing the act must be the polity. The dispersion of the polity is inevitably accompanied by the extinction of the only agent that can inflict the criminal sanction. Hence even if the punishment is 'deserved' by the wrongdoer, there is no agent who may inflict it.

Further, both in the case of the blood feud and in the case of criminal punishment (as understood by Kant), it is not merely impermissible on the part of the wrong agent to perform the act of violence. It is, as a matter of fact, a different act that is being performed, as the act hinges on the status of the agent performing it. A killing performed by the wrong agent is not merely a morally impermissible blood feud; its impermissibility is attributed to the fact that, despite all the good intentions of the perpetrator to perform a blood feud, his act does not (and cannot) count as a blood feud. Similarly, it could be argued that an execution performed by a private individual does not constitute a criminal punishment; it is merely an act of violence. This is not mere semantics. Blood feuds and punishment bring about certain goods, and the goods resulting from both blood feuds and criminal punishment are contingent upon the identity or status of the agent inflicting it. To be properly labelled 'punishment' under this view, it is not sufficient that it hurts or causes displeasure to those who have wronged (as those can result from the actions of a private agent or even of an animal or from natural forces); it must also reflect an authoritative judgment concerning the wrongfulness of an act, and such a judgment can only be made by an authoritative entity—the state. It is false therefore to say that private individuals *ought not* to punish; they simply *cannot punish*, as their acts do not constitute punishment.

These examples establish the moral and political significance of the identity of agents in performing certain tasks. Yet this concern is not merely a concern of moral and political theory. It is also entrenched in

value in the particular case'. See Thomas Hill, 'Kant on Wrongdoing Desert and Punishment', 18 *Law and Philosophy* at 407, 433 (1999). Under Hill's interpretation, after the dispersion of the state, there are no officials who are charged with the responsibility of imposing sanctions prescribed by law. Hence, the infliction of suffering cannot be justified as part of the faithful fulfilment of the officials' duties.

the legal system. Legal rules often assign particular tasks to certain agents. In explaining the rationales for such legal determinations, instrumental theories of law typically maintain that the aim of such restrictions is to identify the body or entity that is most capable of carrying out the particular task at the lowest cost, when the task is defined in a way that is independent of the identity or the status of the agent performing it. When circumstances allow, such legal restrictions ought to be lifted to enable the most capable body or entity to perform the task.[20] Consequently, the entity that ought to provide security is the entity which is more capable of providing security at the lowest possible cost, the entity which ought to provide education is the one that is most capable of providing high-quality education, etc. Furthermore, the characterization of what the task is, is (at least in principle) separable from the identity or the status of the entity which ought to be in charge of performing it. If the task is deterring criminals, providing health or educational services, protecting the environment, or providing defence and security, advocates of traditional legal theories maintain that the policymaker ought to select the agent in accordance with the (contingent) suitability of the agent to perform the task when the task (and, in particular, the criteria for succeeding in performing the task) can be characterized independently of the identity of the agent.[21]

However, legal doctrine cannot be easily reconciled with this position. It is often deeply concerned with the identity of the body making the decision or performing the act. Producing legislation is the job of a public entity—the legislature; and the decision to inflict a criminal sanction is the job of another entity—the courts. Last and more controversially, the execution of criminal punishment and of maintaining security traditionally has also been assigned to a public entity: the police and the army.[22] The insistence that such functions remain in

---

[20] Thus for instance, advocates of private prisons justify the establishment of such prisons on the grounds of 'soaring inmate populations' and the inefficiency of public enforcement. See John J. DiIulio Jr, 'What's Wrong with Private Prisons', 92 *The Pub. Int.* 66, 68 (Summer 1988). See also Steven Shavell, 'The Optimal Structure of Law Enforcement', 36 *J. L. Econ.* 255, 268–9 (1993).

[21] See, e.g., Alon Harel, 'Why Only the State May Inflict Criminal Sanctions: The Argument from Moral Burdens', 28 *Cardozo L. Rev.* 2629, 2634 (2007).

[22] Admittedly though, this is hardly universal. Historically, there are many examples of privatizing various functions of criminal law and criminal law enforcement. It is known that for a very long time English law relied on private prosecution. See Douglas Hay, 'The Criminal Prosecution in England and its Historians', 47 *Modern L. Rev.* 1 (1984); David Friedman, 'Making Sense of English Law Enforcement in the Eighteenth Century',

the hands of public officials is perceived to be a matter of the *legitimacy* of the decision or act, rather than merely of its expected success in achieving its goals.

One case illustrating the significance attributed to the agent making a decision or performing an act is the legal category labelled in the United States 'Inherently Governmental Functions'. This category consists of functions that must be performed by employees of the Federal Government. The Federal Activities Inventory Reform ('FAIR') Act of 1998 defines functions that are inherently governmental, as 'a function that is so intimately related to the public interest as to require performance by Federal Government employees'.[23] In the absence of a clear non-controversial rationale for the doctrine it is not surprising that what falls under this definition remains vague, and many federal agencies use different definitions when deciding which functions or

---

2 *University of Chicago Law School Roundtable* 475, 475–8 (1995). As a matter of fact 'private vengeance of the person wronged by a crime' was a primary feature of the administration of criminal justice in early English law. J. F. Stephen, *A History of the Criminal Law of England* (London: Macmillan and Co., 1883), 245. This system has been transformed only in the nineteenth century. See Philip Kurland and D. W. M. Waters, 'Public Prosecutions in England 1854–79: An Essay in English Legislative History', *Duke LJ* 493 (1959). While the English system was based on private prosecutors, other jurisdictions relied heavily on the private infliction of criminal sanctions. The southern states of the USA had no actual penitentiary and, until the second half of the nineteenth century, prisoners were leased out by the state to private entrepreneurs. See Alex Lichtenstein, 'The Private and Public in Penal History: A Commentary on Zimering and Tonry', 3 *Punishment and Society* 189 (2001). Another example of private infliction of sanctions is the rule prevailing in Roman law under which the person who committed theft and was caught in the act was given up as a slave to the person against whom the theft was committed. See H. F. Jolowicz and Nicholas Barry, *Historical Introduction to the Study of Roman Law* (3rd edn., Cambridge: Cambridge University Press, 1972). Jewish law has a very similar rule. Under Jewish law if the thief cannot afford to return the theft, the thief becomes enslaved to the person against whom the theft was committed. Moreover, some legal systems were almost entirely private. In recent research on medieval Icelandic institutions it was said that Icelandic institutions 'might almost have been invented by a mad economist'. See David Friedman, 'Private Creation and Enforcement of Law', 8 *Journal of Legal Studies* 399, 400 (1979). In the Icelandic system which operated successfully for hundreds of years, 'killing was a civil offence resulting in a fine paid to the survivors of the victim. Laws were made by a "parliament," in which seats were a marketable commodity. Enforcement of law was entirely a private affair.' See Friedman, 'Private Creation', 400. Iceland is not unique in this respect. As Friedman argues: '[T]he idea that law is primarily private, that most offenses are offenses against specific individuals or families, and that punishment of the crime is primarily the business of the injured party seems to be common to many early systems of law.' See Friedman, 'Private Creation', 400; Richard Posner, *The Economics of Justice* (Cambridge, Mass.: Harvard University Press, 1983), 119–43.

[23]   FAIR Act of 1998, Pub. L. No. 105–270, § 5(2)(A), 112 Stat. 2382, 2384–5 (codified at 31 USC § 501 note (2006)).

activities are 'so intimately related to the public interest'. President Barack Obama recently stated that:

[T]he line between inherently governmental activities that should not be outsourced and commercial activities that may be subject to private sector competition has been blurred and inadequately defined. As a result, contractors may be performing inherently governmental functions. Agencies and departments must operate under clear rules prescribing when outsourcing is and is not appropriate.[24]

The drafters of the FAIR have been aware of course that the abstract definition is not sufficient to identify which functions are inherently governmental. Hence, the Act contains, in addition to the definition, a list of functions that are understood to be 'inherently governmental.' These functions include the following tasks:

   (i) to bind the United States to take or not to take some action by contract, policy, regulation, authorization, order, or otherwise;

  (ii) to determine, protect, and advance United States economic, political, territorial, property, or other interests by military or diplomatic action, civil or criminal judicial proceedings, contract management, or otherwise;

 (iii) to significantly affect the life, liberty, or property of private persons;

 (iv) to commission, appoint, direct, or control officers or employees of the United States; or

  (v) to exert ultimate control over the acquisition, use, or disposition of the property, real or personal, tangible or intangible, of the United States, including the collection, control, or disbursement of appropriated and other Federal funds.[25]

The intricacies of the doctrine have been discussed extensively by legal theorists and by courts and they seem to be comprehensible only to doctrinal minds. But the doctrinal nuances are less important than the fact that the rhetoric surrounding the debate suggests that the doctrine is not grounded in instrumental considerations. Even the term

---

[24] Presidential Memorandum of 4 March 2009, Government Contracting, 74 Fed. Reg. 9755, 9755–6 (6 March 2009).

[25] FAIR Act § 5(2)(B), 31 USC § 501 note. Further the next paragraph—section (C)—describes the 'functions excluded' from the definition of Inherently Governmental Functions.

'Inherently Governmental Functions' indicates that the concerns underlying the doctrine are not merely instrumental. The functions are 'inherently governmental'; they cannot in principle be privatized.

A major recent case in which the Israeli Supreme Court decided to
strike down a statute authorizing the establishment of private prisons is
another clear example of the legal insistence in determining not only
how incarceration is being performed or executed but also who performs it. In
this case Chief Justice Dorit Beinisch decided to strike down the law
authorizing the privatization of prisons on the grounds that it is the job
of the state and the state alone to imprison. She rejected explicitly
instrumental arguments against privatization:

[T]he very existence of a prison that operates on a profit-making basis reflects a
lack of respect for the status of the inmates as human beings, and this
violation of the human dignity of the inmates does not depend on the
extent of the violation of human rights that actually occurs behind the
prison walls.[26]

Chief Justice Beinisch continued to explain why her decision does not
rest on instrumental concerns:

Imprisoning a person is the culmination of the criminal proceeding initiated
against that person by the state on behalf of the entire public. The power of
imprisonment and the other invasive powers that derive from it are therefore
some of the state's most distinctive powers as the embodiment of government, and they reflect the constitutional principle that the state has a
monopoly upon exercising organized force in order to advance the general
public interest. ... Indeed, just as the state through the legislature is responsible for regulating criminal legislation, so too it is responsible for enforcing
the criminal law and punishing offenders according to the law through the
executive branch—a responsibility that is realized, inter alia, by imposing the
role of managing and operating prisons on the state.[27]

What could be the reasons underlying the concern for the appropriateness of the agent and, in particular, the insistence that the performance
of certain functions must be done by public agents? In principle

---

[26] HCJ 2605/05 Academic Center of Law and Business v Minister of Finance 76. <http://
elyon1.court.gov.il/files_eng/05/050/026/n39/05026050.n39.pdf>, my emphasis.
[27] n 26 at 69.

there can be three types of justifications: instrumentalist justifications maintaining that public agents are more likely to be better at providing the relevant goods, normative constraints justifications under which there are normative constraints on private individuals, and, last, state-centred justifications which maintain that some of the relevant goods provided by public agents simply cannot be provided by private individuals.

Instrumental justifications consist of two major stages. First, the theorist identifies the goals of the decision or the activity. Criminal punishment can be used to deter people, to rehabilitate them, or to guarantee that they get what they deserve, to express disapproval of the wrongful act, etc. These goals are conceptually separable from the identity of the agent inflicting the sanction. Next the theorist establishes that a particular agent is the most likely to successfully realize these goals. To the extent that the state is more likely or capable of realizing these goals than other agents, it ought to be in charge of performing the task.

The most influential instrumental justification for the claim that only the state ought to punish was made by John Locke. Locke believed that the state should be empowered to inflict sanctions on those who transgress the laws of nature because the state is less partial than other agents in its treatment of offenders.[28] In principle, Locke argued, punishment inflicted by individuals is both possible and permissible in the state of nature.[29] But he also added that private agents inflicting sanctions are likely to be either too lenient ('Self-Love will make Men partial to themselves and their Friends') or too harsh ('Passion and Revenge will carry them too far in punishing others').[30]

Law and economics theorists also defend the involvement of the state in punishing on the basis of instrumental justifications. In their view, punishment should be carried out by the state because the infliction of sanctions involves a collective action problem. An individual who inflicts a sanction has to bear the costs of inflicting the sanction himself, whereas the benefits resulting from the infliction (such as deterrence and incapacitation) are enjoyed by everybody. It follows that individuals will underinvest in the infliction of sanctions.[31]

---

[28] John Locke, *Two Treaties of Government: Second Treatise*, ed. Peter Laslett (Cambridge: Cambridge University Press, 1960), chapter 2.

[29] Daniel Farrell, 'Punishment without the State', 22 *Nous* 437 (1988).

[30] See Locke, *Two Treaties* (n 28).

[31] Dennis Mueller, *Public Choice* (Cambridge: Cambridge University Press, 1989), ii. 9–15.

Other economists dispute the claim that the state is typically the best agent to inflict punishment. It has been argued for instance that states are inclined to increase sanctions above the optimal level in order to 'export' their criminals elsewhere.[32] If so, perhaps states are not the ideal agents to make determinations concerning the size of the sanction, as they are inclined to inflict harsher sanctions than required to deter crime.

Among the most influential claims of legal theorists opposing privatization is that private agents are less likely to be accountable than public officials, and that often they may act in ways that do not promote the goals of government.[33] The conjecture that private agents are not sufficiently accountable is often debated in the literature.[34]

Instrumental justifications require establishing factual claims concerning the performance of the state and the performance of private agents. Once the goals of punishment are identified, it is necessary to show that the state makes better judgments concerning the severity of sanctions, is better able to inflict the sanction, is more likely to calibrate their optimal size, etc. Further, if faced with contrary evidence, an advocate of an instrumentalist argument must be willing to concede that punishment ought to be inflicted by non-state entities. There are no principled grounds why the state ought to inflict criminal sanctions. The desirability of privatization hinges therefore on contingent factors, and such factors may change from time to time and from society to society.

In my view these observations provide the basis for criticizing the instrumentalist view. The instrumentalist justifications fail for reasons discussed in Chapter 1, namely for reasons of insincerity or inauthenticity. Instrumental justifications are mere superficial rationalizations of a different normative sensibility. More specifically, such justifications fail to capture a prevalent intuition, namely that the involvement of the state in the infliction of punishment is not based on its (alleged) ability

---

[32] Doron Teichman, 'The Market for Criminal Justice: Federalism, Crime Control, and Jurisdictional Competition', 103 *Michigan L. Rev.* 1831 (2005). Tomer Broude and Doron Teichman, 'Outsourcing and Insourcing Crime: The Political Economy of Globalized Criminal Activity', 62 *Vanderbilt L. Rev.* 795 (2009). For an accessible summary of this argument, see Alon Harel, 'Economic Analysis of Criminal Law: A Survey', in Alon Harel and Keith Hylton (eds.), *A Research Handbook of the Economic Analysis of Criminal Law* (Cheltenham: Edward Elgar, 2012), 10, 34–5.

[33] Verkuil, *Outsourcing Sovereignty*, chapter 1 (n 1).

[34] Martha Minow, 'Public and Private Partnerships: Accounting for the New Religion', 116 *Harvard Law Review* 1229 (2003).

to 'get it right'. The justification for the role of the state is based on *who it is that punishes* rather than on *what the state punishment is likely to be*.

Echoes for this intuition can easily be detected among political theorists discussing criminal punishment. Theorists often distinguish between the usefulness or the justness of the decision to punish and the permission to punish. Thus, for instance, David Lyons argues that: 'it is not generally accepted that I have the right simply to hurt another who has done something wrong, just because he has done it, where there is no special relation between us.'[35] Further, John Simmons claims that 'neither one's general level of virtue nor one's particular talents in the area of punishing . . . are normally taken to establish any special claim to be the one who should punish others.'[36] Even Locke (who also developed the instrumentalist account described above) agrees with this observation:

Now to justify the bringing any such evil [i.e., punishment] upon any man, two things are requisite. First, That *he who does it has commission and power to do so*. Secondly, That it be directly useful for the procuring of some greater good. Whatever punishment one man uses to another, without these two conditions, whatever he may pretend, proves an injury and injustice. . . . Usefulness, when present, being but one of those conditions, cannot give the other, which is a commission to punish; without which also punishment is unlawful.[37]

Under this view, one ought to separate two questions: (a) whether an agent 'deserves' to be punished or ought to be punished for other reasons, and (b) whether a particular agent is the 'appropriate agent' (namely 'has a commission') to inflict the sanction.[38] To justify the infliction of punishment X by an agent Y on a wrongdoer Z, it is not sufficient to show that X should be inflicted on Z and that Y is the most likely or the most capable agent to inflict it. Something else needs to be shown.

Both normative constraints justifications and state-centred justifications reject the instrumental view and attempt to explain why sanctions

[35] David Lyons, 'Rights against Humanity', 85 *Philosophical Review* 208 (1976).

[36] See, e.g., John Simmons, 'Locke and the Right to Punish', 20 *Philosophy and Public Affairs* 311, 312 (1991).

[37] John Locke, *A Second Letter Concerning Toleration* in *The Works of John Locke* (London: Thomas Davison, 1823). My emphasis.

[38] Hill, 'Kant on Wrongdoing', 407 (n 19).

ought to be inflicted only by 'appropriate' agents and appropriateness, under these justifications, is not merely a contingent fact hinging on contingent qualities of the state. Under the normative constraints justifications, while the infliction of sanctions by 'inappropriate' agents may serve the purposes of punishment (whatever these purposes are), there are normative constraints on the infliction of sanctions that are not grounded in the success of the punishment to realize its goals. Even when the punishment inflicted by an agent X is impartial, effective, and just, it could be illegitimate simply because it is inflicted by X rather than by another agent—the appropriate agent to inflict it.[39] Under the state-centred justifications, sanctions that are imposed by the 'wrong' agent do not constitute punishment at all, as they fail to realize the goods that punishment is designed to realize.

Locke and Nozick defend a justification for punishment which can be classified as a normative-constraints justification. Under their view individuals in the state of nature have a right to punish (which is designed to prevent further wrongdoing on the part of the wrongdoer herself and on the part of others).[40] Further, individuals not only have a right to punish but also a right to transfer or alienate the right to punish. Lastly, both Locke and Nozick believe that we can attribute to individuals a decision to transfer the right to punish to the state (based on the individuals' own concern to protect their natural rights and the greater effectiveness of the state in calibrating the harshness of criminal sanctions). The power of the state to punish is attributable not merely to the 'usefulness' of the state in realizing the goals of punishment but also to its 'commission to punish' based on the voluntary (or constructive) alienation of the right to punish to the state.

State-centred justifications go further and argue that punishment is an agent-dependent activity. Only the state can punish, namely, by acting in a way that realizes the goals of punishment. State-inflicted sanctions are designed to realize goals or perform tasks that punishment is designed to achieve and those cannot be performed successfully by private institutions or individuals. To develop a state-centred justification it is

---

[39] It is even possible that there is no agent for whom it is permissible to inflict a just sanction.

[40] Locke, *Two Treaties*, chapter 2 (n 28); Robert Nozick, *Anarchy, State and Utopia* (New York: Basic Books, 1977).

necessary to develop a theory of punishment—a theory that will explain what is particularly valuable about punishment and, then, establish that the only agent capable of realizing this value is the state. One indication supporting this conjecture is the earlier observation made, namely that sometimes it is not merely that the act performed by the wrong agent is impermissible, but that it is a different act altogether. A 'blood feud' performed by the wrong agent is not a wrongful blood feud; it is not a blood feud at all. Further, the 'goods' resulting from a blood feud, namely the redressing of the injustice, can be brought about only when the appropriate agent performs the killing. Similarly, it could be argued that the successful performance of certain functions, such as the infliction of criminal sanctions, can be realized only if the appropriate agents engage in it. If the criminal sanction is designed to communicate disapproval, successful communication of disapproval must emanate from those entities whose judgment is especially worthy of respect (such as the state), rather than from agents who have no such privileged status (such as other individuals).

To sum up, traditional justifications maintain that the state ought to be in charge of a task to the extent that it is capable of performing it successfully, and successful performance hinges on contingent factors. In the context of punishment, it is merely the (contingent) superior ability of the state to calculate what the just sanctions are and its power to inflict them that results in the conclusion that the state ought to be in charge of punishing. In contrast, both the normative-constraints justifications and state-centred justifications maintain that the state is uniquely placed to punish for non-contingent reasons. State-centred justifications also maintain that the very value of punishment turns upon the identity of the agent inflicting it. It is not that it is impermissible for non-state agents *to punish;* it is rather that no other agent *can punish,* and any attempt to punish on the part of such agents is bound to fail, and constitute a mere (impermissible) act of violence. As the concept of 'inherently governmental functions' indicates, legal practice also provides support for the view that sometimes the agency of the state is crucial for the successful performance of a task. The aim of the rest of this chapter will be to explain the significance of the agency of the state, and develop a state-centred justification for the provision of certain goods. I shall also try to explicate what the public provision of a good means.

C. Two Conceptions of Public Deliberation: Reason-based Deliberation versus Deferential Deliberation

To develop a state-centred justification, one needs to understand what it means for an act or a decision to be performed or made by the state. The key to the (normative) understanding of what the state does is to understand what the term 'public official' means. The primary hypothesis developed here is that to be performed by the state means to be performed by public officials and what characterizes public officials is their mode of reasoning or deliberation. It is the status of public officials that facilitates engaging in a distinctive mode of reasoning which guarantees that their decision or act is attributable to the state.

For a decision to be attributable to the state, i.e., to be done in the name of the state, one must establish that the state made the decision and that the agent which performed the act complied with an order (or deferred to an order) issued by the state. To clarify what this means this section differentiates between two forms of deliberation: reason-based and deferential deliberation. Under the first form of deliberation, agents recruited by the state identify what the public interest or the common good is and act accordingly. Under the second form of deliberation, such agents defer to the sovereign and act in accordance with its will independently of what they judge to be the public interest. I shall argue that what characterizes acts of the state is that they are performed out of deference and that public officials ought to be characterized as agents whose decisions are in essence deferential to the sovereign.

Let me provide a simple example. Suppose that Rex, the governing person serves as a legislator, a judge, and an executive power. Rex enacts a criminal prohibition against murder, coupled with a threat of capital punishment for its violations. Rex, who is an enlightened and benevolent despot, further promulgates this new norm and seeks its enforcement. Rex is also in charge of prosecuting and convicting criminals, in which case he must complete his task of law enforcement by inflicting the death penalty. I shall assume here that Rex is a legitimate authority (either because he was elected democratically or for any other reason).

Certainly, punishment in such a case is the state's doing. This is so because each and every element in the sequence of events beginning with legislation and ending with punishment has been executed by Rex, acting in his capacity of all-in-one-person government. To be sure, not every act performed by Rex can count as the state's doing. Rex, after all, could have published a novel in which he tells the story of Rex passing a law against murder; presided over a moot court competition finding that the accused raped the victim; or shot his neighbour (who happens to be the actual rapist) over a parking space dispute. Rex the sovereign misfires in these cases because he does not reason and act within the proper institutional settings—settings that grant his words and deeds the normative force of the words of a sovereign. In each one of these cases, Rex may have identified the relevant public interests (whatever they are), strike the right balance between them, and apply them to the peculiarities of the case at hand. Yet Rex's words lack the appropriate normative force, as Rex has not acted as a sovereign. It would prove helpful to exploit the case of Rex in order to explore the ways in which privatizing executive powers may run afoul of invoking the public point of view, and thus of constituting state action.

Suppose Rex seeks the assistance of another individual in executing his court decisions and enforcing the laws he gives, more generally. This assistance can take different forms. First, and least importantly, Rex may simply grab the hand of another, forcefully deploying it in the service of executing a convicted murder (say, by pressing the fingers of this person against the gun's trigger). Certainly, this form of assistance makes no practical or moral difference, and the execution remains Rex's doing, as it always has been. To the extent that this execution is administered on the basis of reasons derived from the public point of view (including also the reasons for the particular way in which the execution is performed, e.g., by using bullets of .22 calibre, rather than .3 calibre), Rex's doing and the state's doing are one and the same.

The remaining two forms of assistance (relevant for our purposes) differ from the preceding form in that they involve enlisting other persons as agents, that is, as creatures exercising their capacities to reason, intend, and judge. Assisting persons, on this view, are not just human instruments whose fingers are being pressed against the trigger of a firearm. Instead, the act of pulling the trigger is for them an upshot of a reflective process of deliberation with respect to administering the nuts and bolts of the capital punishment. However, these two forms differ from each other: one features *fidelity by reason*, the other *fidelity by deference*.

Upon the former form of assistance (fidelity by reason), the enlisted person undertakes to execute the official pronouncements of Rex the legislator and/or judge impartially. The underlying conception of fidelity, fidelity by reason, requires the assistant to display an impartial concern for the interest of society, that is, to perform the task in question in a way that is most conducive to the general good (whatever it is). This requirement does not turn on the assistant's motive for acting impartially. Indeed, the motivation for displaying impartial concern may arise from sincere patriotism, though it may equally be the upshot of Rex setting the right structure of economic incentives to influence the conduct of her assistant. Rather, the impartiality requirement reflects a commitment to decide what to do and how to act in connection with the execution of an official pronouncement by reference solely to concerns that merit, from an impartial point of view, appropriate consideration.

Crucially, the challenge on the part of the assistant is not just to set aside irrelevant concerns, such as his private whims, but rather to make *value judgments*—to reason—about the precise content of the concerns at stake and the best way to balance them against one another, say, in deciding which method of execution or bullet calibre is best overall, i.e., promotes the public good. These judgments proceed from the assistant's point of view, because even an attempt to decide on these matters impartially implies a value judgment (again, by the assistant) concerning what impartiality requires. To this extent, impartially executing the official pronouncements of Rex in fact thwarts, rather than reinforces, the possibility of identifying the execution with the state's doing. This is because the assistant, whose deliberation toward action proceeds from his own conception of the general interest, does not approach the task of executing the order from Rex's point of view, which is the public point of view. Indeed, fidelity by reason opens a critical gulf between the judgment of the state (concerning the need to execute the convicted murderer and the method of execution) and that of the executor (concerning whether and how to administer the execution) precisely *because* it demands that the latter makes judgments concerning the general interest as he (impartially) sees it, but not as it is seen from the point of view of Rex the legislature or adjudicator.

Thus, by invoking an impartial concern for the public good, assistants necessarily misfire insofar as they fail to replicate the public interest as seen from Rex's point of view. Of course, it is possible that there is an overlap between the judgment of the assistant and that of Rex. Such an overlap is at best coincidental. There is nothing in the impartiality requirement that can ensure a systematic convergence between the two persons, especially in matters pertaining to justice and political morality, more generally. In contrast to the commonly held view, impartiality (and reason, more generally) need not be threatened by privatization, as it is commonly held; to the contrary, impartiality is a source of the incongruity that privatization might generate between the state and the outsourced services.

The third form of assistance is based on *fidelity of deference*. Fidelity of deference insists that assistants defer to the judgments of Rex in fixing the contours and details of executing official pronouncements. The deference requirement demands that, for the purpose of administrating the execution of official pronouncements, an assistant must suppress his own judgment (concerning execution) and open up to the judgment of Rex, which is the judgment reached from the public point of view. It is a requirement to take at face value Rex's judgment (whatever it is) and pursue it either because Rex is the sovereign or for any other reason, e.g., because this is required by one's commitment to one's job etc., or even because deference to Rex guarantees one's better prospects in the job.

On this conception of fidelity,[41] recruiting assistance amounts to increasing the available *means* by which Rex can govern her subjects on the basis of his, and only his, conception of the general interest and the best ways to bring it about (including, of course, through setting appropriate punitive responses to crimes). Unlike fidelity of reason, deferential fidelity is assessed not by reference to the general interest as impartially identified from the assistant's own point of view, but rather by reference to the assistant's success in retreating from his point of view and in adopting the public point of view, which is Rex's.[42]

Now return to the real world, where determining whether an action is the state's doing defies the tautological fashion of submerging the state and its doings in Rex and his doings. The challenge of any form of government claiming legitimacy is to make decisions and perform actions in the name of the polity—decisions and actions that can be

---

[41] This brief exposition of the deferential conception of fidelity does not seek to specify the conditions under which deferential execution of government decisions can be possible or justified. This issue is discussed in section E.

[42] The assistant may, of course, abuse his authority if he does not retreat from his point of view.

attributed to the state alone. Otherwise, such decisions and actions are not at all the doing of the state, but rather of one person or political elite pretending that their decisions are those of the polity.

This is clearly understood in the case of a democratic legislature. Yet acknowledging the necessity of courses of action that can be attributed to the public is not unique for proponents of democracy. If anything, it is the burden on the part of any government (democratic or otherwise) claiming legitimacy to act in the name of the polity. Democracy is but one regime purporting to act in the name of the polity, and I do not make here any judgments as to whether it is the only regime that can do so successfully.

Further, the preceding discussion helps to show that the concern for misfiring raised by outsourcing executive services is not unique to the hypothetical case of Rex; it remains the same, irrespective of the specific criteria for determining what counts as speaking in the name of a polity. Indeed, the two conceptions of fidelity (by reason and by deference) mentioned above characterize ways of approaching the task of providing service for another entity independently of the theory that informs this entity's shape and content. The next section investigates what deference to the state requires in the real world of politics and whether, if at all, deference to the state is possible.

D. Public Officials, Community of Practice, and Fidelity of Deference

What are the conditions required for an agent 'to act in the name of the state', namely to act in a way such that its act is equated with an act of the state? Who can claim to be acting in the name of the state? This section defends the claim that being a public official requires deference and that for an act to count as 'deferential' only individuals with certain characteristics—'public officials'—must perform them. Being a public official is therefore not merely contingently conducive to the execution of a task which, in principle, can be performed by anybody; it is conceptually necessary for the very performance of certain tasks, in particular tasks which need to be done 'in the name of the state'.[43]

---

[43] Arthur Ripstein claims that, on Kant's political theory, public officials can speak and act in the name of the omnilateral will of the state insofar as they act for the public purposes

Note that this section does not defend the claim that there are indeed tasks that ought to be done 'in the name of the state', only that for a task to be one that is done 'in the name of the state' it must be executed by public officials (and that public officials have certain characteristics that can be rigorously defined). Part E defends the normative claim that there are certain tasks that need to be done in the name of the state. This account of what deference to the state consists of has descriptive and normative implications. Descriptively, it seeks to account for the lived experience of public service. Normatively, it is rationalized as embodying a commitment to certain ideals; in particular, it is essential for the very possibility of legitimate rule.

The crucial dimension required in order to act in the name of the state is to act deferentially, namely to be deferential to the state. But what does deference consist of? Two initially plausible answers should be dismissed from the outset. First, the mere *choice* of persons to support the government's cause, to follow its commands and to act deferentially, is not sufficient. The government cannot simply make a private citizen its agent by asking him to undertake some governmental tasks, such as imprisoning convicted criminals. The reason that the government cannot turn a willing individual into its agent simply by asking that agent to perform a task is that, in reality, the tasks dictated by the state are typically underspecified, and leave broad margins of discretion. Given the underspecified nature of the 'guidance' it would be presumptuous to attribute the act performed by the agent to the state as there are many ways of performing this act, and the choice between the different ways of performing the act is a choice of the agent and not the state. The different ways of performing the act have different consequences in their effects on people's well-being and impact on their rights. Choosing among the different ways of performing the task must be guided or constrained by the state. Given, however, the fact that the guidance of the state is underspecified, an act performed by an individual is (typically) a private act, representing at best the agent's own view as to what the public good dictates. It cannot therefore be attributed to the state.

defined by the relevant legal mandates. See Arthur Ripstein, *Force and Freedom: Kant's Legal and Political Theory* (Cambridge, Mass.: Harvard University Press, 2009), 192–3. As the argument in the main text will show, the Kantian account does not render the connection between omnilateral will and public officials sufficiently precise. In principle, anyone—for-profit and non-profit organizations included—can satisfy the threshold requirement to refrain from pursuing private purposes in the course of enforcing the law.

For a similar reason, deference to the modern state cannot simply mean deference to the actual will of an identifiable natural person. In this respect, the image of Rex is misleading, as in his case what deference is was determined by recourse to the actual mental state of Rex. But, in reality, no such guidance can be elicited.[44] Surely, however, if there is no fact that one can point to which determines what deference requires it follows that fidelity of deference cannot be required of public officials in the modern state. Should we not then turn to fidelity of reason to solve the mystery of what it takes to act in the name of the state?

Avihay Dorfman and I reject this idea.[45] The deferential conception of fidelity can be reconstructed in a way that makes it feasible. On the proposed view, deference requires the existence of a practice that satisfies certain conditions in order for it to count as deference to the state. The deferring agent defers to a community of practice to which she belongs—a community which collectively determines how to act—and takes this determination as a baseline against which to measure what fidelity of deference requires in each particular case. Perhaps ironically, therefore, deference to the state involves collective determination by the deferring agents themselves (*qua* participants in the requisite practice) concerning what choices are dictated by deference. To this extent, a community of practice properly conceived can overcome the difficulty of assessing what impartial pursuit of the public good requires by establishing an *inter*subjective framework through which the enforcement of the law could proceed from the public point of view.

More specifically, two conditions must be satisfied in order for persons successfully to act in the name of the state: (i) the existence

---

[44] On the will or mental-state account, an agent who operates in the name of the state defers to the actual judgments of the sovereign—Rex. There are however reasons to believe that the mental state account of fidelity of deference fails to fit with the realities of the modern state. To begin with, the mental state account presupposes the existence of an identifiable mental state of a sovereign. But typically the agent whose mental state ought to count, namely the sovereign, has no identifiable mental state. Additionally, the tasks typically performed by public official, such as imprisonment of criminals, waging wars, and maintaining public order, require the constant exercise of discretion on the part of the agent performing these actions. The difficulties are not merely epistemic, since they are not just features of a costly process of inferring what Rex wants. The difficulty is that there is no identifiable agent whose 'will' (understood as a mental state) can be fully specified in advance for the purpose of guiding the operation of public officials.

[45] See Dorfman and Harel, 'The Case against Privatization' (n 5).

of a practice dictating what ought to be done; and (ii) the status of the participants in the practice in particular the role that their deliberations have in making decisions. Thus, this section develops an account of fidelity of deference, the centrepiece of which is the claim that speaking and acting in the name of the state requires the existence of a practice which integrates the political and the bureaucratic in the execution of the relevant functions. This practice, because of the integrative form that it takes, is characterized by its principled openness to ongoing political guidance and intervention. Under this view, political offices ought in principle to be able not only to set the practice into motion but also to determine its content, guide its development, and steer its course. Let us explore these two conditions in greater detail.

Community of practice. The first condition involves the existence of an institutional structure in which the general interest as seen from the public point of view is articulated. As mentioned earlier, a person cannot simply choose to approach the world in which she acts from the point of view of the state, since this point of view cannot be specified apart from an ongoing practice of executing government decisions. Execution is never mechanical; it requires ongoing practical deliberation on the part of public officials when determining how to proceed with the concrete implementation of government policy.

According to this view, approaching the task of execution from the perspective of the state depends upon there being an ongoing framework or coordinative effort in which participants immerse themselves together in formulating, articulating, and shaping a shared perspective from which they can systematically approach the implementation and execution of government decisions, thus tackling questions such as how one should proceed in general and in the particular instance. The process takes a coordinative form in the sense that participants are responsive to the intentions and actions of one another as they go along with the execution of government policy and decision. To this extent, a practice places a freestanding constraint on the practical deliberations of its participants. For instance, what an official does in a particular case depends on the ways her co-officials have approached the matter in similar cases. This form of responsiveness is founded on a joint commitment to support the practice of executing laws by taking the intentions and activities of other officials as a guide to an official's own conduct.[46]

---

[46] The precise elaboration of the structure and possibility conditions of social practices is not important for present purposes. Familiar accounts are given by David Lewis, *Convention:*

The existence of a community of practice renders deferential fidelity by executors possible. This is because the rules generated by engaging one another in this practice guide and constrain the decisions of the agents. The next stage of the argument seeks to establish the conditions that the practice ought to satisfy in order to be a practice of the state.

The integrative form of the practice: politics redux. Privatizing the execution of government functions poses a serious challenge even with respect to private entities seeking faithfully to take on the role of public bureaucracy. The challenge is that the newcomers—the private agents of execution—cannot approach the task of execution from the perspective of the state merely by so pronouncing and even by intending to do so. But this shortfall can, in principle, be overcome by forming a practice. This could be a personal practice, in the case of an individual who undertakes to execute government laws, or it may otherwise be a group practice featuring a plurality of individuals jointly committed to deferring to the conception they come to share in the course of deliberating toward action from one case to another in a way that is consistent and intelligible. Can an action dictated by a practice developed by private agents count as an action done in the name of the state? Were the answer positive, it would undermine the claim that privatization is incompatible with acting in the name of the state.

Given that a community of practice can arise between private individuals, its mere existence is not sufficient for the purpose of speaking and acting in the name of the state. The practice must be able to integrate the political offices into the practice's community.[47] This integration, it is important to note, does not limit the role of politicians to that of setting the practice among bureaucrats in motion by determining the basic rules of conduct and the boundaries of the framework within which bureaucrats deliberate toward action. Rather,

---

A Philosophical Study (Cambridge, Mass.: Harvard University Press, 1969); Margaret Gilbert, *Living Together: Rationality, Sociality and Obligation* (Princeton: Princeton University Press, 1996); Michael E. Bratman, *Faces of Intention: Selected Essays on Intention and Agency* (Cambridge: Cambridge University Press, 1999).

[47] It is important to note that integration stands in opposition not only to a private community of practice, but also to a purely political community of practice. The discussion in the text emphasizes the necessity of the practical integration between politics and bureaucracy. The opposite threat concerns the politicization of the community of practice. Indeed, excessive involvement of politicians in and around the execution of government functions might reduce this practice to mere politics (in the pejorative sense of the word, as associated with blatant sectarianism). For more on the latter threat, see Bruce Ackerman, *The Decline and Fall of the American Republic* (Cambridge, Mass.: Harvard University Press, 2010).

integration enables political officials to influence the ongoing deliberations and everyday actions performed by bureaucrats within these boundaries. A practice of public officials that takes the integrative form does not merely operate among bureaucrats (with politicians taking the back seat), but rather includes among its engaging participants both politicians and bureaucrats.

An integrative practice is crucial because otherwise the rules of conduct generated by a practice are no less private (in the appropriate sense) than the rules that a private individual happens to adopt when asked by the government to imprison a convicted murderer in her basement. The inclusion of politicians in the practice of execution is necessary to forge a connection between the rules generated by it and the general interest (as seen from the public point of view). Privatization, insofar as it cuts political officials off from the community of practice, denies the remaining members of this practice—e.g., employees of a firm—access to the state's conception of the general interest.

Normally, outsourcing is inconsistent with the integrative form that a practice must exhibit to count as a practice of the state. Perhaps even the very point of outsourcing in this area is to break with the political-executive integration and, in its stead, to embrace a strict institutional and functional division of labour between law-making (or law-applying) and law-executing. On this view, the government is in charge of setting the desired ends and of imposing basic constraints on the means that the private executor can deploy in pursuit of these ends (whatever they are). It then steps back to make room—*an arena of permissibility*, as it were—for the private entity so that the latter could meet the designated ends with whatever means, provided that they are consistent with the basic constraints set out by the government. In that, outsourcing gives rise to a practice among executors which takes a separatist, rather than an integrative, form.

Consider the case of employees of an either for-profit or non-profit organization faced with the task of imprisoning convicted criminals. Such employees must decide the precise content of the competing interests at stake and their relative weights, as part of determining how to proceed in any particular case. Deferring to the rules generated by the practice in which they—*qua* private employees—act may fall short of deferring to the general interest (as seen from the point of view of the state). They can of course defer to their superiors—the chief executives of the employer-organization. Moreover, they can appeal to the basic principles to which they are committed by virtue of joining the organization—the maximization of stockholders' wealth in the case of a for-profit organization and, in the case of a non-profit organization, the vindication of certain values (as construed from the organization's own point of view regarding the meaning of these values).[48] None of these can justify the attribution of such acts to the state.

Indeed, insofar as they participate in a practice that takes a separatist form, namely one that is not constantly nourished by the interaction with politicians, they may be unable to absorb the views of the relevant political offices and determine what the general interest, properly conceived, requires. Against this backdrop, there is no reason to believe that private employees can act on rules and policies that are articulated from the public point of view simply by virtue of participating in an ongoing practice. The practice that they follow is not sufficiently integrative in the sense that it does not provide politicians the opportunity to shape its contours. It is thus implausible to describe their efforts in executing laws as the doings of the state.

This can be illustrated by turning our attention to the Israeli private prison case. In deciding to strike down the statute that authorizes the establishment of private prisons, Chief Justice Beinish of the Israeli Supreme Court identified the type of powers that employees of the private prison have under the proposed legislation. Such powers include:

the power to order an inmate to be held in administrative isolation for a maximum period of 48 hours; the power to order the conducting of an external examination of the naked body of an inmate; the power to order the taking of a urine sample for an inmate; the power to approve the use of reasonable force in order to carry out a search on the body of an inmate and the power to order an inmate not to be allowed to meet with a particular lawyer.[49]

Such decisions must be made in a prison on a regular basis and they cannot be dictated in advance, as they require responding to evolving circumstances. At the same time it is essential that such decisions be

---

[48] A non-profit organization can surely seek to promote the state's interests. But insofar as this commitment depends on the organization's conception of these interests, it remains fundamentally sectarian. This would be true even when the organization takes an impartial stance toward the realization of these interests as it depends upon the question of what (from the organization's point of view) impartiality requires.

[49] HCJ 2605/05 (n 26).

made in the name of the state. How could such decisions be made 'in the name of the state' if, in reality, they must be made by the prison warden? This is the puzzle which can be resolved by the concept of integrative community. Integrative community guarantees: (i) that the decisions of the warden are not the by-product of his own vision as to the public good but are grounded in a practice; and (ii) that the practice is that of the state, as the community to which the warden belongs is an integrative community. Politicians and bureaucrats participate in determining the rules governing this community. The inclusion of politicians in the practice is necessary to forge a connection between the rules generated by it and the general interest (as seen from the public point of view). The rules generated by the integrative practice—the rules that govern moves within the practice and set the baseline against which to determine what deferential fidelity requires—are the product of practical deliberation that spans the entire range of governmental hierarchy which is to say, all the way up to the highest political office and all the way down to the lowest level prison warden.

Note that this argument does not focus on how much and to what extent politicians make actual use of their power to influence the practice. In some cases and with respect to some spheres of state action, politicians seldom use their power. That said, it is the combination of the potential for intervention and guidance of the practice, on the one hand, and the readiness of the politicians to intervene whenever they are unsatisfied with the ways in which the practice operates, on the other, that counts. Accordingly the realization of this potential is not in and of itself crucial to determine whether the political offices are sufficiently integrated into the community of practice. Instead, what is crucial is the participants' Hohfeldian liability to the power of political officials to place them under a duty to act in certain ways and the willingness to exercise this power whenever politicians are unsatisfied with the ways in which the practice operates.

Nothing in this argument turns on a formal definition of 'public official' or 'private employee'; the spectre of tautology in this respect is hence groundless. Executors are 'public officials' by virtue of being participants in the practice. They are not officials prior to it.[50] Their participation in a coordinated effort (say, to imprison convicted

---

[50] The practice-based account of what is a public official need not apply globally. Indeed, there may be compelling reasons to invoke other definitions of public officials in other contexts (say, for resolving disputes governed by labour law, torts, and so on).
It is evident that some contemporary regulatory schemes that are commonly associated with

criminals) renders the practice possible, to be sure. Accordingly, it is in principle possible that private employees of a private firm would be considered, under this analysis, public officials. This may be in the (fantastic) case in which they satisfy the two conditions articulated above: that of participation in a *practice* which takes an *integrative* form.

One last clarification is in order. The deferential conception of fidelity cannot render excusable or justifiable every instance in which public officials suppress their own respective judgments (concerning how one ought to proceed). Serving the Nazi regime is one obvious example, though other small-scale cases of blatant immorality on the part of the government may be sufficient to count as a compelling reason against displaying the otherwise virtuous commitment to deferential fidelity. The argument developed here sets to one side the sensational cases, focusing instead on the moral concerns that arise in everyday bureaucratic practice.[51] At the same time, this analysis implies that in contrast to the view of some the duties of deference of public officials are broader than those of ordinary citizens.[52]

Deferential execution of government functions may not be practically available to persons in general. The mere choice of persons to support the government's cause by invoking the deferential conception

Max Weber's influential account of bureaucracy and public office are only contingent; they do not capture what is genuinely distinctive and valuable about public officials. For instance, neither the fixed-salary-based structure of official compensation nor the procedural due process and the legal protection against termination of civil service except for cause is necessary for sustaining a community of practice among public officials. It is of course possible that the employment stability and security associated with the Weberian picture of public office plays an important role in sustaining a viable community of practice that takes an integrative form. Other contemporary aspects of public office, such as qualified immunity, may be tightly connected to acting on behalf of the state. However, while such aspects may be conducive to the sustaining of a community of practice, they are not defining features of such a community. The main themes of Weber's account appear in Max Weber, *Economy and Society*, ed. Guenther Roth and Clause Wittich (Berkeley: University of California Press, 1978), 220–1, 235–6, 958–79, 988, 1028–38; cf. Nicholas Parrillo, 'Testing Weber: Compensation for Public Services, Bureaucratisation, and the Development of Positive Law in the United States', in Susan Rose-Ackerman and Peter L. Lindseth (eds), *Comparative Administrative Law* (Cheltenham: Edward Elgar, 2010), 47.

[51] On the limitations of deference, see Harel, 'Outsourcing Violence?' (n 7). See also the discussion in section F.

[52] For an attempt to defend the view that public officials and citizens do not differ in their duties of obedience, see Kimberley Brownlee, *Conscience and Conviction: The Case of Civil Disobedience* (Oxford: Oxford University Press, 2012). For a critique along the lines set in this chapter, see my review in *Notre Dame Philosophical Books* (29 February 2013) at <http://ndpr.nd.edu/news/37833-conscience-and-conviction-the-case-for-civil-disobedience/>.

of fidelity is not sufficient to turn them into public officials. Public officials can be characterized as those individuals who may act out of deference to the state and its institutions. This section identified two conditions which must be fulfilled for a person to be a public official, i.e., to be capable of reasoning deferentially and therefore to be capable of acting successfully in the name of the state: the existence of a practice and the intimate proximity of the community of practice with political authority.

E. Why Some Goods Must be Publicly Provided: Intrinsically Public Goods

As observed at the outset, many proponents and opponents of privatization (implicitly) hold in common the assumption that the execution of government functions can in principle be performed by either private or public bodies. From their perspective, the only live question is which, between the two bodies, is capable of performing these functions better. In that, they implicitly keep separate the question concerning the quality of performing the function at stake from the one concerning the identity of the agent performing this function. Once again, on this view any agent can, at least in principle, perform the relevant function so that determining who is more capable of performing it turns on purely contingent considerations.

Indeed, the argument thus far has shown that privatization of certain government functions is not merely a (desirable or undesirable) instance of relocating state power of execution from public to private entities. For privatization in this context transforms this power into a purely private one. Accordingly, private entities that are formally vested with 'state' powers of execution nonetheless act in their own name (and not that of the state). More specifically, such bodies inflict *their* own punishment on a convicted criminal, wage *their* own war, and maintain *their* own (private) order. By contrast, public officials, acting under the necessary conditions, can display fidelity of deference to the state, in which case their acts of execution are, in fact, those of the state.

Thus, to the extent that the goods resulting from the acts of public officials depend on their being done in the name of the state, it follows that such goods cannot be realized by private agents. The rest of this section defends the claim that some goods indeed depend upon the public nature of their provision and, consequently (given the analysis in section D), they must be provided by public officials. In other words these goods are *intrinsically public goods*.

That privatization cuts the government off from the privately executed activities carries two important implications. First, to the extent that some goods can only be provided by the state it follows that privatization changes dramatically the character of the goods, rendering the privately provided goods worthless. Second, privatization may be detrimental to the core liberal and democratic commitment to human dignity. In what follows I identify these implications, focusing on the cases of (a) punishment and (b) war.[53]

1. Punishment as an Intrinsically Public Good

This subsection explores first the radical change in the character of public goods associated with a morally deserved punishment once the responsibility for its provision is handed over to private entities. It argues that the success of the infliction of sanctions to communicate the wrongfulness of the action is contingent upon its public provision.

Certainly, private entities can accomplish a variety of desirable goals by exerting violence on their addressees. Thus, for example, privately run prisons can promote deterrence by subjecting convicted criminals to harsh treatment; they also can incapacitate prisoners; and certain retributive concerns can also be promoted by private bodies. To the extent that one such concern is the infliction of deserved suffering on criminals, private bodies can contribute to the promotion of retributive justice. Lastly, with the right structure of incentives in place, a minimal humane treatment of prisoners can also be provided by these bodies.

That said, there exists one respect in which the private provision of violence runs afoul of being what it purports to be, namely, punishment for the public wrong done. Indeed, the infliction of 'punishment' by a private entity is inherently defective.[54] After all, sanctioning a wrongdoer is an expressive or a communicative act of condemnation. It is a public manifestation of condemnation and disapprobation of the

---

[53] This section is also based on the analysis in Dorfman and Harel, The Case against Privatization (n 5).

[54] I do not argue that the exertion of violence by non-state actors can never count as punishment. Parents seem to be able to punish their children; and even the law in certain cases allows for victims of torts (private wrongs) to exert punitive damages from tort-feasors. The argument in the text picks out the case of punishment *for crimes* (*public* wrongs).

criminal deeds.[55] Unlike deterrence and perhaps other conventional goals of punishment, public condemnation is possible in the first place only if it emanates from the appropriate agent. Condemnation is ineffective unless done by an agent who is in a privileged status to that of the one subjected to the condemnation, one whose judgments concerning the appropriateness of the behaviour is worthy of attention or respect.[56] Otherwise, an infliction of 'a sanction' amounts to an act of violence which cannot express or communicate censure for the culpable and wrongful acts done.

To see this, recall that on this account, the privatizing state cuts itself *off* from the privately executed activities (of inflicting 'punishment', waging a 'war', or maintaining 'public' order). These privatized activities are not the doings of the state; private entities vested with the formal authority to execute the activities in question cannot speak and act *in the name of* the state. However, the ability to speak and act in the name of the state is crucial for justifying a violent act (say, that of incarcerating a person), as it is necessary for the punishment to communicate a judgment (concerning the wrongfulness of the act) by the state.

Under this view, the private provision of 'punishment' in fact amounts to the mere imposition of pain and suffering by one private person on another, necessarily failing to realize punishment's intrinsic good of expressing, not to mention conveying, condemnation for

---

[55] This view is shared by many contemporary legal theorists. An early articulation of this claim was developed by Robert Nozick who believes that '[r]etributive punishment is an act of communicative behaviour', and that retribution achieves two goals. The first is 'to connect the criminal to the value qua value', and, the second is to connect the wrongdoer to the value in a way 'that value qua value has a significant effect in the criminal's life, as significant as his own flouting of correct values'. See Robert Nozick, *Philosophical Explanations* (Cambridge, Mass.: Harvard University Press, 1981), 370. Joel Feinberg believes that: 'Punishment is a conventional device for the expression of attitudes of resentment and indignation and, of judgments of disapproval and reprobation.' See Joel Feinberg, *The Expressive Function of Punishment* in *'Doing and Deserving'* (Princeton: Princeton University Press, 1970), 95, 98. Anthony Duff believes that punishment is a 'communicative practice' designed to communicate to offenders the censure or condemnation that they deserve. See Anthony Duff, *Punishment, Communication, and Community* (Oxford: Oxford University Press, 2001).

What is shared by all of these views is the conviction that punishment differs from the mere infliction of harm on the criminal; it is a practice that is meant to convey certain moral judgments and, in this respect, it differs from other practices used by the state to induce individuals to behave in a desirable manner, e.g., taxation.

[56] The respect that is owed to these judgments is not necessarily because they are more likely to be correct. The likelihood of correctness is clearly relevant, but it need not be the only relevant consideration.

public wrongs. Alternatively, the person inflicting the sanction conveys his own judgment concerning the act, rather than that of the state. But his own judgment deserves no greater attention than that of the person who is subjected to the sanction. It follows that there is an interdependence between the provision of the good resulting from punishment—censure—and the agent performing it such that providing the good is contingent upon its being provided by a public official. Other agents simply cannot make legitimate judgments concerning the wrongfulness of the act and therefore cannot punish.

The second implication of the argument follows from the previous one. If the punishment is not a state punishment, it is attributable to the agent inflicting it. But it is unjust to confer upon private entities an official mandate to subject other private persons (be they convicted criminals, residents of an enemy state, or persons threatening to disrupt public order) to physically violent treatment.

Since on this account, criminal punishment is designed to convey condemnation, rather than merely to inflict pain or to deter, the activity of a private individual incarcerating a convicted criminal violates the criminal's dignity. This is because the private warden, who seeks to give effect to the state's condemnation of the inmate, speaks and acts in his name (or his employer's name). His condemnation, therefore, presupposes the privilege of subjecting the inmate to the private warden's judgment concerning how to proceed with expressing condemnation, including judgments concerning what treatment is due at any given moment and in response to every given situation.[57] Since, as argued above, fidelity to the public good depends in the case of the private warden on his own view of what the public good requires, subjecting the inmate to private powers of condemnation offends against the moral equality that exists between the two by virtue of their being private persons. The private warden lacks the moral standing to speak and act in the name of the state. Whereas a public warden, by virtue of participating (in the right way) in the relevant community of practice, can claim that he acts in the name of the state and that 'his' judgments are not his but fundamentally those of the

---

[57] The warden engages her inmates in virtually everything, to be sure, and the engagement ranges from substantially invasive searches and disciplining measures to everyday routine and down to the most technical matters regarding the governance of those living behind bars (such as the selection of the ketchup brand that inmates could get at lunch). For illustrations, see HCJ 2605/05 76 (n 26).

state, a private warden cannot make such a claim, as his judgment emanates from his reasoning and not from that of the state.[58]

Now, to make this case even worse, consider the implication of the state's official endorsement of wardens acting in conformity with the fidelity conception of reason. Indeed, by siding with the private warden in the case just mentioned, the state indicates that it presumes the superiority of this private individual by giving priority to his judgment over the judgment of the inmate (or, for that matter, of any other member of the political community). To this extent, the privatizing state not only allows for the violation of the dignity of its citizens by their peers; but by outsourcing its special power of inflicting criminal punishment, it actively stamps the moral inferiority of those subject to the rule of private entities with a public seal.

2. War as an Intrinsically Public Good[59]

Conventional wisdom suggests that waging a war in furtherance of the state's legitimate interest reflects a special case of inflicting deadly violence on a large scale. Unlike many other instances of mass killings, war is a quintessential expression of political sovereignty. Indeed, war-making is typically about asserting the very existence of sovereignty: the state on the defence purports to regain or preserve its very sovereignty, at least with respect to some areas within its pre-war territory, while the other state seeks to establish sovereignty in its stead. On this characterization, the practice of (just or unjust) war is a political manifestation of force in the service of promoting the general interest as judged by the state.

---

[58] This qualitative difference between public officials and private individuals underlies Max Weber's familiar observation that the public official 'takes pride in . . . overcoming his own inclinations and opinions, so as to execute in a conscientious and meaningful way what is required of him . . . even—and particularly—when they do not coincide with his political views'. Max Weber, 'Parliament and Government in Germany Under a New Political Order', in *Weber: Political Writings*, (ed.) P. Lassman and R. Speirs (Cambridge: Cambridge University Press, 1994), 160.

[59] To forestall misunderstanding, note that the claim that fighting a war ought to be done out of fidelity of deference does not cover every conceivable case of warfare. Instead, this section deals only with wars that are justified on the grounds that they promote a legitimate state-relative interest such as the case of waging a war in self-defence. Thus, this account does not seek to address wars that are grounded in state-independent ends. Such wars can (and perhaps, must) be executed regardless of the identity of the agent who acts for the sake of these ends—the paradigmatic case being wars justified by reference to the demands of humanitarian intervention.

Accordingly, every act taken in the process of waging a war can and should, in principle, be justified by resort to that interest. To the extent (and only to the extent) that the troops deployed by the state act out of fidelity of deference (in the precise manner explained above), the judgments of the troops concerning the means that are both necessary and appropriate to deploy in general and in any particular instance in the war count as judgments made by the state itself.

By contrast, the privatization of the armed force opens a critical gulf between the judgments that might be made by members of this force and those actually made by the state. This is just another way to say that a privatized task force that purports to give effect to the state's decision to go to war in fact speaks and acts in its own name. Its various operations, taken severally and as a whole, cannot express the judgment of the state with respect to their justness. Thus, participants in this private military subject their potential victims to their judgments of how to proceed with the war—what violent measures to apply in every given situation against potential victims—in light of what they judge to be the overall balance of reasons behind the state's decision to go to war. It follows that private soldiers—mercenaries, really—assume a normative power that individual persons normally lack, namely, the standing to subject other human beings to their private judgments, including judgments concerning the justness of killing and maiming them. Perhaps in some extraordinary cases, there may arise good reasons to excuse (or even justify) these apparently criminal acts. The point of this argument, however, is that such considerations cannot be grounded in the law (and ethics) of war, but rather in the law (and ethics) of criminal law *simpliciter*.

The preceding analysis bears directly on one of the most profound debates among non-pacifists regarding the ethics of war. Dorfman and I introduced the terms of the debate and identified the distinctive way in which the account here can illuminate this debate.[60] To begin with, there exist two different approaches to the morality of war.[61] On the

---

[60]   See Dorfman and Harel, 'The Case against Privatization' (n 5).

[61]   For a critical survey of contemporary debates, see Seth Lazar, 'The Morality and Law of War', in Andrei Marmor (ed.), *The Routledge Companion to Philosophy of Law* (New York: Routledge, 2012), 364–79. It would be worth emphasizing that most disagreements revolve around the morality, rather than the legality, of the just war doctrine. Thus, moral critics of the traditional approach to the just war doctrine can (as some of them actually do) concede that this doctrine may be the second-best legal regime that we can furnish at this point. See J. McMahan, *Killing in War* (Oxford: Oxford University Press, 2009), 109–10.

traditionalist approach (most famously associated with Michael Walzer), the practice of engaging in a war picks out a special moral practice, one which is irreducible to ordinary morality; in particular, the thought is that troops are morally governed by principles of action that are qualitatively different from the principles that would apply to them in their non-military, private lives. Traditionalists consider the content of soldiers' moral practice by reference to the question of what it is that soldiers think soldiers ought to do in war circumstances. Walzer, for one, takes this first-person perspective, arguing that 'I [i.e., the soldier] find in them my moral equals,'[62] by which he means that soldiers normally conceive of themselves as governed by rules that are either the upshot of 'mutuality and consent' or of 'shared servitude' between them.[63] Other proponents of the traditionalist approach pursue a contractarian approach. The latter endorses the basic premise made by Walzer, namely the claim denying the application of general morality to the war context while embracing the freestanding morality of professional roles.[64]

The most immediate implication of the traditionalist approach is twofold: first, there exists a strict separation between the morality of deciding to go to war (*jus ad belum*) and the morality of executing this decision in practice (*jus in bello*). Second, as has already been noted, soldiers are morally equal so that just and unjust combatants share precisely the same moral permissions and restrictions in connection with fighting wars.

The revisionist approach (most famously associated with the work of Jeff McMahan), by contrast, insists that there is nothing morally significant about the practice of war that could detach it from the rest of morality. Thus, in a typical statement, revisionists criticize the traditionalist approach for putting forward a 'normative structure that is fundamentally incoherent with the structures that govern our lives in the realm of private violence'.[65] Accordingly, for revisionists, soldiers are people too, and the moral rules of engaging in a war are set by reference to the question of what a private individual who happens to

[62] Michael Walzer, *Just and Unjust Wars* (3rd edn., New York: Basic Books, 2000), 36.

[63] Walzer, *Just and Unjust Wars*, 37 (n 62).

[64] See, e.g., Thomas Hurka, 'Liability and Just Cause', 20 *Ethics & Int'l Aff.* 199, 210 (2007); Yitzhak Benbaji, 'The Moral Power of Soldiers to Undertake the Duty of Obedience: A Contractarian Case for the War Convention' (unpublished manuscript).

[65] Christopher Kutz, 'Fearful Symmetry', in David Roden and Henry Shue (eds.), *Just and Unjust Warriors: The Moral Status of Soldiers* (Oxford: Oxford University Press, 2008), 69, 70.

serve in the army ought to do. This way of approaching the morality of war leads revisionists to deny the two basic tenets of traditionalists' just war theory—that *jus ad bellum* and *jus in bello* are independent and that combatants, just and unjust, are morally equal. The basic thought here is, once again, that the practice of war should be assimilated into ordinary, individual morality. Soldiers can never leave behind, as it were, their basic responsibility for acting from a morally impartial point (be that the execution of war or the keeping of a promise).

But here is the problem. The insistence on moral impartiality gives rise to a counter-intuitive result: the revisionist approach seems to be making the strongest (i.e., non-instrumental) case for the privatization of militaries. Revisionists are not self-consciously aware of this possibility. There is a head-on collision between the application of personal morality to the war context, on the one hand, and the ability of soldiers to speak and act in the name of the state, on the other. Indeed, to say that soldiers are morally obliged to approach the world impartially (as they would ordinarily do outside the context of war) is just another way to say that they are required to act from fidelity of reason. But those who pursue the execution of government decisions out of fidelity of reason in fact speak and act in their private names, rather than that of the state. A war, including in particular a just war, which is executed by private individuals as opposed to soldiers who are public officials, can only be governed by the moral rules that govern private violence, which is to say the moral rules behind criminal law *simpliciter*. To put it blatantly, this view turns the soldiers—including soldiers who are formally drafted and employed by the state—into mercenaries and the war into private acts of killing.

The revisionist view maintains that it is immoral on the part of a soldier fighting in an unjust war to kill another soldier even when this is done in accordance with the rules of *jus in bello*. Under this view there is no reason for a soldier fighting an unjust war to be exempted from responsibility for killing a person who fights in a just war. The soldier should judge the justness of the war prior to his decision to kill, since if the war is unjust so is the killing. In contrast, Dorfman and I have argued that the killing of the soldier can be considered just only insofar as the person who does the killing does not judge the justness of the war.[66] Making this judgment, after all, is what renders the war

---

[66] It is, of course a different question whether the state's judgment is correct, so that the war can be consistent with the demands of just war (whatever they are).

unjust, as the justification for the decision to kill rests on a private judgment concerning the justness of the war.

It is not denied of course that the killing on the battlefield could sometimes be just for reasons that have nothing to do with it being a killing in a war. It could be justified on the part of individuals to kill in order to prevent genocide or other serious violations of human rights. But it cannot be justified as an act of war of a sovereign state designed to protect its integrity as a political community. The justness of such a war is contingent upon its being carried out in the name of the state; the private judgment of the soldier concerning the justness of the war ought to play no role in the soldier's deliberations.[67]

Soldiers (like wardens and public officials, more generally) are also political creatures who assume an important role in the political order. Indeed, they hold a distinctive position in the process of resolving political disagreements among sovereigns. War is no mere exertion of deadly violence (although it surely is that as well). War also constitutes an assertion of sovereignty and therefore belongs to a set of political institutions that purport to regulate the practical affairs of states and their citizens despite, and indeed because of, the deep moral disagreements that arise between them. A successful reconstruction of the practice of war (as well as that of punishment) must account for the irreducibly political nature of this practice and, by implication, the moral importance of the political order.

F. The Limits of Justifiable Deference

The chapter so far has identified the virtues of deference of public officials, focusing attention to cases where deference of public officials is a virtue. It was also shown that there are some goods that cannot be provided in the absence of such deference on the part of public officials—intrinsically public goods. Further, deference was defined as requiring complete suppression of the judgment of public officials as to what the public interest dictates. Public officials are required to defer, i.e., act in accordance with 'integrative practices', rather than make independent evaluations as to what public interest requires.

---

[67] Note that it does not follow that citizens ought not to refuse to join the war in the first place, if it is unjust; only that once they fight in the war the justness of the war ought not to be relevant to their deliberation.

But what are the limits of such deference? After all, every person in the twenty-first century can be expected to acknowledge the limitations of justified deference of public officials. The history of deference is too often the history of evil, while the history of resisting deference since Antigone is the history of admirable heroism and goodness. To the extent that the analysis herein is incompatible with this observation it must be rejected.

To do so let me identify two limitations on the justifiable deference of public officials. Public officials are not exempted from making normative judgments. Prior to their decision to defer, public officials should make two types of moral judgments. First, public officials are required to fill only public offices which are necessary for the performance of legitimate state functions. Public officials ought therefore to make a moral judgment concerning the appropriateness of the public office they fill. A guard in a concentration camp is not a public office necessary for performing a legitimate state function. It would therefore be impermissible for a person to become a public official of this sort, as the functions performed by such a public official are not legitimate state functions.

This however is not enough. The delineation between different types of public officials is not always clear. A public official who serves a legitimate state function may at times be asked to perform tasks that fall outside of the scope of responsibilities of the legitimate public office. Fidelity of deference requires a public official to defer to those orders that fall within the scope of the responsibilities of the public office. A soldier is assigned the task of protecting the state, not the task of killing citizens. A soldier thus ought to make a judgment whether the decision he is about to execute promotes the state functions that the role is designed to promote.

This observation may raise the suspicion that some of the concerns voiced here are merely semantic. After all, one can always define the scope of responsibilities of the public office in normative terms, such that the public official would be required to make normative judgments including judgments such as whether the sanction he inflicts is proportionate to the crime committed, or whether the war he fights is a just one, etc. Thus, McMahan's view under which soldiers ought to make moral judgments concerning the justifiability of the war could easily be 'translated' into the proposed conceptual framework by stating that the public office of a soldier requires soldiers only to fight just wars. Hence, fighting unjust wars is no longer 'a legitimate state function' and, therefore, fighting such wars is beyond the tasks of the public office of a soldier.

I do not deny that at times identifying the scope of responsibilities of the public office may involve normative judgments, such as whether the act promotes the public interest. Yet, I believe that, most typically, the moral scrutiny required of a public official in identifying the scope of responsibilities of the (legitimate) public office is significantly less demanding than the moral scrutiny required of the state in establishing the public office in the first place, defining the scope of responsibilities of the public office, and issuing orders to the officials occupying it. A prison guard ought not in most cases to release a prisoner simply because he believes (even justifiably believes) that the sanction is too harsh. There is therefore a discrepancy between a moral judgment concerning the justifiability or permissibility of an order of the state to engage in a task and the justifiability or permissibility of the act of an official of the state following such an order. It is often the case that it is permissible or even required for a public official to act in accordance with an order, although it is impermissible or unjust on the part of the state to issue such an order. This discrepancy is not a matter of an excuse granted to an official (although such excuses may at times be relevant to the judging of the behavior of the public official). Instead such a discrepancy is founded on the irreducibility of political morality to private morality.

G. Conclusion

The contemporary debate concerning privatization rests typically on factual conjectures concerning efficiency and accountability of the different agents. More specifically this debate is grounded in an attempt to identify agents who are more capable of performing a state function in the furtherance of the public interest. The success and failure conditions against which the decision or the act is measured are, in principle, independent of the identity or the status of the agent making the decision or performing the act. The basic premise of this debate is that determining who ought to perform the function is grounded in answering the question of who is more capable of performing it and the criteria of success do not hinge on the identity or the status of the agent. This chapter inverses the order of this reasoning: it is not that *who ought to do the task depends upon who can succeed in doing it;* rather, it is that *who can succeed in doing it depends upon who ought to do it.* The traditional justifications provided by both friends and foes of privatization are mere rationalizations. In reality the opposition to privatization is not grounded in contingent facts concerning the foresight and the loyalty of the agent; it is founded on more foundational principles of political theory.

Inversing the reasoning in the way suggested exposes a primary flaw in the dominant reasoning concerning privatization. Political practices such as punishment and war promote a variety of desirable ends (such as deterrence and security). But their justifications depend not merely on the successful realization of these ends; rather it depends on the ability to attribute the realization of these ends to the agent whose judgments counts, i.e., to the state. The trouble with conventional theories of punishment and war is that in rushing to guarantee the realization of these respective ends they fail to take seriously the concern for political legitimacy and such legitimacy is contingent upon the agent to whom the decision can be attributed.

4

Necessity Knows No Law[1]

A. Introduction

Chapter 3 established that there are some decisions and actions that are valuable only if they are performed by the state. It is the task of this chapter to establish that some decisions and actions must be performed by private individuals. It is shown that dignity requires that some acts often characterized as 'public' ought to be reconceptualized as private acts. This is because certain forms of deliberation can only be performed by private individuals and not by public officials.

Why would an act ever offend dignity if performed by a public official rather than by a private individual? The argument developed here is based on a normative distinction between acts performed under the direction of principles or rules and unprincipled, context-generated acts—acts performed not under the guidance of rules, but under the force of circumstances. The decisions or actions required in extreme cases ought to be performed strictly as acts of necessity. More specifically the agents who perform them ought not to be guided by general rules, principles, or precedents. Instead they ought to make particular rule-free judgments, not guided by norms. Given that public officials must operate on the basis of rules, such decisions cannot be made by public officials.

The use of rules or principles in exceptional cases of the type I discuss here presupposes the commensurability of human lives: some human lives may have to be sacrificed for the sake of protecting others. But, as

[1] This chapter is based on Alon Harel and Assaf Sharon, 'Necessity Knows No Law', 61 *University of Toronto LJ* 845 (2011).

human life in the Kantian terminology has value but no price, no such exchange value can be fixed and, consequently, the use of rule-based reasoning is impermissible. Dignity requires that in cases of emergency, sacrificing the lives of one person for the sake of others is permissible only when it is perceived to be exceptional and unprincipled, i.e., when it does not indicate a commitment to comparative evaluation of the lives of one person against another. A private act in cases of emergency does not offend dignity because it is not authoritative; it does not purport to establish a fixed exchange rate between the lives of different people. This is not so in the case of an official acting in the name of the state.

To establish my claim Assaf Sharon and I use a decision of the German Constitutional Court, in which the Court declared a prominent provision of a new German anti-terrorism law unconstitutional and void. Section 14 of the Civil Aviation Security Act[2] enacted in the Bundestag in June 2004 authorized the Minister of Defence to order that a passenger airplane be shot down, if it could be assumed that the aircraft is being used against the lives of others and if downing it were the only means of preventing this danger. This section was explicitly drafted with the attacks of 9/11 in mind.[3] The German Constitutional Court declared the provision unconstitutional on the grounds that it violates the constitutional right to dignity (Article 1 of the German Constitution) and the constitutional right to life (Article 2 of the German Constitution). In particular, the court emphasized that the provision treated the innocent passengers aboard such a plane as objects without providing them due legal protection.[4] Indeed, something seems amiss in permitting the killing of innocent civilians under these circumstances. Yet the idea that no action ought to be taken to protect the lives of others—most likely many more in number—seems equally disturbing.

This is but one of a large class of policies and measures that have been vigorously debated anew in the wake of the attacks of 11 September

---

[2] 11 January 2005 BGBl 1 at 78.

[3] For a useful summary of the case, see Oliver Lepsius, 'Human Dignity and the Downing of Aircraft: The German Federal Constitutional Court Strikes Down a Prominent Anti-terrorism Provision in the New Air-Transport Security Act', 7 *German LJ* 761 (2006).

[4] Bundesverfassungsgericht (BVerfG—Federal Constitutional Court), 59 Neue Juristische Wochenschrift (NJW) 751 (2006). An English translation is available at <http://www.bundesverfassungsgericht.de/entscheidungen/rs20060215_1bvr035705en.html?Suchbegriff=luftsicherheitsgesetz> (*German Plane Case*).

2001. Does the threat of mass suffering and death justify torture, pre-emptive strikes, invasions of privacy, extraordinary rendition, and other violations of fundamental rights? How are we to adjudicate such questions from a theoretical moral perspective?

These doubts are new expressions of old disputes. The object of dispute, although probably of a more general scope, is often treated in relation to a family of legal and moral phenomena Sharon and I called *extreme cases*.[5] These are cases characterized by radically irregular circumstances, typically involving catastrophic consequences, avoidance of which requires severe measures. The leading examples all involve situations in which actions that are normally regarded as illegal and immoral are necessary to prevent great harms, such as the death of many people. Extreme cases evoke a familiar dilemma. On the one hand, there are strong deontological sentiments—sentiments which imply that we ought not to torture or kill innocent individuals even if this is likely to save lives.[6] The prohibitions on killing and torturing are grounded in the sacredness of life (or life's intrinsic value), which is sometimes used to justify the claim that the life of a person ought not to be sacrificed even for the sake of saving the lives of several others.[7] On the other hand, there is an equally powerful conviction that when the threat is grave and when the consequences might be catastrophic, lives may have to be sacrificed and rights may have to be infringed upon. The case of the rogue plane brought before the German court triggers the same dilemma. The killing of innocent civilians by the state seems morally and constitutionally intolerable. Yet, at the same time, allowing a plane to crash into a densely populated area is clearly an unacceptable alternative.

Two positions reject the existence of the dilemma entirely, thereby indicating the outer limits of the debate, while another traditional view represents an intermediate stance. The first position rejects the deontological intuition and claims that consequences—and consequences

---

[5] Harel and Sharon, 'Necessity Knows No Law' (n 1).

[6] The deontological intuition can also be phrased in terms of rights—agents ought not to violate rights even if doing so is likely to lead to more rights being respected. See, e.g., Robert Nozick, *Anarchy, State and Utopia* (New York: Basic Books, 1974). For a survey of the literature, see Alon Harel, 'Theories of Rights', in Martin P. Golding and William A. Edmundson (eds.), *The Blackwell Guide to the Philosophy of Law and Legal Theory* (Malden, Mass.: Blackwell Publishing Ltd, 2005), 191.

[7] Note that I do not maintain that intrinsic value always implies prohibitions of such a type. It is not therefore intrinsic value *as such* that generates the prohibitions, but the distinctive characteristics of the intrinsic value of human life.

alone—are to determine what ought to be done in all cases, extreme cases included. The other extreme is occupied by the position often called absolutist deontology. This position rejects the intuition that deontological rules must sometimes be violated to prevent catastrophic outcomes. According to the absolutist deontologist, one is never allowed to kill the innocent or to violate rights, *come what may*. A notable intermediate position between consequentialism and absolutist deontology is threshold deontology. Threshold deontologists maintain that deontological constraints apply so long as the awfulness of the consequences remains under a certain threshold. Once the threshold is reached, consequentialist considerations should apply.

Section B rejects each one of these three traditional positions, as it shows that none recognizes the seriousness of the dilemma of extreme cases. Instead, section C proposes a new position reconciling the conflicting sentiments. Unlike threshold deontology, this solution is not merely a compromise that lies between the extremes of consequentialism and absolute deontology. The proposal turns on the idea that, correctly understood, what is most pernicious for deontology is (at least sometimes) not merely the violation of moral rules as such, but their *principled* or *rule-governed* violation. Analysing the distinction, this section explicates the conception of deontology on which this proposal rests. The fundamental idea is the rejection of the identification of deontology with rules that have no exceptions. Deontological constraints are not incompatible with exceptions; in fact exceptions can be required by deontology. Under this understanding, deontology is based on the idea not of absolute moral rules allowing no exceptions, but rather of unconditional duties and prohibitions. Maintaining a normative distinction between acts performed under the direction of principles or rules and unprincipled, context-generated acts—acts performed not under the guidance of rules, but under the force of circumstances— allows for accommodating the necessity of infringements in extreme cases within a deontological framework. The actions required in extreme cases ought to be performed strictly as acts of necessity. More specifically, the agents who perform them ought not to be guided by general rules or principles. Instead, they ought to make particular judgments, not guided by norms. Part D applies this framework to the case of rogue planes and also shows how the category of exceptional cases and the distinctive modes of reasoning required in such cases can be shown to follow from the Kantian conception of human dignity. The use of rules or principles in exceptional cases presupposes the commensurability of human lives: some human lives may have to be sacrificed for the sake of protecting others. But, as human life in the Kantian tradition has value but not a price, no such exchange value can be fixed, and consequently, the use of rule-based reasoning is impermissible. Section E establishes that in extreme cases reasoning cannot be conducted by the state, as it cannot be performed by public officials. Only private individuals can reason. Unlike the deliberation characterizing public officials the reasoning of private individuals in such cases does not constitute part of a practice and is not responsive to precedents or rules. This is precisely what renders such reasoning permissible (or even mandatory) in cases of emergency. Section F draws some further consequences and conclusions elaborating on and extending these arguments.

B. Deontology: Categorical and Absolute Impermissibility

What shall we do when the only way to prevent calamity involves doing what would otherwise be clearly and quintessentially wrong? Are we permitted, or even required, to shoot down a civilian plane threatening to crash into an urban centre? Within a deontological framework the answer, it seems, is simple. If the prohibition on killing the innocent is a deontological prohibition, it must always be wrong to shoot down a plane containing innocent civilians. In its ruling on legislation authorizing such action, the German Constitutional Court expresses this thought:

Such a treatment ignores the status of the persons affected as subjects endowed with dignity and inalienable rights. By their killing being used as a means to save others, they are treated as objects and at the same time deprived of their rights; with their lives being disposed of unilaterally by the state, the persons on board the aircraft, who, as victims, are themselves in need of protection, are denied the value which is due to a human being for his or her own sake.[8]

---

[8] See *German Plane Case*, para 122 (n 4). Note that the deaths of the plane's passengers are foreseen but unintended effects of the act of preventing the plane from being used to kill. Yet, the mere fact that this is a foreseen rather than an intentional killing does not imply that there are no serious moral concerns about shooting the plane. The case of the plane is similar to the

One natural way of understanding this paragraph is as an affirmation of an absolute deontological prohibition forbidding the downing of a plane under these circumstances.

Before proceeding let me mention only one important qualification to this deontological prohibition. Many deontologists have argued that if it is possible to kill people who are destined to die anyhow for the sake of saving others, this action is permissible.[9] The so-called principle of secondary permissibility suggests that shooting the plane down may be permissible, as the passengers of the plane are destined to die anyhow.

To overcome this problem one can simply modify the case such that the principle of secondary permissibility is inapplicable. One can assume for instance that shooting the plane down may kill a few unfortunate persons on the ground that would not die otherwise. Alternatively one can assume that some of the passengers on the plane would not die unless the plane is shot down or, at least, that the passengers' chances of survival are higher if the plane is not shot down. Under such circumstances it is evident that many deontologists would maintain that shooting the plane is impermissible.

Is it, however, impermissible to down a plane under circumstances in which it threatens the lives of innocent victims? Similar questions have of course been debated by contemporary moral theorists, particularly in the context of the debates concerning deontology.[10] It seems that consequentialists would be more favourably disposed towards the view that it is permissible (or even mandatory) to take such action under extreme circumstances, while (some) deontologists would be committed to the position that it is never permissible to do so. Yet most committed deontologists would oppose the view that it is never permissible to take actions of this sort.

---

case known in the literature as the grenade case—a case in which an agent starts a grenade to stop a trolley foreseeing that it will kill innocent bystanders. In such a case we cannot say that the bystanders are used as a means (as their presence, like the presence of the passengers in the plane, is not necessary for the saving of lives) and yet, it is commonly assumed by deontologists that starting the grenade is impermissible. See, e.g., Frances Kamm, *Morality Mortality* (Oxford: Oxford University Press, 1996), ii. 173.

[9] See Kamm, *Morality Mortality*, ii. 198–200 (n 8). The court is not oblivious to this concern. See *German Plane Case*, para 130 (n 4).

[10] See, e.g., Shelly Kagan, *The Limits of Morality* (Oxford: Clarendon Press, 1989); Samuel Scheffler, 'Introduction', in Samuel Scheffler (ed.), *Consequentialism and its Critics* (Oxford: Oxford University Press, 1988).

Even orthodox advocates of deontological prohibitions concede that certain significant risks warrant the infringement of rights—including the right to life.[11] A leading strategy for dealing with the dilemma of extreme cases is what has come to be known as *threshold deontology*. Thus, most contemporary deontologists agree that deontological injunctions can be overridden under certain circumstances. Even if one concedes that shooting down a plane carrying fifty passengers in order to save fifty victims is not justified, the numbers can surely be fiddled with until an acceptable ratio is achieved. What about shooting down fifty passengers to save 1,000 victims? What about 10,000? And what about shooting down two to save fifty? The issue surely must not hinge on playing with the numbers. As a matter of principle, there must be some ratio of victims to potential victims that would indeed justify the downing of the plane.[12] This is not merely an abstract observation of moral philosophers. The duties to protect are an established component of many constitutions, including the German Federal Constitution. This duty entails a duty to protect the potential victims of a terrorist attack, and such a duty, enshrined in the constitution, may require under certain circumstances infringing some people's rights.

Some of the difficulties faced by threshold deontology are familiar, and need not be rehearsed here.[13] One difficulty, however, has not received proper attention. Threshold deontology is not faithful to the underlying values and commitments of deontology of at least one central brand—Kantian deontology.

The basic challenge faced by threshold deontology is to address the following question. If the life of one person cannot be sacrificed for the sake of saving one other person, or two, or even one hundred, why can it be sacrificed to save one thousand, or ten thousand, or one million? The natural answer of a Kantian threshold deontologist is to maintain that while sacrificing one person to save two or three violates the

---

[11] The best-known deontologist who makes this concession is Robert Nozick in his famous footnote. See Nozick, *Anarchy, State and Utopia*, 30 n.* (n 6); see also Thomas Nagel, *Mortal Questions* (Cambridge: Cambridge University Press, 1979), 56.

[12] The literature concerning threshold deontology is vast. For a useful review of the literature, see Eyal Zamir and Barak Medina, 'Law, Morality and Economics: Integrating Moral Constraints with Economic Analysis of Law', 96 *Cal. L. Rev.* 323 (2008).

[13] See, e.g., Eyal Zamir and Barak Medina, *Law, Economics, and Morality* (Oxford: Oxford University Press, 2010), 51–6; Larry Alexander, 'Deontology at the Threshold', 37 *San Diego L. Rev.* 893 (2000).

victims' dignity, the sacrifice of one to save a thousand does not violate the victims' dignity. In other words, there is a threshold above which the sacrifice of life does not constitute a dignity violation.

This answer however fails because Kantian deontology opposes not merely the crude consequentialist metric of exchange; it abhors the very process of exchanging lives *as such*. The concept of dignity is at the foundation of the deontological theories examined here. Yet, dignity as Kant phrased it, 'admits no equivalent' and therefore the willingness to sacrifice one for the sake of two or one for the sake of ten lives or a thousand lives raises the same type of questions and concerns. Allowing consequences to determine whether dignity was violated or not seems inconsistent with the notion of dignity as understood by Kant. As dignity 'admits no equivalent', sacrificing the lives of one in exchange for a thousand lives is not more respectful of dignity than sacrificing the lives of one in exchange for a hundred. It is the very sacrificing of one life *in exchange* for other lives (and not the number of lives sacrificed) that compromises dignity.

It follows therefore that if threshold deontology is to be justified, it is not because sacrificing a life of one person for the sake of saving a million does not violate dignity, but because the compromising of the dignity of the victim is sometimes justified. The threshold deontologist may maintain that there are two principles at play here: a dignity-based deontological principle forbidding the killing of innocent people, and another principle mandating the saving of innocent people. The latter principle may at times override the former. So when the first principle is outweighed by consequences, it is outweighed by a different principle with a different rationale, i.e., one that is not deontotological and is not dignity based. This is a possible answer but it remains somewhat ad hoc, unless it is explained how it is that consequences come to matter. In other words if, as deontology assumes, consequences do not always determine the rightness and wrongness of actions, why does this change when their weight increases? Further, incorporating consequences in this way certainly deviates from the Kantian framework for which, as dignity forms a foundational value of this system, it must override any other non-foundational principles. It seems therefore that while threshold deontology triggers decisions that seem reasonable on their face, it is difficult to justify it (at least to the extent that one is inclined to use a Kantian framework).

This difficulty seems to be mirrored in the literature on threshold deontology. Threshold deontologists commonly profess that they cannot provide us with a clear statement of the threshold; they cannot provide us, that is, with a rule determining when a threshold has been crossed. Moreover, we are not even provided with a clear list of criteria for making such determination. This renders the idea of a threshold an unprincipled compromise between the horns of the dilemma, since it remains unclear why consequences start to matter all of a sudden.

Threshold deontology seems to conflict with the Kantian foundations of deontology, in particular it conflicts with the value of dignity as understood by Kant. The challenge therefore is to provide an account that will justify using force in cases of emergencies and yet be respectful of the Kantian insight that dignity 'admits no equivalent'. Section C is devoted to addressing this challenge.

C. Necessity Knows No Law

In his discussion of law in the *Summa Theologiae*, Aquinas addresses cases of emergency in which 'the observance of [a] law would be hurtful to the general welfare' and says that in such cases the law 'should not be observed'.[14] He argues that if:

the perils be so sudden as not to allow of the delay involved by referring the matter to authority, the mere necessity brings with it a dispensation, since necessity knows no law.[15]

What does it mean that 'necessity knows no law', and how does this claim justify acting contrary to law in cases of necessity? Aquinas's dictum can be interpreted in two ways: an instrumental (pragmatic) way and a principled way. Under the first, the law is simply not rich enough to capture the complexity and diversity of circumstances, whilst consequentialist reasoning requires admitting exceptions to the law. As Aquinas says: 'All law is ordered to the common well-being of men and gains the force of law precisely from this fact. To the degree that it fails in accomplishing this end, it loses its binding force.'[16] On the other hand, the principled, non-consequentialist interpretation requires differentiating between rule-based and non-rule-based behaviour,

---

[14] St Thomas Aquinas, *Summa Theologica* (trans. Fathers of the English Dominican Province, Christian Classics 1981) (1948), pt. I-II q. 96, art. 6.

[15] Aquinas, *Summa Theologica* (n 14).　　[16] Aquinas, *Summa Theologica* (n 14).

independently of the desirability of the actions resulting from such reasoning. There are circumstances under which it is simply wrong to use rule-based reasoning. Aquinas may have acknowledged this when he observed, 'He who in a case of necessity acts besides the letter of the law, does not judge the law; but of a particular case in which he sees that the letter of the law is not to be observed.'[17]

This ambivalence between pragmatic and principled justifications for resisting rule-based reasoning can also be seen among jurists. Many contemporary jurists oppose the incorporation of exceptions into legal rules. Often this sentiment is based on the pragmatic concern that by codifying exceptions, one provides incentives to abuse the codified exception.[18] Yet, in other contexts the opposition to codification is grounded in a more principled position, which is expressed in somewhat vague or metaphorical terms. Incorporating exceptions into the law, it is claimed, is against the 'genius and spirit of our law';[19] it is alien to any system of law;[20] it threatens to deform or stretch the law.[21] Incorporating provisions designed to address exceptional situations is destructive to the very spirit of the law and its underlying values. What, for instance, seems particularly offensive to the opponents of legalizing the 'ticking bombs' exceptions to the prohibition against torture is the fact that:

an effort is also being made to see whether something like torture can be accommodated *within the very legal framework that purports to prohibit it*. The American executive seems to be interested in the prospects for a regime of cruel and painful interrogation that is legally authorized or at least not categorically and unconditionally prohibited.... An effort is being made to see whether the law can be stretched or deformed to actually authorize this sort of thing. The administration does not just take the prisoners to the waterboards; it wants to drag the law—our law—along with them.[22]

---

[17] Aquinas, *Summa Theologica* (n 14).

[18] See, e.g., Richard Posner, *Not a Suicide Pact: The Constitution in a Time of National Emergency* (Oxford: Oxford University Press, 2006), 85–6; Oren Gross, 'The Prohibition on Torture and the Limits of Law', in Sanford Levinson (ed.), *Torture: A Collection* (Oxford: Oxford University Press, 2004), 229, 240.

[19] See, e.g., Jeremy Waldron, 'Torture and Positive Law', 105 *Colum. L. Rev.* 1681, 1719 (2005).

[20] Waldron, 'Torture and Positive Law' (n 19).

[21] Waldron, 'Torture and Positive Law', 1741 (n 19).

[22] Waldron, 'Torture and Positive Law', 1741 (n 19).

Metaphors such as 'drag[ging] the law . . . to the waterboards' seem to capture an important and a valuable sentiment. Yet these are metaphors, and to provide the basis for a normative argument, metaphors must be unpacked. To explicate these metaphors, it is not enough to invoke pragmatic considerations such as the concern that incorporating exceptions invites abuse and manipulation. Instead, principled considerations ought to be appealed to. Such considerations focus, for example, on the permissibility and impermissibility of certain forms of reasoning. In extreme cases, the agent ought not only to *act* in a different way than she acts in non-extreme cases, but she also ought to *reason* differently.

Extreme cases of the type discussed here constitute a distinctive category,[23] characterized by circumstances that command not only actions which are normally impermissible, but also forms of reasoning which are not acceptable in non-extreme cases. Before we establish this, two complementary observations ought to be noted. First, if a threat arises to the lives of a great number of people, then if one has the power to prevent it, one ought to do so. The imperative to save life (when this involves no significant risk to oneself) is itself a deontological imperative.[24] When catastrophe threatens, it does not matter what the law dictates—whoever can prevent it ought to do so. Second, the actions characteristic of extreme cases are such that when unjustly performed, their being permissible, or even ordered, by the legal system cannot serve to exculpate the agent. Thus, if a plane does not constitute a genuine threat to many innocents—if, so to speak, there is no ticking bomb—then the fact that one was ordered to down the plane or torture the prisoner does not justify one's actions. Legislation or legal authorization of such acts plays no justifying role in extreme cases—neither in exculpating the agent when wrongly performed, nor in justifying her inaction when action is necessary. In extreme cases, therefore, legal directives should not impact the agent's reasoning. An agent capable of acting to prevent a calamity must do so regardless of legal direction and authorization. And, when no such threat exists or cannot reasonably be avoided, the agent must refrain from the action regardless of legislation or any other forms of legal authorization.

---

[23] This of course is not to deny that there are vague cases.

[24] If I see a person drowning and can save her (without risking my own life), I ought to do so, even if I know she will crash her car and kill ten people in the future.

In general, the law ought to guide the behaviour of individuals by influencing their practical deliberations. When conducting themselves, individuals ought to incorporate the law into their practical reasoning and follow the laws which apply to them. Legislation of extreme cases cannot, or should not, be incorporated into one's reasoning in this way and is therefore inert. Moreover, the codification of extreme cases can also infect reasoning in non-extreme cases. 'Dragging the law to the waterboards' is an apt metaphor for describing the effects of incorporating exceptions into the legal rules because it suggests the *spreading* of the poisonous effects from extreme cases to the entire array of cases. What it seems to imply is not only that it is epistemically impossible to have perfect laws, i.e., laws that bring about correct directives in each and every case. It also suggests that it is wrong to amend our laws in light of extreme cases (by introducing exceptions) even when this can improve the performance of agents, i.e., generate better decisions on their part, since agents ought not to be guided or instructed by such legal rules or, for that matter by any rules.

These conceptions regarding legislation can be grounded in and explained by moral considerations. Put crudely, the claim is that the incorporation of the exception into the law is wrong because it 'normalizes' the exception and corrupts the law. Codification of extreme cases puts them on a par with other legal directives. The law prohibiting the killing of innocents and the law permitting it are on a par, separated merely by variations of circumstance. But this undermines a crucial difference: only the prohibition on killing innocents is an acceptable principle. Only the forbidding of torture is an acceptable rule. Such actions are in principle wrong. Although particular instances of these types may constitute unavoidable exceptions, rules allowing them cannot be accepted as norms. By legislating them, their status as exceptional—as cases that exceed the reach of principled, rule-like directives—is undermined. And the legal system becomes one that incorporates and places on equal footing directives forbidding mistreatment of individuals and directives allowing it. By incorporating it the exceptional becomes part of a routine requiring agents to consider each and every time whether the circumstances specified in the law justify the killing.

These ideas might have a basis in Kant. In his *Lectures on Ethics* and his essay 'On the Supposed Right to Lie from Philanthropy', Kant expresses two opposite positions regarding the apparently similar cases of the robber at the door and the murderer at the door. In the *Lectures on Ethics*, Kant presents the case of a 'necessary lie'. This is a case in which a robber appears at one's door asking whether one's money is in the house. In this case, Kant says, 'the lie is a weapon of defence' and, hence, allowed.[25] In his polemical article 'On the Supposed Right to Lie from Philanthropy', he presents the case of a murderer asking about the whereabouts of an innocent person for the purpose of killing him. In such a case, Kant surprisingly says, it is forbidden to lie.[26] These apparently irreconcilable positions have triggered a wealth of literature proposing solutions, emendations, or criticisms of Kant's views.[27] This chapter however does not aim to survey these works nor to take issue with them, but merely to present one way of thinking about the issue that may help in mitigating the conflict between these two texts.

In his essay 'On the Supposed Right to Lie', Kant's main concern is to reject the idea advanced by Constant against his theory of morality according to which duties are secondary to rights. That is to say, A has a duty to B to ϕ only if B has a right to be ϕ'ed to by A. Thus, to one who has forfeited his right to be told the truth (by threatening to harm another), there is no duty of truthfulness. Countering this view, Kant urges that because moral duties are unconditional, they cannot depend on there being a corresponding right. Duties, says Kant, precede rights, for otherwise they would not be unconditional (as they must if they are to constitute moral duties at all). The question, then, is what makes a duty conditional. Without going into the intricacies of Kant's exegesis, Sharon and I suggest that a proper understanding of this notion requires distinguishing it from an absolute duty. An absolute duty is one to which there can be no *exception*. An unconditional duty, on the other hand, is a duty that is not conditioned by anything contingent, such as the agents' desires. The duty to tell the truth irrespective of how much the lie may serve the social good is unconditional because it includes no clauses conditioning it on consequences. The duty not to torture *so long* as it serves the greater good of society is conditional because it includes such a conditioning clause.

---

[25] Immanuel Kant, *Lectures on Ethics* (1781), ed. Peter Heath and J. B. Schneewind, trans. Peter Heath (Cambridge: Cambridge University Press, 1997), 204.

[26] Immanuel Kant, *On a Supposed Right to Lie from Philanthropy*, in Immanuel Kant, *Practical Philosophy*, ed. and trans. Mary J. Gregor (Cambridge: Cambridge University Press, 1996), 611–15.

[27] For some recent accounts see Tamar Schapiro, 'Kantian Rigorism and Mitigating Circumstances', 117 *Ethics* 32 (2006); Allen W. Wood, *Kantian Ethics* (Cambridge: Cambridge University Press, 2008), 240–58.

In the *Lectures*, on the other hand, Kant is concerned not with questions of moral principles and the relation between rights and duties, but rather with the practical moral questions of what is to be done in cases of necessity. In this context what is at issue is a practical matter: if one is put in a position where acting according to the dictates of moral principles will cause unavoidable harm, can one stray from the principles? The question is not about which principles one ought to adopt in the first instance, and Kant nowhere in this discussion suggests that the duty not to lie should be amended such that it does not apply to cases of necessity. This certainly does not alleviate the tension between Kant's texts since he (at least) seems to maintain in the essay on lying that one is forbidden to lie to the murderer at the door. Yet Assaf Sharon and I have expressed the view that this is a possible way of making sense of both texts.[28] As far as moral principles go, duties are unconditional and, hence, the only acceptable principle regarding lies is that they are forbidden. When it comes to practice, there can arise cases in which this duty ought not to be upheld. But while this can warrant deviation from the rule, it does not warrant its replacement by another rule, nor its emendation.

For the Kantian-inspired position just presented, the focus of the discussion is the agent's reasoning. By incorporating lying as an exception to the rule which dictates truthfulness—i.e., by making the duty of truthfulness conditional—an agent who considers whether to follow the rule of truthfulness has to consider the possibility that lying is permissible under our norms. Even when lying is eventually rejected on the grounds that the circumstances do not call for it, the idea that lying is permissible has been admitted into one's system of moral laws. But, under the present proposal, the moral duty dictates not only not to lie, but rather not to consider the possibility that lying is permissible by our rules. In other words, the prohibition on lying is characterized by unconditionality. Incorporating rule-governed exceptions into deontological rules, as Kant says, undermines their unconditional status.[29]

---

[28] Harel and Sharon, 'Necessity Knows No Law' (n 1).

[29] This view contradicts of course the views of many contemporary philosophers who deny that the reasoning of an agent (and in particular the agents' intentions) can ever affect the rightness of the act. See, e.g., Judith Jarvis Thomson, 'Self Defense', 20 *Philosophy and Public Affairs* 20 (1991). Yet although this view gained popularity in recent years it is by no means self-evident or universally endorsed. See, e.g., Jeff McMahan, 'Intention, Permissibility, Terrorism and War', 23 *Philosophical Perspectives* 345 (2009).

It follows that there is a compelling reason not to incorporate exceptions to unconditional duties. But does it also follow therefore that it is never permissible to violate such duties? If killing innocents is always prohibited by the rules, how could it ever be permissible to actually do so? How could the duty remain unconditional when it is sometimes permissible (or even mandatory) to violate it?

D. By Force of the Circumstances

Extreme cases require action that is taken out of necessity and not under the direction of law. Under the circumstances of the particular case, agents ought to act on the basis of the concrete factual necessity, the condition of things, the force of specific circumstances, the necessity of the moment, and similar situation-specific necessitating considerations. These cases resist rule-governed normativity; to put it crudely, being inherently irregular, they cannot be regulated by general rules. It is the force of the circumstances—circumstances in light of which (some of) our principles collapse—that necessitate the action, not any mitigating principles.[30]

What makes a case extreme is precisely the definite and common conviction that it is one where following the laws is unacceptable. The question then becomes, what is to be done when faced with such a case? One option is to jettison or, at least, emend the law. But given the Kantian thought about deontological rules as unconditional, this cannot be the answer. The alternative is to think in terms of rules and exceptions. If something is a genuine exception to a rule, it is not just that the rule doesn't apply to it but that some other, emended rule does. An exception is an instance of the type to which the rule applies, which is not governed by the rule.

---

[30] In his discussion of torture, Christopher Kutz develops an idea that bears some similarity to this analysis and argues that 'in the hypothetical, ideal case, the ticking bomb example does confront us with real necessity, not in our imaginations. Confronted by real, existential necessity, we find that our principles yield. But we must be precise about what this means. The image of ourselves torturing, or authorizing torture, is not a *deduction* from ethical principles. It is rather a *recognition* that our principles could imaginably be unable to withstand the pressure from concrete opposing values.' See Chris Kutz, 'Torture, Necessity and Existential Politics', 95 *California L. Rev.* 235, 264 (2007). Kutz concludes that necessity in such a case is not necessity as justification but necessity as fact.

From a deontological point of view, there is a distinction to be made between performing an unlawful or impermissible act and doing so under a rule or a principle permitting such acts. On the basis of this claim, it is possible to articulate a conception of action in extreme circumstances that is respectful of deontological tenets yet attentive to the gravity of the consequences. To get a clearer view of this, consider again the reasoning of the agent. When downing a rogue plane, for example, the agent may reason from the normative premiss that there is a principle directing him to down a plane threatening many lives, and from the factual premiss that a particular plane does threaten that number of lives, to arrive at the conclusion that he ought to shoot it down. Such reasoning clearly involves a principle according to which shooting at civilians is permissible in cases in which the ratio of those killed and those saved is appropriate. If such principled exceptions are excluded, however, the agent will reason in another way. He will start with the premiss that saving innocent lives is his duty (at least insofar as he is in a position to do so) and, recognizing the factual truth that the only means to achieve this is by downing the plane, conclude that this is what he ought to do. Notice that in this mode of reasoning, no principle permitting the harming of innocents is employed.[31]

On the face of it, this may seem like mere sophism: an empty analytic distinction carrying no genuine moral weight. But this appearance is misleading. Within a proper deontological conception, the reasoning of the agent is a key factor in the determination of the moral status of his actions. Thus, an action's moral status can differ depending on whether it is done as a permissible act under the rules or as an exceptional one. Specifically, there is moral significance in the difference between harming innocents as a principled, permissible act and doing so as an exceptional, unavoidable measure in order to save lives.

This analysis is grounded in a key concern shaping deontology. Kant famously voices this concern in the *Groundwork of the Metaphysics of Morals* when he claims that:

---

[31] For Kant, this should not be described in terms of means–ends reasoning, but as rendering the action itself one of saving lives. For, as Kant says, a categorical imperative 'represents an action as objectively necessary and makes it necessary not indirectly, through the representation of some *end* that can be attained by the action, but through the mere representation of this action itself (its form), and hence directly'. Kant, *The Metaphysics of Morals* ed. and translated by Mary J Gregor (Cambridge, UK: Cambridge University Press, 1996), 15.

everything has either a *price* or a *dignity*. What has a price can be replaced by something else as its *equivalent*; what on the other hand is raised above all price and therefore admits of no equivalent has a *dignity*.[32]

This conception of dignity as incommensurable need not entail its absolute inviolability. A more reasonable interpretation of Kant's thought is that dignity is not to be considered as a currency to be traded, as a replaceable resource to be weighed against equivalents. Deontological morality consists in an aversion to the treatment of human life as having a 'market value', as Kant puts it, as capital to be weighed and traded. Human life and perhaps other comparably fundamental values must not be treated as a good to be maximized, as an asset that can be quantitatively measured and traded against equal or higher quantities of goods. The weighing of lives against lives is what, under this conception, the deontologist primarily aims to avoid. Fundamental values and rights must shape the way we deliberate by setting constraints on the ends we may morally endorse.[33] Harming the innocent under such circumstances can never be justified, although it may be an unavoidable consequence of a necessary action.[34]

In extreme cases, the urgent need to avoid catastrophic consequences clashes with the stringency of deontological constraints. Absolute deontology sacrifices the former element to uphold the latter. Consequentialism and threshold deontology, on the other hand, both try to resolve the conflict by administering a procedure of comparison between the competing considerations in each case. But if they can be weighed against consequences, deontological constraints are no longer unconditional and the values underlying them are mere instruments, goods of 'market value' not 'dignity'. Thus, by entering the weighing game, both consequentialism and threshold deontology (albeit in different ways) sacrifice the gist of deontology—the idea of treating human beings as ends in themselves and of constraints on deliberation and action stemming from their intrinsic value, or 'dignity', as unconditional. The alternative sketched here, on the other hand, allows for

---

[32] Kant, *The Groundwork of the Metaphysics of Morals* ed. and translated by Mary J Gregor (Cambridge, UK: Cambridge University Press, 1998), 426.

[33] Similar aversion to reasoning by weighing is expressed by Nozick, *Anarchy, State and Utopia* (n 6), and echoed by Rawls in John Rawls, *A Theory of Justice*, revised edn. (Cambridge, Mass.: Harvard University Press, 1999), 3.

[34] Note that this essay focuses exclusively on Kantian dignity which, as Kant himself explicitly maintains, cannot be traded; it is not necessarily a general feature of other intrinsic goods.

addressing the urgency of avoiding catastrophic consequences while preserving these deontological sensitivities. Extreme cases might require practical infringements of deontological norms, but do not warrant (nor require) their normative perversion. Extreme cases truly are exceptional.

Let me explore one possible objection to this proposal. According to the deontological conception proposed here, there are circumstances under which planes ought to be downed. And of course agents are called upon to shoot the planes under such circumstances and not to shoot them under different circumstances—circumstances in which the rules prohibiting the downing of planes apply. It follows that agents should identify those circumstances and judge whether the exceptional circumstances prevail. To do so it seems that that the agent ought to construct a rule identifying the exceptional circumstances. But constructing such a rule and acting on its basis are precisely what is impermissible.

Assaf Sharon and I denied the second premiss of this argument. Exceptional cases ought to be identified by the agent, but their iden- tification does not have to be based on rules. In fact, there cannot be a rule specifying what is to count as an exception, for then it wouldn't be an exception. The claim that the distinction between standard cases, to which the rules apply, and exceptional cases, to which they don't, must itself be based on rules, is a position that falls into familiar difficulties. In fact, even when rules can be articulated for our judgments, we often reason on the basis of particular judgments, not rule-like generaliza- tions. Just as the mathematical calculations of the ballistics of a thrown ball are a redescription of our mental process when catching a ball, rather than properly what we do, so the description of reasoning and judgment in terms of rules is sometimes a redescription. There is no difficulty in claiming that a judgment that some rule is inapplicable is not one that is guided by rules; it is simply made without the guidance of rules.[35]

The fact that the downing of the plane ought not to be governed by rules has important implications. An agent cannot use her former actions (or actions of others) as precedents or as guidance for her future

---

[35] This claim does not presuppose that the judgment whether the rule applies or not is easy, or that the correct answer is evident, nor that mistaken decisions cannot occur. It is perhaps somewhat consoling for those who are concerned about moral errors to point out that an error may be excused at times when the judgment, although mistaken, is a reasonable one.

decisions. Every case has to be considered afresh as there is no set of norms governing the decision to down the plane. Establishing precedents, the use of analogies in this respect is no different from using rules to make specific determinations.

It is time now to apply these observations to the case of the plane. Downing a passenger plane is the sort of action that is to be done only when the specific circumstances of the case are such as to make it practically necessary. An agent may only properly perform such actions when she acts merely on the basis of the brute necessity of the circumstances. If the performance is based on the decision of a superior hierarchy authorized by the state, by a precedent or even based on the dictates of law, it is no longer performed strictly on the basis of the necessity of the moment; it becomes part of regular institutional practice. The legal system recognizes necessity as a justification; it exempts individuals from legal responsibility when they act under the circumstance of necessity. But acting on the basis of necessity is dictated by circumstances, not by authorization or specific directives. If it is the right thing to do, downing a passenger plane is to be done regardless of directives, statutes, or rules.

Once legislation authorizing the downing of the plane is reinstated, it permeates the actions of agents acting under its direction even in cases in which these agents judge (or ought to judge) that the plane ought not to be downed. Downing the plane presents itself as a legitimate option that sometimes ought to be chosen and, at other times, rejected. Regardless of whether or not the act of shooting down a passenger plane under extreme circumstances constitutes a violation of the passengers' dignity, the endorsement of such a norm treats the duty not to hurt innocents as conditional and thereby can be said to fail to respect the passengers' dignity. When, on the other hand, the act of downing a plane in exceptional circumstances is dictated by the force of the circumstances rather than governed by a rule, one does not act under the directive of law or under authorization, and thus is not incorporating a principle according to which the lives of the passengers are dispensable or exchangeable. Clearly, downing a plane can be permitted only in circumstances of grave necessity. But—and this is the main point—it can be permitted only *as* an act of necessity, as an act performed strictly from the necessity of the circumstances, and not under the direction of any rules, precedents, or authorizations.

This analysis is grounded in an understanding of deontology as consisting of constraints on moral deliberation—namely, that under the circumstances described here, human lives ought not to be weighed against each other. Specifically, in the extreme cases examined here, there is a prohibition on weighing lives against lives. Under normal circumstances there is no weighing of lives against lives because downing the plane is not a legitimate option. In the exceptional circumstances described here there is no weighing of lives against lives because the shooting is grounded in the urgent need to save lives, which is not guided by any metrics of weighing one life against another.

E. Who Ought to Down a Plane?

In extreme cases agents ought to shoot the plane, and shooting is not rule governed. The agent ought to act on the basis of the concrete factual necessity, the condition of things, the force of specific circumstances, the necessity of the moment, and similar situation-specific necessitating considerations. These cases therefore resist rule-governed normativity.

But whose shooting is it? Is it the individual who shot the plane or is it the state? We saw in Chapter 3 that there are certain forms of reasoning which are not accessible to private individuals—private individuals cannot act on the basis of 'fidelity of deference'. This section develops an analogous argument: that public officials cannot reason in extreme cases 'by force of the circumstances'; acts of the state are practice based. Acting in extreme cases must be an act of a private individual; it can never be attributed to the state.

Chapter 3 established that public officials must be guided by fidelity of deference and such fidelity requires deference to 'integrative practices', namely practices that are shaped and coordinated together by public officials and by persons who hold political office. Given the concept of fidelity of deference and, in particular, the fact that fidelity of deference must be grounded in practices, and that practices are governed by rules, principles, or precedents, extreme cases cannot be addressed by public officials. Hence, when a person who serves as a public official in other contexts may (and in fact should) act in extreme cases, such act must count as a private act; it is not done in the name of the state, as it cannot form part of an integrative practice.

My claim follows directly from the account of who is a public official in Chapter 3. Fidelity of deference requires public officials to 'defer' to the judgments of the state concerning the public good. Deference involves compliance not to a particular decision of a person but to an 'integrative practice': to act deferentially the agent (public official) needs to be constrained by 'a practice'. Practices are characterized by stability, uniformity, and transparency, all of which are essential to the very possibility of deferring to the state. The practice ought to constitute 'an ongoing framework or coordinative effort in which participants immerse themselves *together* in formulating, articulating, and shaping a shared perspective'.[36] Further, 'the process takes a coordinative form in the sense that participants are *responsive* to the intentions and actions of one another as they go along with the execution of government policy and decision.'[37] The responsiveness to previous decisions and to the reasoning of others characterizing a practice presupposes that the agent does not judge the particular case independently of previous and future decisions. Instead, she regards the particular case as fitting into a global normative pattern. Consistency and coherence become central prominent features in making the decision. A decision that forms part of a practice is justified only if it can be rationalized as part of a coherent enterprise.

By participating in a practice (irrespective of whether this practice is an integrative practice or not), the decisions governed by the practice become part of a regular institutional coordinative enterprise and thus defy the inherent irregularity characterizing the deliberation required in extreme cases. Acting 'by force of the circumstances' conflicts with the fundamental principle underlying the acts of public officials. Acts of public officials are embedded in a practice; the justifiability of the acts is always contingent upon their suitability in a more coherent normative order. Decisions of public officials made in their capacity as public officials are dependent upon a practice. Extreme cases defy such reasoning. If public officials are identified as those who operate within a practice and are bound to comply with it, agents facing extreme cases cannot be public officials, as they cannot be guided by a practice. Given this characterization an agent making decisions in extreme cases cannot act as a public official and her act does not count as an act performed 'in the name of the state'.

---

[36] See Chapter 3.   [37] See Chapter 3.

When catastrophe threatens, it does not matter what the law or the sovereign dictates—whoever can prevent it ought to do so. The actions characteristic of extreme cases are such that when unjustly performed, no order can exculpate the agent. Thus, if a plane does not constitute a genuine threat to many innocents—if, so to speak, there is no ticking bomb[38]—then the fact that one was ordered to down the plane or torture the prisoner does not justify one's actions. An order of the minister plays no justifying role in extreme cases—neither in exculpation of the agent when wrongly performed, nor in justifying her inaction when action is necessary. An agent capable of acting to prevent a calamity must do so regardless of legal direction and authorization. And, when no such threat exists or it can reasonably be avoided, the agent must refrain from the action regardless of any orders.

This conclusion may be puzzling to the reader. As in most cases all agents involved in the decision are public officials (a soldier or a minister), it seems natural to assume that the decision to down the plane must be a state decision. A soldier serving in an army shoots a plane. Should it not be enough to justify the conclusion that she is doing it as a public official and that her action is done in the name of the state?

The answer is negative. The fact that an agent serves as a public official does not imply that an act she committed is a state act. Extreme cases are a distinctive category: cases that ought to be governed by a distinctive type of reasoning, which also dictates who the agents capable of engaging in it are. Only private individuals may act in extreme cases and their decisions do not count as decisions of the state.

F. More on the Distinctness of the Exceptional

I have argued that extreme cases constitute a distinct normative category. This distinctness stemming from the exceptionality of the circumstances figures into the forms of reasoning appropriate for them, and restricts the types of considerations that may enter into such reasoning. The leading example thus far has been the case of rogue

---

[38] Or, more precisely, if one is not warranted in believing with overwhelming confidence that such threats exist.

planes. But the analysis applies to numerous current debates including torture, targeted assassinations, and other similar acts.[39]

Torture is strictly forbidden. For some deontologists, no principles permitting torture can be acceptable. And yet when a ticking-nuclear-bomb scenario is invoked, even a deontologist (at least of the brand I have defended) will recognize that torture may be unavoidable. Extreme cases require extreme measures. Violations of our most fundamental norms may be unavoidable. But this does not entail a rejection or modification of our basic rules. What allows the torture is solely the necessity of avoiding catastrophe, not a different law allowing torture in some conditions. Other considerations ought not to be incorporated into the determination of what is to be done in such cases. In particular, long-term considerations such as deterrence and punishment, or institutional considerations such as legal authorization, should carry no weight in extreme cases.[40] When torture, for instance, is necessitated by extreme circumstances, it is to be performed as an act of self-preservation, not as an act of punitive justice or as the implementation of state policy.[41] Further, Sharon and I argued that given the ways the agent ought to reason, such acts ought to be conceptualized as private rather than public acts; public acts are grounded in a rule-governed practice, and being grounded in a practice is incompatible with the nature of the rule-free judgments required of agents in extreme cases.

One significant upshot of this is that extreme cases have little to teach us about the norms we should embrace and policies we should institute. Contemporary debates regarding the legal norms that are to

---

[39] See Assaf Sharon and Alon Harel, 'What is Really Wrong with Torture', 6 *Journal of International Criminal Justice* 241 (2008).

[40] Ironically, it is the leading classical theorist of English constitutional law who understood that, in exceptional circumstances, no relevant distinctions between authorized and unauthorized individuals ought to be made. In his discussion of martial law, Dicey argues that officials can use brutal means to protect the peace, including the infliction of instant punishment, and, 'if need be, put to death persons aiding and abetting the enemy or refusing such aid to the English army. . . . ' Albert Venn Dicey, *Introduction to the Study of the Law of the Constitution* (1897) (London: Elibron, 2005), 506. Dicey however continues and says: 'Let it too be noted that what is true of a general holds good of every loyal subject according to his situation and the authority which he derives from it, e.g., subordinate officer, of a magistrate or even of a private citizen who is helping to resist an invader.'

[41] For more on the irrelevance of the moral status of the potential victim of torture (particularly his or her culpability in creating the threat) and the illegitimacy of considerations of punitive justice which often creeps into the arguments and deliberations regarding torture, see Harel and Sharon, 'What is Really Wrong with Torture', 241 (n 39).

guide the 'war on terror' (most notably the question of torture) have been greatly shaped by examples falling under the category of extreme cases (such as ticking-bomb scenarios). The proposal on offer, however, entails that deliberations about these issues—important and pressing as they may or may not be—should not be swayed by the intuitions invoked by extreme cases. This is not merely due to their rarity or mismatch with reality, but because their inherent exceptionality renders them irrelevant for questions of institutional norms and general instruction.[42]

To conclude, this chapter re-examines the limits of rule-governed behaviour and argues that recognizing these limits may help in maintaining a non-fundamentalist deontological morality attentive to the moral import of emergencies. More specifically, while traditional deontologists characterize deontology in terms of the special strength or even absoluteness of moral directives, a closer examination of the intuitions giving rise to deontological convictions suggests that what actually characterizes deontology is the unconditional nature of moral rules, rather than their special or absolute strength. This conception of deontology shapes a moral stance with regard to extreme cases allowing for the resolution of the dilemma they trigger. Following this reasoning to its further ramification, I have explicated the sense in which extreme cases constitute a unique category.

---

[42] David Luban argues persuasively that the conditions assumed in ticking-bomb scenarios are hardly, if ever, met in reality. See David Luban, 'Liberalism, Torture, and the Ticking Bomb', 91 *Va. L. Rev.* 1425, 1445–52 (2005).

PART III

Why Constitutions Matter: The Case for Robust Constitutionalism

Introduction to Part III

This part defends *robust constitutionalism*, namely the view that the value of binding constitutional directives and the value of the institutional mechanism designed to protect these provisions (namely, judicial review) do not hinge (merely) on their contingent contribution to the substantive merit of the political or legal decisions. In contrast to the prevalent view, constitutions as well as judicial review are not mere instruments to guarantee good, just, or coherent decisions; they are valuable for other reasons and their value does not depend only or primarily on the degree to which they contribute to the substantive merit of the resulting legislation or executive decisions. More specifically, binding constitutional provisions and judicial review are valuable because they transform and restructure the relations between the state and its citizens in various ways. Within a constitutional framework of the type described in Chapter 5, the state has *duties* towards its citizens. The constitutional order consisting of binding constitutional directives facilitates a clear differentiation between duty-based decisions and discretionary decisions. Further, under a just constitutional order citizens have a right that their (justified or unjustified) grievances be heard and be considered by the state. Judicial review, as I show in Chapter 6, is nothing but the institutional embodiment of such a right—the right to a hearing. These features, I argue, are crucial for a just constitutional order.

By 'robust constitutionalism' I refer to two distinct phenomena: constitutional directives that bind the legislature (Chapter 5) and rights-based judicial review (Chapter 6). Chapter 5 defends 'binding constitutionalism'; it argues that the constitutional entrenchment of pre-existing political rights is valuable not merely because such entrenchment contributes to the substantive merit of the resulting norms or decisions. The value of binding constitutional directives is based on the value of the *binding* nature of constitutional norms. Constitutional entrenchment of rights facilitates public recognition that the protection of rights is the state's *duty*, rather than a mere discretionary gesture on its part. I further argue that the popularity of international law and in particular global constitutionalism can also be explained in these terms. Chapter 6 defends judicial review on non-instrumentalist grounds; it argues that whenever a person argues (justifiably or unjustifiably) that her rights are violated, the state ought to provide a hearing. The duty to provide a hearing requires the state (a) to provide individuals with the opportunity to challenge decisions that they believe (rightly or wrongly) violate their rights, (b) to require the state to justify its decisions, and (c) to reconsider its decisions on the basis of the deliberation and act in accordance with the conclusions of this deliberation. Judicial review is valuable not because it is likely to result in 'better' decisions or to better promote or protect rights or minorities, but because judicial review is nothing but a hearing to which individuals have a right.

Both Chapter 5 (defending the entrenchment of binding constitutional directives) and Chapter 6 (defending judicial review) challenge a standard justificatory framework used in constitutional theory: constitutional instrumentalism. Under constitutional instrumentalism, binding constitutional directives and judicial review pose a threat to legitimacy-based concerns, and in particular to fundamental democratic and participatory values. To the extent that binding constitutional directives or judicial review are justified, they must be justified exclusively on the basis of instrumental reasons (concerning, typically the contingently superior quality of the resulting decisions). Binding constitutional directives are desirable because they are likely to be complied with by the organs of the state, and therefore to the extent that these directives are just they are likely to bring about a just society, guarantee better protection of human rights, etc. Judicial review is desirable to the extent that judges typically make superior decisions relative to those of legislatures (with respect to certain spheres such as human rights).[1]

---

[1] More accurately, judicial review is desirable to the extent that the joint efforts of legislatures and courts bring about superior decisions, in comparison to decisions made by the legislature alone.

In both chapters I challenge constitutional instrumentalism and provide an alternative view, namely robust, non-instrumental constitutionalism. Under robust constitutionalism, the goods provided by constitutionalism are not contingent on the substantive merit of the decisions resulting from it. Instead, the constitutional structure ought to be dictated by a distinct concern for legitimacy, and the concern for legitimacy is independent (or, at least, partially independent) of the substantive merit of the decisions resulting from constitutionalism.

The current debate concerning constitutionalism is premised on constitutional instrumentalism. Advocates of constitutionalism (including advocates of binding constitutional directives and advocates of judicial review) rely on instrumentalist arguments, focusing their attention on the (alleged) contingent, superior quality of decisions resulting from constitutionalism. In contrast, critics of constitutionalism typically use both instrumentalist arguments (concerning the allegedly superior quality of legislative decisions) and non-instrumentalist arguments (typically legitimacy-based arguments concerning the value of democratic participation).[2]

Given this state of affairs, it is evident that advocates of constitutionalism fight with one hand tied behind their back: they do not even purport to rely on non-instrumental legitimacy-based considerations; those considerations have become the safe (and exclusive) domain of opponents of constitutionalism—advocates of democratic participation. The challenge of robust constitutionalism is *to level the playing field in constitutional theory*. It aims to add non-instrumentalist legitimacy to the arsenal of instrumentalist arguments favouring constitutionalism—arguments that do not hinge on the contingent claim that constitutionalism is more likely to result in better or more just decisions.

This introductory chapter has two preliminary tasks. First, section B challenges the force of traditional instrumental justifications in constitutional theory. It is therefore a critique of constitutional instrumentalism as such. Constitutional instrumentalism suffers from the defects described in Chapter 1. It rests on factual speculations that cannot be substantiated, and it suffers from inauthenticity or insincerity. Constitutional instrumentalism rationalizes constitutionalism but, ironically, in doing so, it distorts what it purports to rationalize as it fails

---

[2] I do not wish to imply that all legitimacy-based arguments are non-instrumentalist.

to identify and appreciate the sentiments underlying the popular passion for constitutionalism. Second, section C raises objections to the assumption that democratic/participatory concerns always, or at least typically, provide principled presumptive prima facie reasons against constitutionalism. As a matter of fact the conviction that constitutionalism is detrimental to participatory concerns is flawed. I also show that, to the extent that participatory and democratic concerns have some force, they undermine precisely the plausibility of the most influential justifications of constitutionalism: the instrumental justifications of constitutionalism, but they do not affect arguments of the type I defend here.

Before I establish those claims, let me first make an additional observation concerning what I see as one of the contributions of this part to constitutional theory. Constitutional theory has focused its attention in recent years on one component of constitutionalism: judicial review. Yet many of the democracy-based and participatory concerns raised against judicial review could also be raised against the second component of constitutionalism, namely binding (but non-enforceable) constitutional directives.[3] Arguably, entrenchment of binding constitutional norms deprives the majority of its powers to act in accordance with its judgments irrespective of whether courts are authorized to enforce these norms. Hence, in addition to the major conclusions concerning the desirability of robust constitutionalism, this part also contributes to the understanding of a prevalent phenomenon which has been neglected by constitutional theorists—binding unenforceable constitutional directives.

A. The Fallacies of Constitutional Instrumentalism

Constitutional instrumentalism rests on the conviction that the desirability of constitutionalism hinges on the (likely) contingent consequences of constitutionalism, most typically the substantive merit of

---

[3] This was pointed out by Larry Alexander who argued that many of Waldron's arguments against judicial review apply also to the very existence of constitutional norms (independently of whether courts are assigned with the powers of interpreting constitutional norms). See Larry Alexander, 'What is the Problem of Judicial Review?', <http://ssrn.com/abstract= 802807>, 3–4.

the resulting decisions. Under constitutional instrumentalism, the desirability of binding constitutional directives and of judicial review depends upon whether they bring about (or are likely to bring about) decisions that are superior to those that would have been made in the absence of constitutional directives or in the absence of judicial review.

Constitutional instrumentalists differ from each other in the type of values which they argue ought to be promoted and the precise mechanisms which are conducive to the realization of these values. The entrenchment of binding constitutional norms could be instrumentally desirable for various reasons: as will be shown in Chapter 5, binding constitutional directives can influence legislators, affect public opinion, or become part of general societal cultural and moral heritage. To the extent that the entrenchment of such norms brings about such consequences, entrenchment is instrumentally desirable. Similarly, as will be shown in Chapter 6, advocates of judicial review often argue that judicial review is desirable due to its contribution to the substantive merit of the judicial decisions. For instance advocates of judicial review maintain that courts protect rights better than legislatures, or are more congenial than legislatures to the effective protection of democratic and liberal concerns (such as free speech), or their decisions are more principled, coherent, and stable than those of legislatures or even that they protect the choices made by publicly oriented generations, etc.

Under one influential version of constitutional instrumentalism that I have labelled 'epistemic institutionalism', the design of legal institutions and the allocation of powers among these institutions ought to be guided (primarily or exclusively) by epistemic considerations.[4] The institution which ought to be empowered to make decisions concerning the constitution is the institution which is most likely to decide rightly and to act accordingly. Epistemic institutionalism presupposes that there are right answers to constitutional questions and, further, that the question of who is providing the answer has only an instrumental value; what counts is the decision rather than the agent which makes it or the mechanism which brings it about.

The first flaw of instrumentalist theories is simply that without an investigation of the relevant society at stake and its particular circumstances, it is simply too speculative to make judgments as to the

---

[4] See Alon Harel, 'The Vices of Epistemic Institutionalism', 2 *Jerusalem Review of Legal Studies* 2 (2010).

likelihood that a particular institution will 'get it right' or that one institution is more likely to get it right than another. One of the traditional tasks of judicial review is to protect rights. Yet, historical evidence does not support the conjecture that courts, as a general rule, are better protectors of rights than legislatures.[5] Reliable predictions concerning the performance of the courts versus the performance of legislatures can be made only with respect to certain historical and contextual circumstances. These contingencies change frequently in accordance with changes in circumstances, and even with changes in the personal composition of courts or legislatures. Constitutional instrumentalists make use of factual conjectures concerning the quality of institutions. But those are often too crude, resting on anecdotes and speculations. It is not surprising that these factual conjectures are challenged by opponents of constitutionalism. Given these observations, it follows that, at best, constitutional theorists can make recommendations which are specific to a particular jurisdiction at a particular time. Yet this inevitable modesty does not characterize the debates concerning constitutionalism. Advocates of instrumentalist constitutionalism (as well as instrumentalist opponents of constitutionalism) rarely limit their observations to a particular jurisdiction or to a particular period.

Perhaps however, constitutional instrumentalists should simply inculcate the virtues of modesty. Hence, arguably this argument is not against constitutional instrumentalism as such, but against constitutional instrumentalists who simply fail to understand the inevitable limitations of instrumentalism and see the complexity of instrumental arguments and the need to be sensitive to the changing circumstances and their impact on the optimal design of institutional structure.

Unfortunately an attempt to remedy this defect suffers from an additional drawback. Such an attempt radically deviates from the way constitutions are understood by the public and even by those who draft them. Constitutions are typically designed to last for long periods, and the history of the American Constitution illustrates the shifts that take place in the history of such constitutions. It is not an accident that instrumentalists fail to acknowledge the inevitable limitations of

---

[5] David Rabban, *Free Speech in Its Forgotten Years* (Cambridge: Cambridge University Press, 1997); Wojciech Sadurski, 'Judicial Review and the Protection of Constitutional Rights', 22 *Oxford J. Leg. Studies* 275–99 (2002); Adrian Vermeule, *Law and the Limits of Reason* (New York: Oxford University Press, 2009), 231.

instrumentalism. The normative power of constitutions in society S at time T cannot turn on whether the constitution in S at time T is likely to bring about justice, as constitutions generally are meant to last for generations.

Further, even if the instrumental value of the constitution could be established, such a justification fails to be attentive to the real reasons underlying the passion for constitutionalism. In other words constitutional instrumentalism suffers from inauthenticity or insincerity; it fails to identify the real sentiments and rationales underlying the support of constitutionalism. It attempts to rationalize constitutionalism by justifying it on grounds that seem non-controversial: the substantive merit of the resulting decisions. But such grounds cannot explain the public appeal of constitutions.

By doing so, I suggest that constitutional instrumentalists distort what is really valuable about constitutionalism, namely the sense (that advocates of constitutionalism have) that constitutions are a necessary (rather than a contingent) feature of a just or legitimate society. If I am right, there is a gap between what the debate concerning constitutionalism is really about and what instrumentalist arguments can or even purport to establish. The spirit of the debate and the range of participants indicate that the debate concerning constitutional directives and judicial review cannot reasonably be construed as a debate concerning the likely contingent consequences of different systems of constitutional design. The flaw in constitutional instrumentalism is simply its failure to comprehend what is at stake. Constitutional instrumentalism is an exercise in rationalizing constitutionalism, but it fails to capture the more elusive passion underlying the debate: the passion for political legitimacy.

B. Democracy versus Legitimacy

Opponents of constitutionalism often use powerful legitimacy-based arguments. More specifically they argue that constitutionalism deprives individuals of their participatory rights or of their autonomy. Under such a view, at least in the absence of other special considerations, the majority is simply the appropriate or fair or neutral constituency to make decisions concerning the scope of our rights. The conjecture of constitutionalists is that there is at least a strong prima facie case for democratic legitimacy against constitutionalism, as the democratic non-constitutionalist principle is one that is 'fair' and 'neutral'. Jeremy Waldron articulated this view as follows:

Suppose a citizen who disagrees with a legislative decision about rights poses the two questions I have envisaged. She asks: (1) why should this bunch of roughly five hundred men and women (the members of the legislature) be privileged to decide a question of rights affecting me and a quarter billion others?; and (2) even if I accept the privileging of this five hundred, why wasn't greater weight given to the views of those legislators who agreed with me? In democracies, legislatures are set up in ways that provide reasonably convincing answers to these two questions. The answer to the first question is provided by the theory of fair elections to the legislature, elections in which people like *Cn* were treated equally along with all their fellow citizens in determining who should be privileged to be among the small number participating in decisions of this kind. The answer to the second question is given by the well-known fairness arguments underlying the principle of majority decision (MD). It is not my task to defend this here; the fairness/ equality defense of the majority-decision rule is well known. Better than any other rule, MD is neutral as between the contested outcomes, treats participants equally, and gives each expressed opinion the greatest weight possible compatible with giving equal weight to all opinions. When we disagree about the desired outcome, when we do not want to bias the matter up-front one way or another, and when each of the relevant participants has a moral claim to be treated as an equal in the process, then MD—or something like it—is the principle to use.[6]

This claim concerning the rationales underlying democracy is not limited only to opponents of constitutionalism such as Waldron.[7] Moderate advocates of constitutionalism espouse a balancing approach which balances the normative force of democratic decision-making with other liberal concerns for the protection of rights, freedom, and equality. Under the balancing approach proposed by proponents of the moderate view, imposing a binding constitutional directive and,

---

[6] Jeremy Waldron, 'The Core of the Case against Judicial Review', 115 *Yale LJ* 1346, 1387 (2006), footnotes omitted.

[7] Waldron's critique focuses on judicial review but as Larry Alexander pointed out his critique can be directed also against any binding constitutional provisions (irrespective of whether they are judicially enforced). See Alexander, 'What is the Problem of Judicial Review', 3–4 (n 3).

further, granting courts powers to enforce it are always detrimental to important democratic values. Such a loss to democratic values may sometimes be offset by conflicting considerations, namely the importance of protecting rights and promoting autonomy and equality. Consequently, judges ought sometimes to uphold statutes that violate rights in order to promote participatory values.[8]

I wish to deny the presumptive force of democratic concerns and argue that sometimes democracy undermines legitimacy. More specifically I wish to argue that democratic or participatory concerns have force only with respect to some decisions, but not all. Depriving a legislature of the power to violate rights (by entrenching binding constitutional directives or even by establishing a system of judicial review) need not be justified on the basis of balancing pros (liberal values) and cons (democratic or participatory values). Instead, such decisions are not necessarily the type of decisions that ought, in the first place, to be made by the public or by the majority.[9] The presumptive case for majority decisions is illusory. Just as democratic legitimacy is not affected by denying a polity the power to make decisions for other polities, so too democratic legitimacy is not affected by denying the polity the power to violate individual rights.

Take the following analogy. Assume that I owe John $100. Instead of paying, I insist that a vote take place among the citizens of my jurisdiction to decide whether or not I ought to pay John the money. John is outraged. He argues that it is his prerogative to insist that I pay the money. I, on the other hand, argue that it is a matter of balancing conflicting rights. On the one hand, fairness considerations are enhanced by granting citizens or members of a community the power to decide this issue; arguably, members of my jurisdiction are treated as equals if they have a power to participate in all decisions concerning financial debts. On the other hand, granting such a power to the citizens of my jurisdiction may deprive John of his individual right. Perhaps his right to the money weighs more and the citizens ought not to decide whether I ought to pay him or not. But, even if this is so, it is a matter

---

[8] Corey Brettschneider is a primary advocate of this view. See Corey Brettschneider, *Democratic Rights: The Substance of Self Government* (Princeton: Princeton University Press, 2007), 139.

[9] This is true unless of course there are instrumental justifications for authorizing the legislature to make such decisions. For an earlier (and, unfortunately, less careful) defence of the claim that some decisions need not be made by legislatures see Alon Harel, 'Judicial Review and the Value Theory of Democracy', 47 *Representation* 63 (2011).

of balancing John's right to the money and the procedural rights of the citizens of my jurisdiction to political participation.

I think most of us would rightly protest that there should be no balancing there whatsoever. In the absence of special reasons, the decision whether to pay the money ought not to be based on a vote among members of the jurisdiction. To the extent that John has a right to the $100, it is not up to the citizens of the jurisdiction to decide on that matter; to put it somewhat bluntly: it is none of their business.

The reason that this procedure seems wrong on its face is simple. John's reasonable claim in our example is not merely the claim that all things considered I ought to pay him $100. Instead, I believe, John's claim is that the decision whether I ought to pay him or not does not hinge on a vote or a referendum or any other procedure; it hinges only on the substantive merit of his claim. Granting the power to decide to a majority *for the reason that it is neutral or fair procedure* conflicts with John's justified claim that I pay him $100 and, in particular, his justified conviction that his right is not conditional on anybody's good will or preference or judgment. To the extent that we may want to grant the citizens of the jurisdiction the power to resolve the dispute, it therefore cannot be for fairness-based reasons.

Note that this reasoning applies also in cases of uncertainty. While, so far, I have presumed that in fact I owe John $100, the argument would also be relevant in case there is an uncertainty with respect to the question of whether I owe $100 or not. If there is a dispute as to whether I owe $100, it does not seem presumptively appropriate (on fairness or neutrality grounds) to authorize the citizens of the relevant jurisdiction to make decisions with respect to it. Let me examine here two possible objections to this argument.

Under the first objection this claim could be raised against any institution that is assigned the task of settling the dispute between me and John and, consequently, it simply proves too much. After all John also believes that the debt ought not to hinge on the good will or preferences or moral convictions of a court or an arbitrator. Hence it follows that no institution whatsoever can settle the dispute. Needless to say that this is absurd, as the substantive merit of John's claim needs to be evaluated by somebody: a legislature, a court, or an arbitrator or some other agent.

This conclusion does not follow. John's reasonable conviction is that the dispute ought to be resolved on the basis of reason, and that reason dictates that he ought to get his money back. The institution that ought to resolve the dispute ought therefore to be an embodiment of reason. This does not imply that no institution could resolve the dispute, but only that the 'neutrality' or 'fairness' of the institution adjudicating the dispute is insufficient (or even irrelevant). What is relevant is that the institution that settles the dispute uses reason.

Under the second objection, there are numerous differences between the case of John and the case of fundamental political rights. To explore this objection, let me examine an additional case. Assume that you believe in a libertarian system under which the state has the duty to protect property rights. You believe that individuals have a natural right to property which ought not to be violated by the state. Naturally, the implementation (or even the very existence) of such a right may be controversial. We need, therefore, an institution to decide whether a particular norm violates the natural right to property or not. Such an institution may err at times. It may either grant the polity powers it should not have (and, consequently, deprive individuals of their property rights) or, it may deprive the polity of the power to make decisions in cases that do not involve natural right to property (and, consequently violate the right to self-governance). In the latter case, the polity is indeed deprived of a power that it ought to have. But to the extent that you believe in a libertarian system, presumably you also believe that the soundness of the decision to entrench such rights or not to do so does not turn on the fairness or neutrality of the institution, but on the question of whether the relevant institution is likely to make a correct judgment. Thus, precisely as there is no principled fairness-based reason to grant the polity a right to decide whether I owe John $100, so there is no fairness-based reason to grant the public the power to make decisions as to whether a particular norm violates the natural right to property or not.

Opponents of constitutionalism could challenge this analogy and argue that, unlike the case of John, there is a prima facie case against constitutionalism as the establishment of a system of constitutional property rights affects all of us. Each and every one of us would benefit (or be harmed) by such a system. More generally, all of us are affected by the legal rights we have so all of us ought (at least as a presumptive matter) to have a say with respect to what these rights are.

I believe this argument is flawed in two ways. First while all of us are affected by the legal rights we have we are not affected by them to an equal degree. A robust free speech principle protects some (political radicals) more than others (political moderates). If the potential impact of a right is what ultimately justifies democratic participation, it follows that political radicals ought to have a greater say than political moderates in determining the scope of the free speech principle, and this seems wrong. Second and more importantly, what impacts a person in a way that ought to grant that person a say in a decision is ultimately a normative question. Not every consequence that a norm may have on the lives of a person grants that person (even as a presumptive matter) a say. What counts is not merely an impact but an impact of the right kind or the right sort. The mere fact that protecting the right to free expression may affect the interests of all does not imply that all ought to participate in the making of the decision.

If indeed, as suggested above, the question of whether somebody has or does not have a say in a decision does not rest merely on whether it affects her interests, it follows that to establish the case against constitutionalism it is not sufficient to point out that legal rights affect all of us. Most importantly, it suggests that there are no presumptive shortcuts. To establish the case for democratic legitimacy requires a painstaking effort to understand the values underlying democracy and apply them properly. Perhaps there are such values. Perhaps for instance the polity has epistemic superiority, or perhaps granting such powers to the people has important positive consequences in educating the public. But considerations of fairness or neutrality cannot provide such a justification.

There is however one important caveat to this observation. I believe that ironically, there is a strong dignity-based argument against the most popular and influential argument for constitutionalism namely the epistemic justification of constitutionalism. Under the epistemic justification for constitutionalism, constitutionalism is likely to result in superior decisions as individuals are not sufficiently competent to make decisions concerning fundamental rights. Binding constitutional directives and judicial review are likely to bring about better decisions than democratic procedures with respect to these rights.

This argument is based on a distrust of people's normative judgments. Arguably even if the normative judgments of citizens are inferior to those of judges, they still have a right to make them and, relying on binding constitutional directives or appointing a judicial elite to make such decisions for them is an offence to their dignity. Thus while it is not necessarily wrong to deprive citizens of the right to make decisions concerning fundamental rights, it may be wrong to deprive citizens of the power to make decisions concerning fundamental rights *on epistemic grounds* i.e., *on the grounds that they lack sufficient moral knowledge* or *on the grounds that they are inferior in their powers of moral deliberation.* Granting a person rights to make decisions with respect to moral questions simply *because they are superior in their deliberative powers* may raise dignity-based concerns.

Fortunately, I need not explore the soundness of the caveat. If this caveat is sound, it only implies that some of the most influential traditional instrumentalist arguments of constitutionalists are false. This observation should urge constitutionalists to search even more probingly for non-instrumentalist justifications for constitutionalism, which is precisely the challenge of Part III.

C. Summary

Constitutionalism is typically justified on instrumentalist grounds. Constitutional instrumentalism is the dominant position among constitutionalists and non-instrumental legitimacy-based concerns are typically used to reject constitutionalism. In this part I have argued against constitutional instrumentalism. I have also raised doubts concerning the presumptive case for democratic or participatory procedures.

Most importantly, I wish to emphasize again the contribution of robust constitutionalism to the levelling of the playing field in constitutional theory. Advocates of instrumentalist constitutionalism fight with one hand tied behind their back because they start with the premiss that constitutionalism must rest exclusively on instrumental grounds. Principled or legitimacy-based considerations can serve only opponents of constitutionalism. Robust constitutionalism remedies this defect; it adds legitimacy-based arguments to the arsenal of arguments favouring constitutionalism. Chapters 5 and 6 develop the case for robust constitutionalism. Chapter 5 defends binding constitutional directives (and also global binding constitutional directives) and Chapter 6 defends judicial review on non-instrumental grounds.

5

Why *Constitutional* Rights Matter: The Case for Binding Constitutionalism

He who is commanded and fulfills [the command] is greater than he who fulfills it though not commanded.[1]

To be tortured would be terrible; but to be tortured and also to be someone it was not wrong to torture would be even worse.[2]

A. Introduction

The Talmud tells a story of a Gentile who missed a great business opportunity because he did not want to disturb his father by taking a key that was under his father's pillow. The red cow that was his reward for honouring his parents was of immense value at the time. Rabbi Ulla inferred from this story the lesson that if a Gentile, who is not commanded by God to honour his parents, was rewarded so profoundly, a Jew, who is subject to the commandment to honour his parents, would be rewarded even more for so doing. Rabbi Ulla based this conclusion on a statement by Rabbi Hanina that 'he who is commanded and fulfills [the command] is greater than he who fulfills it though not

---

[1] Talmud, Avoda Zara 3a.
[2] Thomas Nagel, 'Personal Rights and Public Space', 24 *Philosophy and Public Affairs* 83, 93 (2005).

commanded'.[3] This chapter applies this lesson to the legislature, and argues that a society in which the legislature honours rights but is not 'commanded to do so', i.e., is not constitutionally bound to do so, is inferior to a society in which the legislature 'is commanded to do so', i.e., bound by constitutional duties protecting individual rights (and complies with them). The latter society is superior for the reason that in such a society individuals do not live 'at the mercy' of the legislature; their rights do not depend on the legislature's judgments (concerning the public good) or inclinations.

Individuals have political rights, and the normative force of these rights is (at least sometimes) independent of the constitutional entrenchment of the rights. The state ought to protect freedoms and guarantee equality independently of whether these are constitutionally entrenched.[4] Some jurisdictions choose to constitutionally entrench these rights while others do not do so. Compare state A in which a benevolent legislature refrains from violating the rights of individuals or even protects these rights vigorously, with state B in which rights are protected to the same extent as in state A, but they are also enshrined in a constitution or bill of rights. Given that there are no other differences between the two states, which scheme (if any) is superior? Is it valuable to constitutionally entrench pre-existing moral/political rights even when such an entrenchment is not conducive to the protection of these rights? Do *constitutional* rights as such matter, and, if so, why?

This chapter addresses that question and maintains that *constitutional* rights matter, as the constitutional entrenchment of pre-existing moral/political rights is valuable (independently of whether such an

---

[3] See n 1. The *Tosafoth*, one of the important Talmudic commentaries, explains the rationale underlying this surprising claim. It argues that one who is commanded is anxious to obey the commandment. Someone who is not commanded obeys because of his own will to do so, and consequently, should not be rewarded in the same way. The *Ritba* (another influential Talmudic commentary) argues that: 'it is the devil who argues when he is commanded, and the devil does not argue when he is not commanded.' A natural understanding of the reference to the 'devil' is the evil residing in every individual, which tempts people to resist what they have been commanded to do. A person's reward is greater when a greater effort is necessary to overcome one's natural inclinations.

[4] Yet, constitutional entrenchment of moral or political rights may change the scope and weight of the pre-existing rights. Constitutional entrenchment changes the expectations of citizens; it may transform the surrounding circumstances in morally relevant ways; etc. See Joseph Raz, 'On the Authority and Interpretations of Constitutions', in Larry Alexander, *Constitutionalism: Philosophical Foundations* (Cambridge: Cambridge University Press, 1998), 152, 173.

entrenchment is conducive to the protection of these rights).[5] I defend what I label 'binding constitutionalism', namely a scheme of constitutional directives binding the legislature. Binding constitutionalism is characterized by the constitutional entrenchment of pre-existing moral and political rights-based duties (constitutional directives). Such an entrenchment of pre-existing moral/political rights need not be accompanied by an effective institutional system of enforcement such as judicial review and, further, it need not be conducive to the greater or more efficacious protection of the rights enshrined in the constitution. Its value is grounded in the fact that constitutional entrenchment of moral or political rights is in itself a form of public recognition that the protection of rights is the state's *duty* rather than merely a discretionary gesture on its part, or that it is contingent upon its own judgments concerning the public good. I extend this analysis also to global constitutionalism and argue that the appeal of international law is attributable not only to its instrumental contribution to the effective protection of rights and the promotion of justice but to the fact that it imposes duties on the state and that the honouring of these duties is not discretionary; it does not depend on the good will of the state or on the discretion of its legislature. The entrenchment of constitutional and international law duties is essential to the protection of freedom. Citizens are freer in a society in which such rights are recognized as duties rather than as resulting from the mere judgments or inclinations of legislatures. This is because in such a society citizens do not live at the mercy of their legislature (or, in the case of international law, at the mercy of the drafters or interpreters of the national constitution) and are not subject to its judgments or preferences.

To justify binding constitutionalism, examine the difference between state A and state B. In state A the legislature refrains (generally) from violating rights. But, given the absence of any constitutionally entrenched rights, there are no publicly recognized limitations on the powers of the legislature. The legislature's decision not to violate rights does not depend upon its publicly recognized duties; instead, it will be shown, it is publicly understood to be contingent on the

---

[5] I do not claim of course that *all* constitutional rights entrench pre-existing moral/political rights. Larry Alexander distinguishes among three ways of conceptualizing constitutional rights. My concern in this chapter is merely with Alexander's second category, namely those rights that incorporate in the constitution real moral rights. See Larry Alexander, 'Of Living Trees and Dead Hands', 22 *Canadian Journal of Law and Jurisprudence* 227, 230 (2009).

legislature's judgments (or inclinations).[6] The citizens of A are 'at the mercy' of the legislature's inclinations (or judgments); they live under the shadow of the legislature's whims. In contrast, in state B, the legislature is publicly bound to conform to the constitutionally entrenched duties and, consequently, citizens' rights do not depend upon the legislature's inclinations; they are publicly understood to be duties to which the legislature ought to conform rather than discretionary decisions on its part.

The rationale underlying binding rights-based constitutionalism is grounded in the significance of the public recognition of rights-based duties binding the legislature. In particular, the rationale is grounded in the publicly salient differentiation between discretionary legislative decisions (namely those decisions that are grounded in the legislature's inclinations/preferences/tastes/judgments), and those decisions that are grounded in the legislature's rights-based duties. While in both state A and state B the fundamental freedoms are protected to the same degree, only in state B are they honoured, i.e., protected *as rights* which bind the state rather than as discretionary measures the protection of which is at the mercy of the state.

Why is the publicly salient differentiation between legislative decisions grounded in rights-based duties and those grounded in mere judgments or inclinations significant? Is it not sufficient to guarantee that rights are adequately protected? As long as the legislature's decision is rights protecting, why should it matter what the grounds for the legislative decision are? This chapter argues that the public recognition of rights-based duties (by means of constitutional entrenchment or by means of international law) is essential for the protection of freedom (understood as non-domination), as freedom does not require merely that the legislature refrains from violating rights but also that it is bound to do so.[7] This implies that the decision to refrain from violating rights should not be based merely on the legislature's judgments or

---

[6] Arguably moral/political rights can also be publicly recognized. Citizens as well as individual legislators can publicly profess their commitment to protect rights and act accordingly. Yet, I shall show in section C that such public recognition is insufficient, as at most it constitutes recognition on the part of individuals/individual legislators and not of the legislature as such.

[7] This observation borrows from the work of neo-republican thinkers. See, e.g., Phillip Pettit, *Republicanism: A Theory of Freedom and Government* (New York: Oxford University Press, 1997). While I rely on Pettit's analysis, my view does not turn upon the particularities of his theory. As a matter of fact it relies on a much broader tradition set by Rousseau, under which freedom is equated with not being subjected to the will of others. See Fredrick

inclinations. While it is possible that (given their existing judgments or inclinations) the legislature in state A refrains from violating rights (and also will refrain from violating rights in the future), individuals in state A are subject to 'domination', namely to the risk of a potential shift in the legislature's judgments or inclinations. Individuals 'are subject to arbitrary sway: being subject to potential capricious will or the potentially idiosyncratic judgment of another'.[8]

While this chapter is theoretical, it explains and rationalizes a prevalent phenomenon which, so far, has not been given sufficient attention, namely the prevalence of unenforceable or under-enforceable constitutional directives. Unenforceable and under-enforceable constitutional directives raise a serious concern for instrumentalist theories of constitutionalism, as it is not evident that such constitutional directives contribute to the greater conformity of the legislature's decisions with its rights-based duties. The prevalence of binding unenforceable and under-enforceable constitutional directives in different jurisdictions (documented in section B3) cannot be easily defended on instrumental grounds. To rationalize it non-instrumental considerations are necessary.

To sum up, I shall defend the view that constitutional rights matter *as such* not merely for instrumental reasons. The constitutional entrenchment of pre-existing moral or political rights-based duties can be justified independently of their (instrumental) contribution to the protection of these rights. Only citizens whose rights are constitutionally entrenched do not live 'at the mercy of' the legislature and, consequently, their rights do not hinge upon the judgments or inclinations of such legislatures.

Section B defines the concept of rights-based binding constitutionalism. Constitutionally entrenched rights differ from mere moral or political rights in that the former are grounded in existing practices, conventions, precedents, etc. This section also establishes that binding unenforceable or under-enforceable constitutionally entrenched directives are a prevalent phenomenon and can be found in many jurisdictions. While this does not imply that such directives are desirable, it provides the motivation to explore whether and why such directives are desirable. Section C investigates the normative foundations of

---

Neuhouser, 'Freedom, Dependence and the General Will', 102 *Philosophical Review* 363, 380 (1993).

[8] See Pettit, *Republicanism*, 5 (n 7).

binding constitutional directives. It argues that binding constitutional directives are necessary for the protection of freedom (understood as non-domination). It also argues that the appeal of globalism (in particular global constitutionalism) can also be explained in the same terms. Precisely as the constitution is a means of protecting individuals from the risks of living 'at the mercy of' the legislature, global constitutionalism is a means of protecting individuals from the risks of living 'at the mercy of' their national constitutions. One of the surprising conclusions of this chapter which will be briefly discussed is that democratic procedures are often detrimental to freedom. This is not merely (as is well recognized) because of potentially oppressive decisions made by the majority but because even when the majority protects rights vigorously, the decision to protect these rights is discretionary. It is based on the judgments or preferences of legislatures and, consequently, it does not acknowledge the binding nature of the state's rights-based duties.

B. Binding Unenforceable or Under-enforceable Constitutionalism

1. Introduction

Binding constitutionalism is a constitutional scheme characterized by the existence of binding constitutional norms constraining the legislature. Such constitutional norms may be enforceable, unenforceable, or under-enforceable. In cases in which a constitutional provision is enforceable, it designates an organ other than the legislature to decide whether the constitutional limitation was observed and empowers such an institution to invalidate legislation. In cases in which the constitutional norms are unenforceable or under-enforceable, the legislature itself is assigned the power of determining the constitutionality of the legislation.[9]

To denote the binding constitutional norms I use the term 'constitutional directives'. In this chapter I focus my attention exclusively on constitutional directives designed to entrench pre-existing moral/political rights (as opposed to constitutional directives which create new rights). Section B2 describes what *constitutional* directives are and in what ways they differ from the moral or political norms binding the

---

[9] I follow here the description of Hans Kelsen, *A General Theory of Law and State* (Piscataway, NJ: Transaction Publishers, 1949), 156.

legislature. Section B3 establishes that binding unenforceable or under-enforceable constitutional directives are prevalent in many legal systems, including constitutions that are typically considered to contain only enforceable directives. Unlike judicial review, the popularity of unenforceable and under-enforceable constitutional directives has not yet triggered a sustained effort on the part of theorists to explore the rationales underlying these directives. This chapter fills this gap.

2. *Binding Rights-Based Constitutional Directives*

Constitutional directives can originate from different sources and be entrenched in different ways. Dicey believed that the constitution consists of two types of rules: constitutional law rules and

> conventions, understandings, habits, or practices which though they may regulate the conduct of the several members of the sovereign power, of the ministry, or of other officials, are not in reality laws at all since they are not enforced by the Courts. This portion of constitutional law may, for the sake of distinction, be termed 'the conventions of the constitution,' or constitutional morality.[10]

Constitutional directives (as I use the term here) can be written or unwritten, enforceable or unenforceable, originating in a custom or in a convention or drafted by the founders of the constitution. In fact the conventions, understandings, habits, and practices are more central to understanding constitutional directives than written bills of rights, as written constitutional norms become 'constitutional' in the relevant sense only by virtue of the fact that they are enshrined in existing practices and conventions. To understand the significance of constitutional norms, let me define what I regard as essential to constitutional directives. The characteristics I find essential to constitutional directives are at least partly a stipulation on my part. They are not identical to other attempts to capture what is distinctive about constitutional norms. Yet they bear sufficient similarity to what is typically referred to as constitutional norms.[11]

---

[10] A. V. Dicey, *The Law of the Constitution* (10th edn., New York: Macmillan and Co. Ltd, 1959), 24.

[11] For another attempt at defining the characteristics of constitutional norms, see Raz, 'On the Authority and Interpretations of Constitutions', 173 (n 4). My primary aim here is to distinguish constitutional norms from mere moral or political norms.

There are three interrelated features of constitutional directives which differentiate such norms from mere moral or political norms. (1) Unlike moral or political norms, constitutional directives are rooted in practices and conventions of certain communities: legislators, lawyers, and judges. To establish that there is a constitutional directive requiring the legislature to legislate or not to legislate, it is necessary sometimes to use past decisions, to investigate existing conventions and practices, and to explore the past behaviour of the legislature. (2) Constitutional directives are typically more determinate and specific than the pre-existing moral or political norms. The existing conventions and practices used in constructing constitutional norms often serve to entrench a duty that is merely one optional norm among the many optional moral or political norms that can legitimately be used to guide the legislature. (3) Given that the content of constitutional norms is partially contingent on existing practices and conventions they typically are accompanied by interpretative privileges of professional institutions/experts.[12] While judgments concerning the content and the scope of the pre-existing moral/political norms are ones that can be made by anybody (and nobody's judgment is privileged), judgments concerning the content and the scope of constitutional directives require some expertise or, at least, privilege those who have some expertise. Let me investigate in greater detail each one of these features of constitutional norms.

First, a constitutional directive is grounded in practices, conventions, and shared understandings of legislators, lawyers, or public officials. To interpret a constitutional norm one has to resort to the way the norm was interpreted in the past, to the conventionally accepted articulations of the norm, and to the ways it was applied in the past. Conformity

---

[12] I do not argue of course that judges or lawyers can *authoritatively* interpret all constitutional norms. After all some theorists (including Dicey) believe that this is precisely what differentiates conventions from legal rules, and as constitutions can contain both conventions and legal rules, it is evident that not all constitutional directives can be authoritatively interpreted by courts. Even if (as many have argued) the sharp distinction drawn by Dicey is flawed and some constitutional conventions can be interpreted by courts, it is beyond doubt that there can be constitutional norms that cannot be interpreted by courts. Yet, as was noted by Nick Barber, even when courts do not authoritatively interpret a constitutional convention, they often indirectly enforce it for various purposes. See Nick Barber, *The Constitutional State* (Oxford: Oxford University Press, 2010), 92–3. Further, even if courts have no role in interpreting constitutional norms, the statements of academics and lawyers concerning constitutional matters have greater impact and influence precisely due to the fact that identifying constitutional norms requires knowledge of past practices and conventions.

with the constitutional directive depends on there being an ongoing framework or coordinative effort in which participants immerse themselves in formulating, articulating, and shaping the meaning of constitutional norms. The task of identifying the constitutional norm takes a coordinative form in the sense that participants are responsive to the intentions and actions of one another as they identify the nature of the duty and its scope. Such a deliberative practice potentially places a constraint on the practical deliberations of the legislature. What a legislature may do in a particular case depends on the ways the legislature has reasoned in similar cases, the ways such decisions have been understood and interpreted by the legal community, etc. As we are speaking of *binding* constitutional directives, it follows that the relevant conventions and practices of the legislature must also reflect the shared understanding that these norms are not discretionary but genuine constraints on the legislature's decisions.[13]

This description of course leaves important questions open such as: who is the requisite community whose views count? To what extent do the norms endorsed by such a community impose real limitations on the decisions of the legislature? Further this description implies that the distinction between social, moral, or political convictions on the one hand and constitutional norms on the other hand is not always clear-cut. At times moral or political norms can be applied and practised while their status as binding constitutional norms may be disputed. Resolving these questions and others like it is not essential for my purposes here; it is sufficient to point out that the constitutional norms differ fundamentally from moral or political norms in that they are grounded in existing practices and the social understandings of these practices.

The extensive reliance on practices and conventions generates a second important feature of constitutional directives. Most typically, the decisions dictated by constitutional directives are more determinate than the decisions dictated by the pre-existing moral/political duties. Constitutional entrenchment of the pre-existing moral/political norms results in greater specificity and determinacy than that characterizing the pre-existing moral/political norms.

---

[13] This observation also applies to new constitutions. In case of new constitutions there are no past constitutional decisions or precedents, but the interpretation of new constitutions relies on existing social understandings and, at times, on foreign practices and precedents.

The pre-existing moral/political norms constrain legislatures; yet there are many ways to honour the moral/political constraints. Constitutional directives typically select one or a few norms among the many morally or politically permissible or acceptable norms. Thus, the constitutionally entrenched norms provide an answer as to which of the moral or political norms that are compatible with the pre-existing moral or political duties will, in reality, govern the decisions of the legislature. Further, once a norm is constitutionally entrenched, it often thereby becomes superior on purely moral or political grounds to other (previously) permissible or acceptable options, as the entrenchment itself creates a set of expectations that, once formed, the polity has good reasons to honour. Constitutions are thus sometimes 'self-validating'; their authority derives from 'nothing more than the fact that they are there'.[14] It follows therefore that even when constitutional directives entrench pre-existing moral or political norms, the constitutionally entrenched norms are not a mere replica of the pre-existing moral or political norms. The requisite polity has to make choices and select among the infinite number of potentially acceptable moral or political norms one specific norm—one that will serve to guide its legislature and, once the norm is constitutionally entrenched, it may become superior (morally or politically) to other norms which potentially could be entrenched.

Third, the two observations above have important institutional ramifications. The fact that the entrenchment of constitutional norms is rooted in conventions, practices, and precedents often provides a justification for professional bodies or experts such as courts and lawyers to have a privileged role in identifying and interpreting the constitutional duties, as such identification requires knowledge of the existing practices and conventions, and such knowledge requires professional training. Even if the system does not grant formal powers to institutions or experts, such as courts or legal experts, institutions and experts have a greater informal role in examining and identifying the content and the scope of constitutional directives than they have in examining and identifying the content and the scope of the pre-existing moral/political norms.[15]

---

[14] Raz, 'On the Authority and Interpretations of Constitutions', 173 (n 4).

[15] Yet, as pointed out to me by my research assistant Eerez Nizan, sometimes legal experts may have a disadvantage resulting from rigid professional convictions based on distorted or flawed past interpretations of the constitutional provisions.

To sum up, constitutional directives differ from the pre-existing moral/political norms in three main respects. (1) Their content is at least partly determined by existing practices, conventions, and precedents. (2) They are typically more determinate than the pre-existing moral or political norms binding the legislature. (3) Given that the identification and interpretation of constitutional norms requires an understanding of the existing practices and conventions, experts are typically granted special privileges (formal or informal) in identifying and interpreting these norms.

Let me add a few words explicating the concept of *binding* constitutional norms. A constitution may contain norms that do not bind the legislature but merely provide it with discretionary guidelines, e.g., identifying certain norms or values as 'constitutionally worthy' or 'constitutionally unworthy', etc. To the extent that a constitution consists of such non-binding norms, such norms may (but need not) be taken into account by legislatures in deliberating. Further, non-binding constitutional directives can also serve non-juridical purposes of a constitution: they may have symbolic significance,[16] or they may serve 'integrative effects', namely serve to solidify the political community and turn it into a harmonious polity.[17] This chapter focuses only on binding rather than discretionary directives.

Naturally, many (and most likely all) legal systems that establish judicial mechanisms to enforce constitutional norms acknowledge the existence of binding constitutional directives. In such systems courts are assigned the power to give effect to the constitutional directives precisely because these directives are binding and courts are expected to better apply the binding norms than the legislature itself.[18] Yet binding constitutional directives exist also in legal systems that have

---

[16] See, e.g., Edward S. Corwin, 'The Constitution as Instrument and as a Symbol', 30 *American Political Science Review* 1071 (1936).

[17] See Dieter Grimm, 'Integration by Constitution', 3 *International Journal of Constitutional Law* 193 (2008). I have doubts whether there are any non-binding constitutional provisions but the question of whether such norms exist or do not exist is a matter of constitutional interpretation. Note that both vague and unenforceable norms can be as binding as any other norm. Preambles of constitutions often have less binding force than the constitutions themselves. For the debate concerning the binding force of the preamble, see Liav Orgad, 'The Preamble in Constitutional Interpretation', 8 *International Journal of Constitutional Law* 714 (2010).

[18] This is the traditional justification for granting courts the power of judicial review. See Alon Harel and Tsvi Kahana, 'Easy Core Case for Judicial Review', 2 *Journal of Legal Analysis* 227, 228 (2010).

no judicial or institutional mechanisms of enforcement. Further, even when such enforcement mechanisms exist, courts are not necessarily assigned with the duty or even the power to enforce *all* binding constitutional directives. Even in systems that establish judicial mechanisms for enforcing constitutional directives, some constitutional directives remain unenforceable or under-enforceable. While the prevalence of enforceable binding constitutional norms can perhaps be justified on instrumental grounds, namely the greater efficacy of enforceable constitutional provisions, the prevalence of constitutional norms characterized by binding unenforceable or under-enforceable constitutional directives is particularly valuable for my analysis, as it is more difficult to justify such directives on instrumental grounds.[19] Section B3 establishes the prevalence of unenforceable/under-enforceable constitutional directives.

3. *Constitutionalism on the Ground: The Prevalence of Binding Unenforceable and Under-enforceable Constitutional Directives*

There are at least three cases that can be classified as instances of unenforceable or under-enforceable binding constitutionalism. (1) Some legal systems, such as Ireland or India contain explicit written constitutional directives that are binding but unenforceable. Neither courts nor any other institution have the power to invalidate statutes on the grounds that they conflict with the (unenforceable) directives. (2) Even in systems that do not contain *explicit* unenforceable/under-enforceable constitutional directives, legal theorists often identify binding unenforceable or under-enforceable directives. (3) Some legal systems endorse binding constitutional directives without determining in advance whether these directives are enforceable or not. The decision to enforce the constitutional directives is a by-product of judicial decisions that took place long after the decision to endorse binding constitutional directives. Hence, while such systems may eventually contain enforceable constitutional norms, the enforceability of these norms was not necessarily envisioned at the time the

---

[19] Of course unenforceable or under-enforceable constitutional provisions can also be efficacious, and their prevalence can also be explained on the grounds of their greater efficacy. Legislatures may be disposed to conform to binding provisions even when they are not enforceable. Yet, at least initially, it seems that enforceable binding constitutional directives are more likely to be efficacious than non-enforceable ones and, consequently, their prevalence can be more easily explained in instrumental terms.

constitutional provisions were entrenched. Each one of these cases indicates that unenforceable or under-enforceable binding constitutional directives are sometimes perceived to be important or desirable. The underlying justifications for such directives will be investigated in section C.

Let me first draw a distinction between unenforceability and under-enforceability of a binding constitutional directive. An unenforceable constitutional directive is one that cannot be enforced at all; no institution can override the legislature's interpretation or understanding of the directive and, further, no institution can provide a remedy in case the legislature violates it. The Indian and Irish 'directive principles' that will be discussed here are examples of unenforceable constitutional directives. An under-enforceable constitutional directive is one that can sometimes but not always be enforced. Thus, the claim that judicial review ought to be used only in cases of clear or blatant violations of constitutional provisions can serve as an example of under-enforceability.[20] Some violations (blatant violations) of a norm can be overridden by courts while others (minor violations) cannot. The constitutional directive is therefore under-enforced, because there are cases (mild violations) where the constitutional directive conflicts with a statute but courts are not authorized to invalidate the statute.

It is time now to examine the three cases of unenforceability/under-enforceability of constitutional directives. First, in some jurisdictions there are binding unenforceable constitutional directives. Two primary examples are the Indian and the Irish Constitutions. The Indian Constitution contains two separate parts: Part III on 'fundamental rights' and Part IV on 'directive principles'. The part labelled 'fundamental rights' protects individual rights and is justiciable while the part labelled 'directive principles' contains a long list of goals that are binding on the legislature and the executive but unenforceable. Article 37 of the Indian Constitution emphasizes both the binding force of the directives and their unenforceability. Article 37 states that the provisions of Part IV of the Indian Constitution 'shall not be enforced by any court'. It asserts also that the provisions in this Part are 'fundamental in the governance of the country and it shall be the duty of the State to apply these principles in making laws'. The standard interpretation of

---

[20] James Bradley Thayer, 'The Origin and Scope of the American Doctrine of Constitutional Law', 7 *Harv. L. Rev.* 129, 144 (1893); Adrian Vermeule, *Law and the Limits of Reason* (Oxford: Oxford University Press, 2009), 96.

this provision is that 'the rights mentioned in the Directive Principles are to be implemented by the executive and legislative branches of the Indian state, and are not to be the subject matter of intervention by the courts'.[21] A notable theorist addressing the Constituent Assembly in 1948 describes the status of the provisions of Chapter IV as follows:

So, the mere fact that they [the directives] are being included in the Constitution shows that every legislature will be found to respect these directive principles in the Constitution, and, therefore, any act which offends the Directive principles shall be ultra vires. Although every citizen will not be able to go to a court of law for enforcement of these principles, yet the President of every assembly will be within his rights to rule out any Bill and say that this Bill cannot be moved because it is against the fundamental directive principles of the Constitution itself.[22]

Interestingly some of the founders of the Indian Constitution were opposed to introducing unenforceable directives and believed that unenforceable directives are nothing but 'political manifesto',[23] or mere 'political propaganda which may safely be ignored'.[24] The great fears were that the non-binding directives would remain platitudes or pious wishes, and would not be effective guides for legislation and policy.[25] Some contemporary constitutional theorists support this claim and argue that the use of unenforceable directive principles 'threatens: 1) to blur the dual-track separation between entrenched constitutional norms and political norms and 2) to undermine the supremacy of the constitution'.[26]

---

[21] See Vijayashri Sripati and Arun K. Thiruvengadam, 'India: Constitutional Amendment Making the Right to Education a Fundamental Right', 2 *Int'l J. Const. L.* 148, 149 (2004). An alternative interpretation is that: 'the fact that the Constitution says the principles "shall not be enforceable by any court" does not mean they are not justiciable, for while enforcement connotes the availability of a remedy only, justiciability entails recognition from the law and validity for all purposes.' See Alex H. Amankwah, 'Constitutions and Bills of Rights in Third World Nations: Issues of Form and Content', 12 *Adel. L. Rev.* 1, 14 (1989–90).

[22] Vol. vii Constituent Assembly Debates 19 November 1948 (<http://164.100.47.132/LssNew/cadebatefiles/C19111948.html>).

[23] Bertus De Villiers, 'Directive Principles of State Policy and Fundamental Rights: The Indian Experience', 8 *S. Afr. J. on Human Rights* 29, 32 (1992).

[24] Ivor Jennings, *The Approach to Self Government* (Cambridge: Cambridge University Press, 1956), 19–20.

[25] J. C. Johari, *The Constitution of India—A Politico-Legal Study* (revised and enlarged edn., New Delhi: Sterling Publishers Pvt. Ltd, 2007), 93.

[26] Jeffrey Usman, 'Non Justiciable Directive Principles: A Constitutional Design Defect', 15 *Mich. St. J. Int'l L.* 643, 645 (2007).

The typical arguments used to justify the entrenchment of binding unenforceable constitutional directives are instrumental ones. One prominent argument in favour of the directives was based on the conviction that the mere fact that the directives are not enforceable in court does not imply that there are no sanctions on their violation. It has been argued that: 'the sanctions attached to the directives are therefore moral, political and judicial to the extent that they provide the framework in which fundamental rights are to be interpreted and understood.'[27] It was also argued that they may have a great effect on public opinion: 'future elections and public opinion would be the main "Implementing" force behind the directives'.[28] In contrast to the fundamental rights enumerated in the constitution that are enforceable in the courts, the directive principles are enforceable by the electorates.[29]

These observations point out some non-juridical impact that the directives have, i.e., their social or political significance. But the Indian constitutional directives also have legal implications. The most important legal implication is that 'fundamental rights can be restricted when the public interest as formulated in the directive principles requires it'.[30] Although the directives of the Indian Constitution cannot be used to nullify legislation, they can be used as an instrument of interpretation and, in particular, they have been used to help the court to uphold laws that otherwise would be regarded as violating the fundamental rights part of the Indian Constitution.[31] Under the view of the Indian court: 'this harmony and balance between fundamental rights and directive principles is an essential feature of the basic structure of the Constitution.'[32]

---

[27] De Villiers, 'Directive Principles of State Policy', 33 (n 23).

[28] De Villiers, 'Directive Principles of State Policy', 33 (n 23).

[29] Mahendra Pal Singh and Surya Deva, 'The Constitution of India: Symbol of Unity in Diversity', 53 *Jahrbuch des Öffentlichen Rechts der Gegenwart, Yearbook of Public Law* 649, 663 (Germany) (2005).

[30] De Villiers, 'Directive Principles of State Policy', 34 (n 23). This view has long been endorsed by the Indian Supreme Court. See, e.g., *State of Bombay v F N Balsara* AIR 1951 SC 318.

[31] As a matter of fact this is part of a much broader doctrine under which 'the judiciary has evolved the doctrine of harmonious construction which implies that it would do its best to harmonise the implementation of the directive principles with the exercise and enjoyment of Fundamental Rights and go to the last extent of invalidating an impugned law if it failed to establish a logical relationship between the two'. See Johari, *The Constitution of India*, 92 (n 25); Peter E. Quint, 'What is a Twentieth-Century Constitution?', 67 *Maryland L. Rev.* 238, 242 (2007).

[32] *Minerva Mills Ltd v Union of India*, AIR SC 1789, 1806 (1980). For an explanation of the significance of the case, see Singh and Deva, 'The Constitution of India', 663 (n 29).

The (limited) juridical ramifications of the Indian directives could be understood to be detrimental to my main claim, as such ramifications suggest that despite the solemn declaration contained in Article 37 that the directives 'not be enforced by any court' the directives influence judicial decisions and thus, at least sometimes, have juridical implications. This conjecture is false. The juridical ramifications of the Indian directives are limited and the directives impose much broader duties than can be effectively enforced by the courts.[33] For my purposes what is important is that the Indian directives have two important features: (1) they are generally unenforceable even if they sometimes have juridical ramifications and (2) the directives bind the legislators (as well as other branches of government); they are not discretionary.

India is not alone in solemnly entrenching binding non-enforceable norms. In fact the Indian legislature imported the concept from Ireland.[34] Article 45 of the Irish Constitution, called Directive Principles of Social Policy, states that: 'The principles of social policy set forth in this Article are intended for the general guidance of Oireachtas [Parliament]. The application of those principles in the making of laws shall be the care of the Oireachtas exclusively, and shall not be cognisable by any Court under any of the provisions of this Constitution.'

One may often find declarations that emphasize the symbolic significance of the directives contained in the 'Irish Directive Principles of Social Policy'. The President of Ireland described these policy directives in the constituent assembly in 1937 as follows:

They will be there as a constant headline, something by which the people as a whole can judge of their progress in a certain direction; something by which the representation of the people can be judged as well as the people judge themselves as a whole ... They are intended to be directives to the legislature. They are not to be determined by the courts ...[35]

Some regard these provisions as 'an indication that the Constitution was more than a legal document: it was the realization of the hopes and

---

[33] Johari, *The Constitution of India*, 88 (n 25). As the Indian Supreme Court asserted: 'The Court cannot make a directive principle justiciable as it does not create a justiciable right in favor of an individual.' See *Gadadhar v The State of West Bengal*, AIR 1963, Cal. 565.

[34] De Villiers, 'Directive Principles of State Policy', 30 (n 23).

[35] Constituent Assembly Debates (11 May 1937) 69 available at: <http://historical-debates.oireachtas.ie/D/0067/D.0067.193705110029.html>.

ideals of the population in general'.[36] These Articles 'show that the Constitution contains more than legal rules: it reflects, in part, aspirations and aims and expresses the political theories on which the people acted when they enacted the Constitution.'[37] At the same time, it is also asserted that these directives contain duties binding the legislature: 'Although the directives are not justiciable they place parliament under a constitutional obligation to promote certain socio-economic ideals.'[38]

Like the case of the Indian Constitution, the Irish 'unenforceable' directives also have some definite juridical implications.[39] The Irish directives are used to interpret the constitution and ordinary statutes.[40] They are also used to determine whether an unspecified right is legally recognized or not.[41] But this does not imply that the Irish provisions are judicially enforceable, only that they have some influence on judicial reasoning.[42] As a general rule these provisions were not designed to be enforced in courts; they are intended to guide the legislatures themselves and to be used by participants in political discourse.[43]

The Indian and the Irish constitutions contain *explicit* binding but unenforceable directives. A second case of unenforceability or under-enforceability rests on writings and conjectures of constitutional

---

[36] Bertus De Villiers, 'Socio-Economic Rights in a New Constitution: Critical Evaluation of the Recommendations of the South African Law Commission', *JS Afr. L.* 429, 429 (1992).

[37] Criminal Law (Jurisdiction) Bill Reference [1976] IR.

[38] De Villiers, 'Socio-Economic Rights in a New Constitution', 429 (n 36). The Irish court asserted that Article 45: 'puts the state under certain duties, but they are duties of imperfect obligation, since they cannot be enforced . . . by any court of law.' *Comyn v Attorney General* [1950] IR 142.

[39] *Landers v Attorney General* 109 ILTR 1 (1975); *Kerry Co-operative Creameries v An Bord Bainne* [1990] ILRM 664; Robert F. Heuston, 'Personal Rights under the Irish Constitution', 11 *U. Brit Colum. L. Rev.* 294, 301 (1977); A. E. Dick Howard, 'The Indeterminacy of Constitutions', 31 *Wake Forest L. Rev.* 383, 408 (1996).

[40] *Landers v Attorney General* 109 ILTR 1 (1975). De Villiers, 'Socio-Economic Rights in a New Constitution', 429 (n 36).

[41] De Villiers, 'Socio-Economic Rights in a New Constitution', 430 (n 36); *Byrne v Ireland* IR 1972 (241); *Murtagh Properties v Cleary* IR 1972 (330).

[42] As a matter of fact the non-justiciable status of Article 45 led some Irish commentators to argue that Article 45 is ineffective. It was said that 'Article 45 has unfortunately proved successful in keeping socio-economic rights largely beyond the remit of the courts and the cases where it has been considered are very much the exception.' See Ciaran Lawor, 'The Conscience of the Nation: Socio-Economic Rights and the Irish Constitution', 5 *UC Dublin L. Rev.* 34, 40 (2005).

[43] Lawor, 'The Conscience of the Nation', 40 (n 42); V. T. H. Delany, 'The Constitution of Ireland: Its Origins and Development', 12 *U. Toronto LJ* 1, 26 (1958).

theorists. Some constitutional theorists believe that even constitutions that do not explicitly entrench non-enforceable binding constitutional provisions contain such provisions. A prime example is the US Constitution that famously contains enforceable binding constitutional duties. Yet prominent American theorists believe that in addition to the enforceable provisions there are 'pockets' or spheres of unenforceable or under-enforceable binding constitutional directives.

In a classic article on American constitutionalism, James Bradley Thayer defended the view that the US Constitution is under-enforceable. Thayer maintains that the courts 'can only disregard the Act when those who have the right to makes laws have not merely made a mistake, but have made a very clear one, so clear that it is not open to rational question'.[44] He further maintains that a person who is a member of the legislature may vote 'against a measure as being in his judgment, unconstitutional' and later vote to uphold this same measure when it comes in front of him in his capacity as a judge.[45] This seemingly strange statement can be explained on the basis of Thayer's conjecture according to which there is a gap between what is unconstitutional and what courts can (or ought to) declare as unconstitutional. Thayer also argues: 'It was then all along true, and it was foreseen, that much which is harmful and unconstitutional may take effect without any capacity in the courts to prevent it, since their whole power is a judicial one.'[46]

Thayer believed that judicial enforceability of constitutional directives is limited to cases of manifest violations of such directives. In principle, under his view, constitutional directives are enforceable but they are enforceable only when the legislature committed a grave or a manifest violation of the directives. Violations that are not grave or manifest are unenforceable. Some contemporary constitutional theorists support this view on instrumental grounds. Adrian Vermeule for instance claims that courts are less likely to decide correctly than legislatures on constitutional matters in cases that do not constitute manifest constitutional violations.[47] Hence, under his view, constitutional provisions are enforceable in courts only when the court is more

---

[44] Thayer, 'The Origin and Scope', 144 (n 20).

[45] Thayer, 'The Origin and Scope', 144 (n 20).

[46] Thayer, 'The Origin and Scope', 137 (n 20).

[47] Vermeule, *Law and the Limits of Reason*, 2–4 (n 20). For a critique, see the symposium on Vermeule in 2 *Jerusalem Review of Legal Studies* 5 (2010).

competent or more inclined to conform to the constitutional directives than the legislature.[48] Judicial enforceability may be detrimental to the quality of legislative decision-making. To sum up, according to one influential view, the US Constitution is under-enforceable; its provisions are judicially enforceable only when violations are 'blatant' or 'manifest'.[49]

Larry Sager developed an alternative view under which the US Constitution contains pockets of unenforceable provisions. Under his view, there are certain constitutional norms that are never enforceable (irrespective of how grave or manifest the violation is).[50] More specifically, he argues that there is a gap between the scope of binding constitutional directives and the scope of enforceable constitutional directives. Unenforceable binding constitutional directives are ones that are not fit for judicial determination. Sager also identified the spheres in which such unenforceable constitutional directives exist. In his view, the American Constitution contains two prominent unenforceable rights: a right to minimum welfare and a duty to reform structurally entrenched social bias and redress historical injustice.[51] While these provisions are unenforceable, Sager also believes that they are constitutionally binding, precisely as any other part of the constitution. In his view: 'the unenforced margins of under-enforced norms should have the full status of positive law which we generally accord to the norms of our Constitution, save only that the federal judiciary will not enforce these margins.'[52]

---

[48] Thayer made a similar argument and said that: 'much which will seem unconstitutional to one man, or body of men, may reasonably not seem so to another.' Under this view, institutional competence ought to determine the limits of enforceability of courts and legislatures. See Thayer, 'The Origin and Scope', 144 (n 20).

[49] Thayer's position has been highly influential. See Wallace Mendelson, 'The Influence of James B. Thayer upon the Works of Holmes, Brandeis, and Frankfurter', 31 *Vand. L. Rev.* 71 (1978); G. Edward White, 'Revisiting James Bradley Thayer', 88 *Nw. U.L. Rev.* 48, 48–9 (1993). As was recently pointed out, Thayer's theme is merely one theory belonging to 'discrete yet interrelated models governing the proper judicial conduct'. See Zachary Baron Shemtob, 'Following Thayer: The Many Faces of Judicial Restraint', 21 *BU Pub. Int. LJ* 61 (2011). Yet, it has also been criticized and many constitutional theorists reject it. See, e.g., Shemtob, 'Following Thayer', 66–7. See also Mark Tushnet, 'Alternative Forms of Judicial Review', 101 *Michigan L. Rev.* 2781, 2797–801 (2003).

[50] Larry Sager, *Justice in Plainclothes: A Theory of American Constitutional Practice* (New Haven: Yale University Press, 2004), 84–92; Larry Sager, 'Fair Measure: The Legal Status of Underenforced Constitutional Norms', 91 *Harv. L. Rev.* 1212, 1250–3 (1978).

[51] Sager, *Justice in Plainclothes*, 85 (n 50).   [52] Sager, *Justice in Plainclothes*, 88 (n 50).

Sager's conjecture that there are unenforceable binding constitutional directives follows naturally from his conviction that the
American Constitution ought to be equated with political justice.[53]
Given that there are requirements of political justice that cannot be
effectively enforced by the courts (as the courts are incapable of
enforcing them efficaciously), there must be constitutional directives
that are unenforceable. Sager believes therefore that there is a systematic under-enforcement of constitutional norms in the American Legal
system and that one ought to distinguish sharply between the 'Constitution proper' and the 'adjudicated Constitution', namely those parts of
the constitution that are enforceable by courts.[54] Such a gap between
the constitution and the enforceable constitution is not an indication of
a deficiency in the constitution. It is simply a by-product of pragmatic
limitations resulting from the institutional limitations of the courts.[55]

The views of Thayer or Sager are by no means accepted by all
constitutional theorists.[56] Yet even if one rejects these views there is
a third aspect of American constitutionalism that testifies to the prevalence of unenforceable or under-enforceable constitutional provisions.

Both the American and the Israeli legal systems currently have a
system of judicial review designed to enforce (all or some) of the
constitutional norms. Yet, at their inception, it was unclear whether
courts would ever incur such powers.[57] Both systems were founded on

---

[53]   Sager, *Justice in Plainclothes*, 70–83 (n 50).

[54]   Sager, *Justice in Plainclothes*, 86 (n 50).

[55]   For an attempt to expand and strengthen Sager's observations, see Abner S. Greene,
'Can we be Legal Positivists without Being Constitutional Positivists', 73 *Fordham L. Rev.*
1401, 1406–8 (2004–5).

[56]   For critiques of Thayer, see Shemtob, 'Following Thayer', (n 49); Tushnet, 'Alternative
Forms of Judicial Review' (n 49). For a critique of Larry Sager, see Larry D. Kramer,
'Undercover Anti-Populism', 73 *Fordham L. Rev.* 1343 (2005).

[57]   For a brief discussion of the view that the American Constitution does not grant courts
powers of judicial review, see Edward S. Corwin, 'Marbury v. Madison and the Doctrine of
Judicial Review', 12 *Michigan L. Rev.* 538 (1914). Most famously Richard Spraight—one of
the framers—argued that: 'as [the judges] would have operated as an absolute negative on the
proceedings of the Legislature, which no judiciary ought ever to possess: and the state, instead
of being governed by the representatives in general assembly would be subject to the will of
three individuals.' Cited in Larry Kramer, *The People Themselves: Popular Constitutionalism and
Judicial Review* (Oxford: Oxford University Press, 2004), 275. For a contemporary advocate of
the view that American courts were not designed to have the power to review legislation, see
Larry Kramer, 'Forward: We the Court', 115 *Harv. L. Rev.* 5 (2001–2); Larry D. Kramer,
'Putting the Politics back into the Political Safeguards of Federalism', 100 *Columbia L. Rev.*
215, 233–78 (2000). For a recent discussion of the historical origins of judicial review in the
US, see Saikrishna B. Prakash and John C. Yoo, 'The Origins of Judicial Review', 70 *U. Chi.
L. Rev.* 87 (2003).

an explicit acknowledgement of the limitations on the powers of the legislature. But, despite this conviction, the powers of courts to give it effect have been disputed. In the US context one commentator has argued that 'the power [of the Supreme Court] to pass upon the constitutionality of acts of Congress...owes its existence to an act of sheer usurpation by the Supreme Court itself, in the decision of *Marbury v. Madison*.'[58] It was not clear at all that such duty-imposing constraints are enforceable. It was only the decision in *Marbury v. Madison* that solidified the powers of the courts to invalidate statutes. As a matter of fact even today there are prominent theorists who believe that courts do not have as many powers as they purport to have in enforcing the constitutional directives.[59]

Similarly in Israel, even before the groundbreaking case in *Bank Hamizrachi v. Migdal*, that established the powers of Israeli courts to invalidate legislation, section 8 of the Israeli Basic Law: Human Dignity and Liberty imposed constitutional duties on the legislature. Section 8 declares that: 'There shall be no violation of rights under this Basic Law except by a law befitting the values of the State of Israel, enacted for a proper purpose, and to an extent no greater than is required.' Yet, the decision of the Israeli Supreme Court to use the Basic Law: Human Dignity and Liberty to strike down legislation was not inevitable as opponents of the decision were quick to point out.[60]

In both the American and in the Israeli system, there are currently judicial mechanisms for enforcement of constitutional limitations on the legislature. Yet, in both cases, the decision to endorse binding constitutional directives preceded the decision to establish institutional mechanisms for their enforcement. As a matter of fact, the later decision (to have judicial mechanisms of enforcement) was not inevitable; both the Israeli and the US courts could have interpreted the constitutional provisions otherwise.

Unenforceable and under-enforceable binding constitutionalism is therefore a more prevalent phenomenon than is often recognized by constitutional theorists. Some jurisdictions such as Ireland or India contain explicitly binding but unenforceable constitutional directives.

---

[58] See Corwin, 'Marbury v. Madison', 537 (n 57).

[59] See the discussion in Prakash and Yoo, 'The Origins of Judicial Review' (n 57).

[60] Ruth Gavison, 'Not a Reality but an Attempt at Self Fulfilling Prophecy', 28 *Mishpatim* 21–2 (2008) (in Hebrew); Hillel Sommer, 'Richard Posner on Aharon Barak: The View from Abroad', 49 *Hapraklit* 523, 528 (2007) (in Hebrew).

Even constitutions that do not contain explicit unenforceable binding constitutional directives, e.g., the US Constitution, have been understood to contain unenforceable or under-enforceable binding constitutional norms. Finally, some constitutional provisions could have developed to be ones that are unenforceable but, given the ambiguity of the language of the constitutional provisions, courts have eventually acquired the power to enforce the constitutional directives. Despite the prevalence of such directives, the dominant theoretical controversy has been for many years the controversy over enforceability, in particular judicial enforceability. Proponents and opponents of judicial review fail to acknowledge the prevalence of binding *unenforceable* constitutional directives and to ask how (and whether) such binding directives can be rationalized. Section C fills this gap and defends the view that such directives can indeed be justified, and that their justification is not contingent upon instrumental considerations.

C. The Non-instrumental Justification for Entrenching Constitutional Rights: The Case for Binding Constitutionalism

1. Introduction

What is the value of binding unenforceable or under-enforceable constitutionalism? Why would unenforceable or under-enforceable binding directives have any value whatsoever? What may prompt a framer of a constitution to entrench certain moral or political duties without, at the same time, guaranteeing that such duties be effectively enforced by establishing enforcement mechanisms?

One natural explanation is instrumental: constitutionally entrenching moral or political duties (even unenforceable/under-enforceable ones) prompts legislatures (and other branches of government) to conform to these duties. Alternatively one may resort to debunking explanations, arguing that unenforceable or under-enforceable directives are nothing but a verbal pretence to protect rights and thus to gain popularity without paying the necessary price and without genuine willingness to be guided by the constitutional duties. This section develops an alternative hypothesis under which constitutional directives are desirable on the basis of principled non-instrumental grounds.

Constitutional entrenchment of the pre-existing moral/political duties is a form of public recognition of the legislature's rights-based duties. Such a public acknowledgement is necessary to protect freedom (understood as non-domination).

To establish the value of constitutional entrenchment of pre-existing moral and political rights I establish in section C2 the banal observation that the absence of legally binding constitutional directives does not imply the absence of binding moral and political constraints on the legislature. In fact a presupposition that underlies my analysis is that there are moral and/or political restrictions on the powers of legislatures irrespective of whether these restrictions are constitutionally entrenched. Under 'the limitations hypothesis': 'the legislature is morally and/or politically constrained, namely there are normative limitations on its powers.'[61] I then argue in section C3 that the limitations on the powers of the legislature ought to be constitutionally entrenched. To be free, I claim, it is not sufficient that legislatures refrain from violating their rights-based duties. In addition it is also necessary that in cases in which the legislature violates its duties, public condemnation ought to follow and such condemnation cannot be contingent on the moral convictions of individuals. Otherwise, I claim, citizens are not free; they live 'at the mercy of their legislatures'. What guarantees freedom is not the mere fact that the legislature protects the rights but that it is *duty-bound* to do so and the duties that bind it are constitutional duties. This view, I finally argue, has implications not only with respect to constitutional law but also with respect to international law and in particular the debates concerning the recent expansion of rights-based international law duties.

2. *The Limitations Hypothesis*

To establish the rationale for entrenching constitutional directives one ought first to establish the 'limitations hypothesis', namely the hypothesis that legislatures are morally or politically constrained and then to establish the distinctive contribution of constitutionally entrenching the pre-existing moral or political limitations.

The limitations hypothesis is perhaps the least controversial conviction among political theorists. The belief that the sovereign is morally or politically constrained was already prevalent in medieval times. The

---

[61] Alon Harel, 'Rights-Based Judicial Review', 22 *Law and Philosophy* 247 (2003).

divine right of kings did not presuppose that kings have no duties towards their subjects, only that the king is accountable to God alone and no human institution has any power to challenge its commands:

The state of monarchy is the supremest thing upon earth . . . Kings are justly called Gods, for that they exercise a manner or resemblance of divine power upon earth. For if you will consider the attributes to God, you shall see how they agree in the person of a king. God has power to create, or destroy, make or unmake at his pleasure, to give life, or send death, to judge all, and be judged nor accountable to none: to raise low things, and to make high things low at his pleasure, and to God are both soul and body due. And the like power have Kings; they make and unmake their subjects: they have the power of raising, and casting down: of life, and of death: judges over all their subjects, and in all causes, and yet accountable to none but God only.[62]

Indeed all contemporary opponents of constitutionalism concede that the legislature has duties that ought not to be violated.[63] The debate concerning constitutionalism is founded on the premiss that there are rights that ought to be protected and that those rights impose duties on legislatures. I shall develop therefore the case for the constitutional entrenchment of moral and political limitations on the basis of the (non-controversial) assumption that legislatures are bound by moral and/or political obligations.

3. The Case for Constitutional Entrenchment of Political Rights

Section B3 established that many jurisdictions have unenforceable or under-enforceable constitutional directives. As stated above, the prevalence of such directives could be justified on instrumental grounds. The primary task of this subsection is not to challenge the instrumental justifications but rather to raise an independent non-instrumental justification.[64] Under this justification, constitutional directives are valuable independently of whether they trigger better decisions

---

[62] See Extracts from speech to Parliament 21 March 1609 by King James in <http://www.historyguide.org/earlymod/james1609.html>.

[63] See, e.g., Jeremy Waldron, 'The Core of the Case against Judicial Review', 115 *Yale LJ* 1376–86 (2006).

[64] For an attempt to challenge the instrumental justifications to constitutional entrenchment, see the introduction to Part III. An opponent of binding constitutional directives may raise empirically grounded objections to the instrumental conjecture and argue that legislatures that are constitutionally constrained are less rather than more likely to conform to the

(i.e., decisions that are more in conformity with the moral or political limitations) on the part of the legislature. This is in line with the Kantian approach to the problem of authority in general, which 'does not depend on any claims about an authority's ability to generate the correct result in every case, or even on the greater reliability of its chosen procedures, measured against some external criterion'.[65]

To establish the non-instrumental justification, I use a republican understanding of freedom. Under the republican understanding of freedom, to be free it is not sufficient that the person is not coerced or is unlikely to be coerced; to be free it is also necessary that the potential victim not live 'at the mercy of' the potential violator's inclinations.[66] 'Living at the mercy' of another implies that 'it is up to the potential violator' to decide whether or not she will interfere with the right. I also argue that in order for people not to 'live at the mercy of' the legislature, the legislature itself ought to be constitutionally bound. If the legislature is bound by constitutional directives (or international law norms) the citizens do not live 'at the mercy of' the legislature. Constitutional directives are ones that are embraced not only by the legislature itself but also by the polity at large, or at least by powerful components of it.[67] So, even if the legislature violates its

underlying moral/political limitations. In fact constitutional entrenchment may erode respect towards the law if legislatures fail to conform to it or merely pay lip service to it.

Jeremy Waldron—the most vocal opponent of judicial review—is quick to note that judicial review can be detrimental to the quality of decision-making. In his view: 'the written formulations of a Bill of Rights... tend to encourage certain rigid textual formalism.' Jeremy Waldron, 'A Right-based Critique of Constitutional Rights', 13 *Oxford J. Leg. Studies* 18, 26–7 (1993). As courts typically use written canonical formulations the quality of judicial decision-making is lower than the quality of legislative decision-making as the legislature is less concerned with the precise wording and is (at least typically) more concerned with the underlying values at stake.

Waldron's concern that written formulations of a Bill of Rights are undesirable may apply also to binding unenforceable constitutional directives. As constitutional directives sometimes use canonical linguistic forms, they may distract attention from the underlying moral/political values and place too much weight on the specific language of the constitutional directives rather than on the values underlying these directives. Larry Alexander has pointed out that many of Waldron's arguments against judicial review apply also to the very existence of constitutional norms (independently of whether courts are assigned with the powers of interpreting constitutional norms). See Larry Alexander, 'What is the Problem of Judicial Review' <http://ssrn.com/abstract=802807>, 3–4.

[65] Arthur Ripstein, *Force and Freedom: Kant's Legal and Political Philosophy* (Cambridge, Mass.: Harvard University Press, 2009), 197.

[66] See Pettit, *Republicanism*, 5 (n 7).

[67] This follows from the analysis in section B2 under which constitutional directives are ones that are constituted by practices and convictions of legislatures, lawyers, and/or courts.

duties, it is subject to public condemnation, and such public condemnation also implies that citizens' rights are not 'at the mercy' of the legislature.

I shall defend here the view that even if citizens' rights are not better (or at least are equally) protected by constitutionally entrenching moral of political norms, citizens are freer under such a scheme, as they are not subject to the judgments or inclinations of the legislature. In contrast, in the absence of constitutional entrenchment, conformity of the legislature with its moral/political duties is not sufficient as it does not represent sufficient recognition or acknowledgement of the state's duties. The effective protection of the duties in such a case can naturally be attributed to the legislature's judgments or inclinations and not necessarily to its duties. While in a system which has no binding constitutional directives the basic freedoms can be effectively protected, such a system fails to protect these freedoms as rights which bind the legislature, and it is therefore inferior to a system of binding constitutional directives.

To establish the argument consider first the following analogy: A needs $100 to cover some urgent costs. Fortunately B owes A $100 and A turns to B to get his money back. B denies that he *owes* A the money, but, as a gesture of friendship, is willing to grant A $100 'as a present', as B professes to understand that A faces economic hardship.

A is justifiably resentful and possibly even furious. A cares not merely that the $100 be given to him to cover his urgent costs, but also that it be given to him as a repayment of a debt rather than as a present. A wants B to *repay a debt*, rather than merely to get the money. But why should A care? Why should it matter to him whether B gives him a present or repays his debt?

There may be several answers to this question: the granting of a present changes the relations between A and B in certain ways. If B gives the money as a present rather than as a repayment of a debt, it follows that A ought to show gratitude towards B, and such gratitude would inevitably change his future relations with A. If fortune changes and, suddenly, B needs money that A can provide, gratitude may require that A helps B. Further, if B owes A money, A can demand repayment of the debt. If, on the other hand, B does not owe A money, A can, at most, request rather than demand the money. It is evident therefore that the question of whether B 'repays a debt' or gives 'a present' is a crucial question that has significant repercussions for the future relationships between A and B. The reluctance of B to concede his debt harms A, as it implies that A is 'at the mercy of' B's good will, i.e., that it is up to B to decide whether or not to give A the money.

Even if B insists on giving the money as a present, A may find some consolation in the willingness of the community to support his demand, impose sanctions on B, and punish B for his reluctance to acknowledge his debt. Thus, A may not merely justifiably insist that B concede the debt but also insist that if B fails to repay his debt to A (or even repays but insists on giving A 'a present'), then the community at large reproaches B. As long as such a public condemnation is as a general rule intense and effective, then it would be appropriate to say that A is not 'at the mercy of B'. In other words, there is a sense in which it is reasonable to say that A is not 'at the mercy of B', to the extent that B is subjected to social and even legal sanctions in the event that B fails to repay his debt. In such a case, it is not 'up to B' to make the decision. So in order not to be at the mercy of B, it is sufficient that B acknowledges the debt, and that, in case he does not, the community reproaches B in a way that is generally effective.

There are two claims concerning this example which I wish to highlight here. First, in order not to be 'at the mercy of' B it is not sufficient that there are moral norms requiring B to repay his debt. There also must be effective social norms requiring B to do so. In such a case it is the public understanding that counts, not merely the binding force of moral norms. In the absence of such a public understanding, it can be plausibly said that the debt is 'up to B' in the sense that the repayment of the debt hinges on B's judgments or inclinations to repay and, therefore A is not free.

Second, under this view, in order 'not to be at the mercy of B' it is not required that B would indeed be forced to acknowledge his debt. Precisely as I am not 'at the mercy' of criminals if I live in a state that effectively enforces the law (even in a case where a crime is committed against me), so A is not at the mercy of B simply because B refuses to acknowledge his debt so long as there is a general system of sanctions or at least stigma attached to people who refuse to acknowledge their debts. A failure of the system to enforce the debt of B in a particular case does not imply that it is 'up to B' to pay or not to pay his debt or that A is 'at his mercy'. Further, for certain purposes even if I am very vulnerable to outside interference, there is a fundamental difference between different types of vulnerability. As Louis Phillipe Hodgson noted: 'If I live in a particularly nasty part of town, then it may turn out that, when all relevant factors are taken into account, I am just as vulnerable to outside interference as are the slaves in the royal palace, yet it does not follow that our conditions are equivalent from the point of view of freedom.'[68] To borrow with slight modification what Thomas Nagel said: to be enslaved would be terrible; but to be enslaved and also to be someone it was not wrong to enslave (like the slaves in a royal palace) would be even worse.[69]

I shall argue that the relations between A and B can be analogized to the relations between a legislature and its citizens. When a legislature bound by rights-based constitutional directives conforms with the constitutional directives, it can be described properly as bound by its duties. This observation necessarily follows from the way constitutional directives were defined in section B2. The consequence is that the rights of citizens living in such a system are not at the mercy of the legislature. Even if at times the legislature may violate its constitutional duties, it does not imply that individuals live at its mercy.

What does it mean to live 'at the mercy of' another agent, and why is it so important not to live 'at the mercy of another agent'? Proponents of the concept of 'republican freedom' shed light on this concept.[70] Neo-republicans reject 'the key assumption of classical liberalism to the effect that force or the coercive threat of it constitute the only forms of constraint that interfere with individual liberty'.[71] Instead, they identify liberty with non-domination. Domination is understood in terms of the *potential* for arbitrary interference: 'One agent dominates another if and only if they have a certain power over that other, in particular a power of interference on an arbitrary basis.'[72] One is deprived of republican freedom if one lives in 'a condition of dependence'.[73] Dependence renders a person vulnerable to the whim of others; it exposes a person to the potential interference of a dominant agent. In

---

[68] Louis Philippe Hodgson, 'Kant on the Right to Freedom: A Defense', 120 *Ethics* 791–819 at 816 (2010).

[69] Nagel, 'Personal Rights and Public Space' (n 2).

[70] See, e.g., Frank Lovett, 'Republicanism', in Edward N. Zalta (ed.), *The Stanford Encyclopedia of Philosophy* (summer 2010 edn.) <http://plato.stanford.edu/entries/republicanism/>.

[71] Q. Skinner, *Liberty before Liberalism* (Cambridge: Cambridge University Press, 1998), 84.

[72] Pettit, *Republicanism*, 52 (n 7).

[73] Skinner, *Liberty before Liberalism*, 84 (n 71). See also Maurizio Viroli, *Republicanism* (New York: Hill and Wang, 2002), 10.

Pettit's view: 'Being un-free consists rather in being subject to arbitrary sway: Being subject to the potentially capricious will or the potentially idiosyncratic judgment of another.'[74] In describing what it means to live in conditions of political dependence Skinner says: 'The very fact, however, that your rulers possess such arbitrary powers means that the continued enjoyment of your civil liberty remains at all times dependent on their good will.'[75]

The literature on republican freedom is vast.[76] Opponents of 'republican freedom' have argued that the notion of 'republican freedom' is used in different ways by its proponents and, further, that some of its main claims are indefensible.[77] I do not wish to defend here the notion of republican freedom or Pettit's own version of such freedom. The claim that I rely on is the one endorsed by Rousseau, under which freedom consists in some form of independence from the choices of others. Non-interference as such is not sufficient; what is needed in addition is not being subject to the will of others. As Rousseau famously said: 'Freedom does not consist so much in doing one's will as in not being subjected to the will of others.'[78] Hence, the free individual is one who *obeys* his own will, or more explicitly, *one who obeys no will* other than his own.[79] It rests on the conviction that 'I am free insofar as no one gets to decide for me.'[80] I use Pettit therefore to highlight some of the concerns raised more generally by proponents of freedom as independence without necessarily endorsing the particularities of his view.[81]

Phillip Pettit described the predicament of domination as follows:

The grievance that I have in mind is that of having to live at the mercy of another, having to live in a manner that leaves you vulnerable to some ill that the other is in a position arbitrarily to impose ... It is the grievance

---

[74] Pettit, *Republicanism*, 5 (n 7).   [75] Skinner, *Liberty before Liberalism*, 70 (n 71).

[76] For references, see Lovett, 'Republicanism' (n 70).

[77] Kramer, for instance argues that the concerns of theorists of republican freedom are fully and satisfactorily addressed by advocates of negative freedom. See Matthew H. Kramer, 'Liberty and Domination', in Cecile Laborde and John Maynor (eds.), *Republicanism and Political Theory* (Malden, Mass.: Blackwell Publishing, 2008).

[78] Cited in Neuhouser, 'Freedom', 380 (n 7).

[79] See Neuhouser, 'Freedom', 381 (n 7). See also Hodgson, 'Kant on the Right to Freedom', 806 (n 68).

[80] Hodgson, 'Kant on the Right to Freedom', 806 (n 68).

[81] For an analysis and an effective Kantian critique of Pettit, see Hodgson, 'Kant on the Right to Freedom', 809–16 (n 68).

expressed by the wife who finds herself in a position where her husband can beat her at will, and without any possibility of redress; by the employee who dare not raise a complaint against an employer, and who is vulnerable to any of a range of abuses, some petty, some serious, that the employer may choose to perpetrate; by the debtor who has to depend on the grace of the moneylender, or the bank official, for avoiding utter destitution and ruin; and by the welfare dependent who finds that they are vulnerable to the caprice of a counter clerk for whether or not their children will receive meal vouchers.[82]

Pettit continues and says:

[W]hether or not they avoid interference, they certainly have a grievance. They live in the shadow of the other's presence, even if no arm is raised against them. They live in uncertainty about the other's reactions and in need of keeping a weather eye open for the other's moods. They find themselves in a position where they are demeaned by their own vulnerability, being unable to look at the other in the eye, and where they may even be forced to fawn or flatter in the attempt to ingratiate themselves.[83]

Some of the assertions of Pettit here are misleading as they seem to rely on the future prospects that the right will be violated and the psychological anxiety resulting from such prospects. Yet, it is also evident that there is a deeper insight here. One way of understanding what it means to be vulnerable or dominated ought to be equated with the public shared normative understanding, and, in particular, with the way the potential violator's decisions are publicly understood by the potential violator itself and by the community as a whole. A person is vulnerable or unfree not primarily by virtue of the fact that a violation has taken place or that it is likely to take place, but by virtue of the fact that a violation is not labelled by the potential violator and/or publicly recognized and identified by the community as a violation. The potential violator in Pettit's examples—the husband, the employer, or the clerk—may not feel inclined to violate the right, as they may be good-hearted, generous, or compassionate. The potential victim may be aware of it and consequently may be confident that her rights will not be violated. But the mere fact that 'it is up to them' to decide whether or not to do so, is in itself oppressive. A slave suffers from

---

[82] Pettit, *Republicanism*, 4–5 (n 7).   [83] Pettit, *Republicanism*, 5 (n 7).

deprivation of freedom even if his master does not exercise his legal right to issue orders. More generally, a person suffers from deprivation of freedom (understood as non-domination) when the potential violator and the relevant community surrounding her refuse to properly label or classify the behaviour as a violation, and insist that it is up to the potential violator to decide how to behave. To the extent that it is publicly classified as a violation, it is not 'up to the violator to decide' even though the violation may indeed take place.

To borrow this insight and apply it to the constitutional context let us return back to the two states described in the introduction, and compare state A governed by a benevolent legislature with state B in which the same rights are enshrined in a constitution. In both states, let us assume rights are protected to the same extent. Further, assume that in both states rights are also likely to be protected in the future to the same extent. The (benevolent) legislature in state A is as likely to effectively protect rights without a constitution as perhaps the less benevolent legislature of state B that is constrained by binding constitutional directives. Yet, I wish to argue that the status of the citizens in both states is different, and that only citizens in state A live 'at the mercy of the legislature'. In contrast, in state B the legislature is constrained; its decisions are not 'up to it' and consequently individuals do not live 'at its mercy'.

To establish these claims it is necessary to turn back to our definition of a constitutional directive, and show in what ways constitutional directives constitute a public acknowledgement on the part of the legislature itself and on the part of the relevant community in the legislature's duties. More specifically, I aim to show that a legislature bound by constitutional directives is analogous to a lender whose debtor acknowledges the debt, or at least, a lender living in a community which reproaches the debtor for her refusal to acknowledge her debt.

To see why, it suffices to examine the way constitutional directives were defined. As constitutional directives are (by definition) grounded in the practices and conventions of the legislature itself, the legislature can properly be described as accepting the authority of these directives, i.e., acting from its duties. This of course does not imply that the legislature never violates constitutional rights, but merely that in general its behaviour is governed by constitutional directives (as otherwise these directives would not count as constitutional). Further, as constitutional directives reflect the convictions of a community of policymakers, lawyers, and other relevant elites, even when the legislature does not honour the rights, it is (generally) subjected to effective condemnation. In contrast, a legislature that is not bound by constitutional directives may conform to its pre-existing moral or political duties, but its conformity is grounded in its judgments or inclinations; its conformity is not publicly understood by it and by others to bind it. Such a legislature can therefore be analogized to B who is willing to give money to A but insists that it be given as a present rather than as a repayment of a debt. Citizens living in a state with no constitutional directives live therefore 'at the mercy of' their legislature, in the same way as A lives at the mercy of B.[84] Let me defend this claim against what seems to be compelling objections.

One obvious difference between the case of the loan and the case of a state is that when legislatures legislate they do not act on the basis of unfettered discretion. Their decisions therefore do not resemble the giving of a present. Instead, arguably they make judgments concerning the public interest. Hence it is false to say that in the absence of a constitution citizens simply live 'at the mercy of the whims of legislatures', as enlightened legislatures do not operate on the basis of their whims but on the basis of judgments concerning what ought to be done, and those judgments consist also of judgments concerning what their rights-based duties are. On all matters the legislature has to operate on the basis of a judgment concerning the human good and such judgments consist both of judgments concerning the public good and judgments concerning individual rights. This challenge is most lucidly expressed by John Finnis, who argued that there is no fundamental difference between matters of principle and matter of policy and/or public interest as both are grounded in human goods. In his view: 'nowhere here do we find a collective welfare determinable apart from individual rights which define, shape and constitute the common good, the public interest.'[85]

This observation is correct, but it does not undermine my claim. There is still a fundamental difference between a legislative decision designed to promote the public good *as understood by the legislature* and a decision that is mandatory—one that is not subject to the judgment of

---

[84] Individual legislators can of course regard themselves as bound by a duty but this is not a duty of the legislature as such but of the individual legislators.

[85] John Finnis, 'Human Rights and their Enforcement', in John Finnis, *Human Rights & the Common Good: Collected Essays* (Oxford: Oxford University Press, 2011), iii. 19–46 at 34.

the legislature. Thus I concede that even in the absence of a constitution or a bill of rights, the citizen does not live at the mercy of the whims of the legislature. Instead, she lives at the mercy of the judgments of the legislature concerning the public good, and, under the view I espouse here, being subjected to the legislature's judgments is (at least sometimes) detrimental to freedom.

An opponent could challenge this conjecture and argue that acknowledgement on the part of a legislature does not require a constitution or a bill of rights. A legislature could acknowledge its duties by solemnly declaring their commitment to their duties, and this would be sufficient to protect freedom understood as non-domination. This would be a simple and intuitive extension of the Kantian view of what it means to act from duty. Kant believed that only acting from duty has moral worth; the key to the good will is to act dutifully from an interest in the rightness of the action and not (merely) from self-interested reasons or from contingent inclinations, such as sympathy or antipathy. The key to the good will is to be found in an examination of the motive, as good will requires the agent to perform a dutiful act *for the sake of duty*.[86]

A natural extension of the concept of 'acting from duty' to the institutional context is to maintain that what it means for an institution (including the legislature) to act from duty is that the individual members of the legislature act from duty. Thus, when (many or all) individual legislators reason from their (moral or political) duties, the institution of the legislature as such is said to act from duty, and this would be sufficient to justify the conclusion that the citizens are not at the legislature's mercy. Further, it could be argued that prevalent moral or political convictions that are not constitutionally entrenched can also serve to discipline the legislature and, thus, such convictions would be sufficient to guarantee that citizens do not live 'at the mercy of their legislatures'.

---

[86] See Barbara Herman, *The Practice of Moral Judgment* (Cambridge: Cambridge University Press, 1993), 3. What it means for a person to act from a duty is highly controversial in the philosophical literature. Some believe that to act from duty entails that respect for the duty was present at the time of the act and would have sufficed by itself to produce the dutiful act. This view was challenged and an alternative proposal under which to count as an act performed from duty it is required that the action be performed 'because the agent finds it to be the right thing to do and take its rightness or requiredness as his reason for action.' Herman, *The Practice of Moral Judgment*, 12. But these controversies are irrelevant for our purposes.

This extension of Kantian individual morality and, in particular, Kant's analysis of what it means to act from duty into the field of politics, is flawed. To the extent that it is worthy that legislatures act from duty (rather than merely in accordance with duty), the question of whether they did or did not act from duty ought to be public knowledge, as it ought to be judged by citizens and provide the basis for evaluating the performance of the legislature. In other words, whether the legislature acted or did not act from duty ought, in principle, to be observable by citizens. The reasoning of individual legislators, and in particular whether they (as individuals) acted from duty or not, cannot serve as a criterion to determine whether the legislature as a collective body acted from duty. Further even if the legislature solemnly and publicly declares that it is obliged to act in certain ways, such declarations are not binding. Legislatures can legislate but they cannot typically legislate the grounds for their legislation.[87] Constitutional directives as characterized above are ones that can account for the behaviour of the legislature; they are ones that are generally adhered to and endorsed by the legislature as binding, and ones that it is also expected to honour. Further, to the extent that the legislature fails to honour these directives, it is subjected to effective condemnation. It is not up to the legislature to make decisions with respect to its rights-based duties, as there are effective (constitutional) limitations on its powers.

To establish the distinctive nature of constitutional directives, let me reiterate the characteristics of constitutional directives as identified in section B2. In section B2 I argued that constitutional directives have three main features: (1) they are grounded in existing practices and conventions; (2) they are typically more specific and determinate than the pre-existing moral/political norms; (3) the identification of constitutionally entrenched norms requires expertise.

Constitutional directives, I argued, are grounded in practices, conventions, and shared understandings of legislators and lawyers. Interpretations of the constitutional norms are done by examining how they have been understood, applied, and interpreted in the past. It is past conventions, practices, and customs that determine how such constitutional norms are to be understood.[88] Constitutional directives can

---

[87] This could of course be institutionally changed, and perhaps such a change would open the possibility of a different form of public recognition that can substitute the need for constitutional entrenchment of rights. I will not discuss this possibility here.

[88] See section B2.

therefore be accurately described as norms that (as a general rule) govern legislatures' decisions and guide their reasoning. Embracing these norms by the legislature does not result from the legislature's mere official solemn declarations about justice or political morality or in the good will of the individual legislators. Instead its commitment to constitutional directives results from the legislature's own past decisions, and the ways these decisions are publicly understood and justified. The legislature's own practices, conventions, and understandings as well as the norms used to criticize it determine the content and the scope of the constitutional norms. The description of the legislature as 'acting from duty' is grounded therefore in the realities of its operation; more particularly, it is grounded in the past practices and decisions of that legislature—practices and decisions that are embodied in the constitutional directives.

This does not imply that the legislature always conforms to the constitutional directives. Even if the legislature is generally guided by constitutional directives it may at times violate them. Yet, if it does so it is subject to public criticism on the grounds that it has violated its duties. Such a condemnation on the part of relevant elites is part of the way constitutional directives were defined. Hence, given this effective public reaction to such violations, the legislature's decision to comply with constitutional directives is not at its mercy.

Further, as I have argued, constitutional directives are typically more determinate and specific than the pre-existing moral or political norms underlying them. Constitutional entrenchment of the pre-existing moral or political norms triggers greater specificity and determinacy than that characterizing the pre-existing moral or political norms. Specificity and determinacy of constitutionally entrenched norms is necessary, as it is a prerequisite for publicly evaluating the degree to which the legislature's decisions conform to the pre-existing moral or political norms. Determinacy and specificity of the norms is essential as, otherwise, the determination as to what the constitutionally entrenched norms are and whether the legislature conforms to them cannot be publicly made. In the absence of constitutional entrenchment, the pre-existing moral or political duties are too vague and indeterminate to serve as meaningful guidance to the legislature. This does not mean of course that the language of constitutional rights is precise and determinate, but only that the evolving practices of the legislature and the public reactions to it eventually make the content of the constitutional norms more determinate and precise than that of moral and political norms.

Prior to constitutional entrenchment, the conformity of a legislature can be plausibly interpreted as grounded in its inclinations or, perhaps, in its judgments concerning the public good. Even if the legislature solemnly declares its conviction that it is morally or politically bound to legislate in certain ways, its declaration could be challenged by future legislatures or by the citizens. Further, it could be maintained that even if there are social norms that are not entrenched constitutionally, they are vulnerable to shifting public opinion. What turns these norms into a solid foundation under this view is the constitutional entrenchment of these norms, namely the shared understanding that those norms bind the legislature and that it is not free to act otherwise. Binding constitutional directives constitute a publicly verifiable commitment on the part of the legislature as such, and not merely on the part of individual legislators. Further, being (by definition) accepted by the community of lawyers, policymakers, and judges, deviations from the constitutionally entrenched rights trigger condemnation. Such condemnation is not subject to fluctuating moral convictions. It is grounded in the practices and conventions of the legislature itself and the public understandings of how it should act. Consequently, in such a society, citizens do not live at the mercy of the legislature, as the legislature itself generally embraces the constitutional directives and, even in the event that it violates them, the legislature is subjected to reproach on the part of the community.

A real-life example taken from the abortion debate in Germany could help us to appreciate the significance of constitutional entrenchment.[89]

In 1975 the German Constitutional Court declared that the law which allowed abortion on demand during the first trimester of pregnancy was unconstitutional as it violates Article 2 section 2 of the German Basic Law protecting the right to life.[90] The Constitutional

---

[89] For the history of this debate and its significance, see Donald P. Kommers, 'The Constitutional Law of Abortion in Germany: Should Americans Pay Attention?', 10 *J. Contemp. Health L. & Pol'y* 1 (1994); Gerald L. Neuman, '*Casey* in the Mirror: Abortion, Abuse and the Right to Protection in the United States and Germany', 43 *Am. J. Compa. L.* 273 (1995).

[90] See 39 BVerFG 1 (1975). For an account of the case and its significance, see Donald P. Kommers, 'Liberty and Community in Constitutional Law: The Abortion Cases in Comparative Perspective', 3 *BYU L. Rev.* 371 (1985); Felix Lange, 'American Liberalism

Court emphasized that abortion is an act of killing which the law is obligated to condemn. As one commentator emphasized the state had not only the right but also the *duty* to protect developing life in the womb.[91]

As a result of reunification, the Constitutional Court had to address the matter again and in its later 1993 decision the court reiterated its commitment to the view that abortion is indeed a violation of the right to life and that the state has the obligation to protect life, including the life of the foetus.[92] Yet the court also declared that while abortion ought to remain criminal, the state could substitute 'normative counselling' for criminal punishment as a way of fulfilling its obligations to protect foetuses. The court also asserted that the mandated counselling ought to protect life and that the future provisions of any law would have to be specifically crafted so as to preserve the life of the unborn child and to convince the pregnant woman not to have an abortion. As one influential expert said: 'the statutory scheme may include ... compulsory counseling (i.e., plans that would leave the final decision to the pregnant woman) so long as the regulatory scheme as a whole "effectively and sufficiently" protects unborn life.'[93]

I do not wish to scrutinize the reasoning of the German court; nor do I want to discuss the issue of whether foetuses have or do not have a right to life. I shall assume (contrary to my view) that foetuses have indeed such a right. I will argue that the insistence of the German court that abortion remain criminal (even though unpunishable) can be justified on the grounds that in the absence of a criminal prohibition, the life of the foetus is 'at the mercy of' the pregnant woman. Further, it is not only that the decision to abort ought not to be 'at the mercy of' the mother; the decision *whether to criminalize abortion* ought not to be 'at the mercy of' the legislature. The right to life requires therefore not merely the need to *protect life* (by reducing as much as possible the number of abortions or the likelihood that abortion takes place) but also to protect *the right to life* by criminalizing abortion (even when such

and Germany's Rejection of the National Socialist Past: The 1973 Roe v. Wade Decision and the 1973 German Abortion Case in Historical Perspective', 12 *German Law Journal* 2033 (2011).

[91] Kommers, 'Liberty and Community', 395 (n 90).

[92] 88 BVerfGE 203; Kommers, 'The Constitutional Law of Abortion in Germany', 19 (n 89).

[93] Kommers, 'The Constitutional Law of Abortion in Germany', 19–20 (n 89).

a criminalization is not conducive as an empirical matter to the protection of life).[94]

Assume that evidence is provided to the Bundestag convincing it that decriminalizing abortion would, in fact, reduce the rate of abortions in society and, consequently, more lives would be saved if abortions were decriminalized. In addition, assume that the Parliament concludes therefore that while foetuses have a right to life, criminalizing abortions is detrimental to the protection of life and, consequently, it declares that decriminalizing abortion is constitutionally permissible.

Under my analysis, such a decision on the part of the Bundestag is unjustifiable, as it subjects foetuses' lives 'to the mercy' of their mothers. When a pregnant woman decides not to abort, her decision is based on her inclinations (or even her judgment that it is permissible), not on a publicly recognized right of the foetus. Further, under my interpretation of the court's reasoning, it is not only that the decision to abort ought not to be left to the discretion of the pregnant woman, but the decision to criminalize abortions ought not to be left 'to the mercy of' the Bundestag. If the decision to criminalize is at the mercy of the Bundestag, it follows that the life of the foetus is ultimately contingent upon the inclinations of the Bundestag. The insistence of the German Constitutional Court to maintain that abortion is a crime (even though not punishable if normative counselling is conducted) can be rationalized precisely on the grounds that protecting the foetus's right to life is to be left neither to the mercy of the pregnant woman nor to the inclinations of Parliament.

The abortion debate in Germany has much deeper significance than is often recognized. It is not merely about the right to life, or whether the foetus is a human being whose life ought to be protected. More specifically, this debate highlights the sharp difference between *protecting life* and protecting *a right to life*. Life can be protected in a state without protecting *a right to life*. Further, protecting a right to life may even be detrimental to the protecting of life when criminalization of killings leads to a greater number of killings. Under the interpretation provided here, the abortion case can be justified on the grounds that

---

[94] In a discussion with Arthur Ripstein, Ripstein raised the conjecture that perhaps criminalization is not sufficient and that to effectively protect the right to life it is also necessary to inflict criminal sanctions. I do not disagree with this conjecture, and it is possible that in its 1993 decision the court has been more lenient than it should have been given its commitment to the view that abortion is a violation of the right to life.

life and basic freedoms ought not merely to be protected; they ought to be protected *as rights*.

But, arguably, this analysis raises a problem. Given that the right to life is constitutionally entrenched, it could be argued that the foetuses are at the mercy of the constitution, or at the mercy of the constitutional court. Section C4 examines this challenge and suggests that the turn to global constitutional order provides a partial solution for this problem.

4. The Case for Global Entrenchment of Rights: The Rise of Global Constitutionalism

Arguably a constitution cannot solve the problem of freedom, as a constitution is also a human creation. Somebody after all has to draft it and somebody has to interpret it. It follows that even if constitutional rights are entrenched citizens still live at the mercy of the drafters or the interpreters of their national constitutions. It is easy to see that this argument implies that republican freedom can never be realized. Whatever constraints designed to protect individual rights are imposed, it is always the case that there is some entity which imposed it (or which can amend it): e.g., founders of a constitution, interpreters of a constitution, the United Nations, or an international court. Our rights are therefore inevitably at the mercy of the entity which is in charge of drafting and/or interpreting these constraints. Further, while some of these entities are more trustworthy than others, it is unclear that they are more conducive to republican freedom. In other words it is not clear why living at the mercy of a constitution (or at the mercy of a constitutional court) is more conducive to freedom than living at the mercy of a legislature.

I think this challenge that can be labelled the infinite regress challenge is important and misguided at the same time. It is important because (as I show here) it can serve in explaining the appeal of global constitutionalism. It is misguided because it proves too much. To return to our debtor example, we would not say that A, who expects to be repaid by B is unfree as long as there is a generally effective social or legal norm requiring B to repay his debt. But, to the extent that the objection is sound an identical argument applies in this case. Arguably an effective social or legal norm is not sufficient to protect republican freedom. While such a norm guarantees that A does not live at the mercy of B, A lives at the mercy of the social (or legal) norm and, consequently (according to this objection) A is unfree.

But this conclusion seems false. A is not unfree (or at least not unfree in the same way) if there are effective social or legal norms requiring B to repay his debt.

This observation raises the question of identifying the entities that one can be at their mercy without becoming unfree. Why is it the case that to live at the mercy of constitutions (or constitutional courts) is typically considered less detrimental to freedom than living at the mercy of legislatures? When can we justifiably raise the grievance that we are unfree?

I am not going to provide an answer to this question. Judgments of this type are often contextual; they require an understanding of traditions and practices. Yet there is one important observation to make. The answer to this question cannot rest on the greater prospects that legislatures violate our rights than that the drafters of the constitution or its interpreters violate our rights. The answer cannot rest on such contingent grounds for two reasons. First, it is unclear that legislatures are as a matter of fact more likely to violate rights than constitutional courts. Second, even if this is shown, the analysis in section C3 established that to live at the mercy of somebody in a way that is detrimental to republican freedom is not a matter that can be explained in terms of such considerations.

Even if living at the mercy of a drafter or an interpreter of a constitution is better than living at the mercy of a legislature, it may not be sufficient for republican freedom. As scepticism concerning the national constitution grows there is a greater need for an additional layer of norms that will bind the state. The turn to globalism can be regarded as a way to overcome the concern of living at the mercy of national constitutions. Precisely as constitutionalists insist that living at the mercy of the constitution is less detrimental to freedom than living at the mercy of the legislature, so arguably living at the mercy of global norms is less detrimental to freedom than living at the mercy of national constitutions (or at the mercy of constitutional courts). Before I develop this idea, let me first contrast it with the more traditional view of globalism.

The advocates (as well as opponents) of globalism are often instrumentalists. They believe that globalism is conducive to the protection of rights and/or the promotion of justice. To illustrate in a recent article, Ronald Dworkin advocated greater role for international institutions in governing states on the grounds that national norms are not sufficient to guarantee the legitimacy of states.[95] Dworkin identified several failures which in his view could be effectively resolved by establishing authoritative international institutions. He argued that often states fail to protect the rights of their citizens, to coordinate their actions in ways that serve the interests of their citizens, and to guarantee a reasonable degree of democratic participation in the governance of the polity. To resolve all these, Dworkin argued, one needs to establish authoritative and powerful international institutions.

Dworkin is hardly the only instrumentalist advocate of a global normative order. Mattias Kumm has argued also in favour of a global constitutional order. Kumm identified 'justice-sensitive externalities', namely contexts in which states have strong incentives to act unjustly. As examples Kumm mentions the decision of a state to intervene militarily in another country, the decision to embrace nuclear power stations near the state borders, decisions concerning environmental issues, and decisions concerning the investment in combating international crime. The fear of bias against outsiders on matters concerning justice is in his view the primary concern that justifies international legal order.[96] I provided here just two recent examples of influential globalists who rest their arguments on instrumental considerations. A complete list of such arguments would be much longer.

I wish to raise here the conjecture that my arguments against instrumentalism in constitutional theory apply also in the context of globalism, and further that my arguments in favour of binding constitutionalism could serve as a better grounding for global constitutionalism than instrumental arguments. The turn towards globalism should be understood in terms of republican freedom.

In the absence of global norms, individuals live at the mercy of the provisions and interpretations of their national constitutions. The establishment of an additional normative layer (a global one) contributes to the protection of freedom in the same way that adding a layer of constitutional norms contributes to republican freedom. Individuals who live in a global order are free not (only) because their rights are better protected but because the protection of their rights does not depend upon the good will of national courts or other national

---

[95] Ronald Dworkin, 'A New Philosophy for International Law', 41 *Philosophy and Public Affairs* 2 (2013).

[96] Mattias Kumm, 'Global Constitutionalism and the Cosmopolitan State: An Integrated Conception of Public Law' (forthcoming in *Indiana Journal of Global Legal Studies*, 2013).

institutions in charge of interpreting the constitution. Precisely as the turn to constitutionalism protects us from the prospects of living at the mercy of legislatures, so the turn to globalism protects us from the prospects of living at the mercy of the drafters and interpreters of national constitutions.

Further the relationship between global norms and constitutional norms could be a reciprocal relationship. The establishment of a layer of global norms contributes to republican freedom in that the protection of rights does not depend on the good will of national courts or other national institutions and, at the same time, the establishment of constitutional norms contributes to republican freedom in that the protection of rights does not depend on the good will of the international community. Thus the protection of rights is neither at the mercy of national courts (because of the existence of a global order or a global constitution); nor at the mercy of the global community (because of the existence of national constitutions and national courts). Precisely as houses are supported both by internal walls and by external framework whereas each provides support to the other, so the two layers of norms (constitutional and global) mutually support each other. The coexistence of the two layers is justified not (only) by its instrumental contribution to the protection of rights but also by the fact that the protection of rights is neither at the mercy of national constitutional courts nor at the mercy of the global community.

D. The Case against Democracy

This chapter defends the entrenchment of binding constitutional directives on non-instrumental grounds. More specifically, I argue that constitutional directives are justified not merely on the basis of the conjecture that they are likely to be conformed to by the legislatures. Instead, constitutional entrenchment is a form of public acknowledgement of the legislature itself and of the political community that the legislature is duty bound. In the absence of a constitutional duty, legislative decisions could always be attributable to the legislature's judgments or inclinations rather than to its duties and, consequently, the rights are 'at the mercy of' the legislature. I also extended this analysis to explain the appeal of global constitutionalism. Global constitutionalism is designed to guarantee that we do not live at the mercy of the drafters or interpreters of the national constitutions.

One implication of this analysis is the oppressive potential of democracies. In pointing out the oppressive nature of democracy, theorists often point out that democracy may prioritize the interests of majorities over those of minorities (and, at times, the interests of well-organized powerful minorities over those of dispersed unorganized majorities). Yet the analysis in this chapter has exposed an additional concern: the rights of individuals in a democracy are contingent on the judgments and inclinations of the majority. Even if the majority protects these rights vigorously (and is likely to do so in the future), it is still the case that individuals' rights are a by-product of choice or discretion rather than that of duty. This is a non-contingent deficiency of democratic institutions. Even if the legislature is highly enlightened and is devoted to the protection of rights and justice, the mere fact that our rights are 'at its mercy' is a deficiency that needs to be addressed.

It would be natural to extend this analysis also to judicial review. After all, judicial review is an important mechanism that also serves to differentiate sharply between the state's duties and its inclinations. A court declaring that a statute is invalid on the grounds that it conflicts with basic rights makes a clear and non-ambivalent statement that the state is bound to act in certain ways. By invalidating a statute the court affirms that the state has a duty, namely that it is bound to act in certain ways. Thus, it is wrong to maintain that a legislative decision to protect my right to burn the flag ought to be equated with a judicial decision invalidating a statute prohibiting the burning of a flag. Admittedly in both cases I can burn a flag without being subjected to criminal sanctions. Yet, the grounds of the former decision can be that the legislature has indeed a power to prohibit the burning of the flag but it decided not to use its powers. In contrast, the grounds of the latter decision are that the legislature itself is bound to protect the right to burn the flag.[97]

I find this line of reasoning compelling, and I believe that a sound theory justifying judicial review could be grounded in such concerns. Judicial review is an important tool facilitating the differentiation

[97] Note that one may argue that there is an additional difference as once the Court made a decision, it cannot be changed. This however is false as the Court can change its own constitutional interpretations. It is not necessarily the case that legislative decisions are more likely to be changed than judicial ones.

between those concerns that are discretionary and those that are mandatory. By striking down a constitutional directive the court acknowledges a duty on the part of the legislature. Yet it would be tedious to develop such an argument, as it would be too closely related to this chapter. Hence, Chapter 6 pursues a different route and provides a different argument in favour of judicial review.

6

The Real Case for Judicial Review

Judicial review is a present instrument of government. It represents a choice that men have made, and ultimately we must justify it as a choice in our own time.[1]

A. Introduction

Constitutional theory has been obsessed for many years with an attempt to provide an adequate justification for judicial review. This chapter joins the search for a rationale for judicial review. It also wishes to defend judicial review against the recent numerous rising voices that either wish to abolish judicial review altogether or to limit or minimize its scope.[2] Its main task is to expose a critical flaw shared by both advocates and opponents of judicial review and to propose a framework for addressing this difficulty. The critical flaw of the debate concerning judicial review is the conviction that judicial review must be *instrumentally* justified, i.e., that it be grounded in *contingent* desirable

---

[1] Alexander Bickel, *The Least Dangerous Branch: The Supreme Court at the Bar of Politics* (2nd edn., New Haven: Yale University Press, 1986), 16.

[2] The most influential contributions include: Jeremy Waldron, *Law and Disagreement* (Oxford: Oxford University Press, 1999); Mark Tushnet, *Taking the Constitution away from the Courts* (Princeton: Princeton University Press, 1999); Mark Tushnet, *Weak Courts, Strong Rights: Judicial Review and Social Welfare Rights in Comparative Constitutional Law* (Princeton: Princeton University Press, 2008); Larry Kramer, *The People Themselves: Popular Constitutionalism and Judicial Review* (New York: Oxford University Press, 2004); Adrian Vermeule, *Law and the Limits of Reason* (New York: Oxford University Press, 2009).

features of the judicial process (for example, the superior quality of decisions rendered by judges, the superior ability (or willingness) of judges to protect rights, the special deliberative powers of judges, the greater stability and coherence of legal decisions, and so on).[3] Once the critical flaw of traditional theories is understood, this chapter turns to develop a new proposal to defend judicial review that overcomes the difficulties faced by instrumentalist justifications. Under this proposal, judicial review is designed to provide individuals with a right to a hearing or a right to raise a grievance. More particularly, I argue that judicial review is indispensable because it grants individuals opportunities to challenge decisions that impinge (or may have impinged) upon their rights, to engage in reasoned deliberation concerning these decisions, and to benefit from a reconsideration of these decisions in light of this deliberation. Under this view, judicial review is intrinsically rather than instrumentally desirable; its value is grounded in procedural features that are essential characteristics of judicial institutions per se. The right to a hearing as understood in this chapter is grounded in the fundamental duty of the state to consult its citizens on matters of rights, and to consult those who complain (justifiably or unjustifiably) that their rights have been violated.[4]

In contrast to traditional theories, establishing the case for judicial review does not require establishing complex empirical assertions, such as the claim that courts render better decisions or the claim that courts' decisions are more protective of democracy, rights, or stability and coherence. Establishing the case for judicial review requires merely establishing that courts are faithful to the values embodied in the adjudicative process. It is the adjudicative process itself, and not any complex contingent consequences of this process that are sufficient to justify judicial review. Further, I argue, the adjudicative process is not an instrument designed to protect the right

---

[3] Very few of the constitutional theorists examine or even mention the non-instrumental concerns. Even when these concerns are mentioned they are typically dismissed. Adrian Vermeule maintains that: 'In principle, these consequentialist premises exclude a domain of (wholly or partially) nonconsequentialist approaches to interpretation. It turns out, however, that this is not a very large loss of generality, because very few people hold views of that sort. Interpretative consequentialism is an extremely broad rubric.' See Adrian Vermeule, *Judging under Uncertainty: An Institutional Theory of Legal Interpretation* (Cambridge, Mass.: Harvard University Press, 2006).

[4] The analysis is based mainly on two previous papers: Yuval Eylon and Alon Harel, 'The Right to Judicial Review', 92 *Va. L. Rev.* 991 (2006); Alon Harel and Tsvi Kahana, 'The Easy Core Case for Judicial Review', 2 *Journal of Legal Analysis* 227 (2010).

to a hearing or to 'maximize' the amount of hearing or the degree of recognition citizens receive at a hearing. Instead, the right to a hearing is constitutive of the adjudicative judicial process; adjudication is in reality a realization or manifestation of the right to a hearing. Hence, the case for judicial review does not depend on judicial review being an efficient instrument in guarding democracy or rights, or indeed even in effectively protecting the right to a hearing itself. Consequently, in contrast to previous (instrumental) justifications of judicial review, the soundness of the right-to-a-hearing model of judicial review does not turn on complex (and dubious) empirical conjectures.

Once it is evident that judicial review is valuable because at its essence it is a hearing the chapter turns to explore the justifiability of intermediate review systems—systems of constrained judicial review. Constrained judicial review rejects legislative supremacy, as it affirms that courts have a privileged status in interpreting the constitution. At the same time, it also rejects judicial supremacy, as it maintains that judicial privileges should be constrained and greater constitutional responsibilities ought to be given to the legislature. Systems as diverse as weak judicial review, popular constitutionalism and departmentalism can be classified under this heading. This chapter argues that such systems can, under certain conditions, be legitimate; their legitimacy hinges on their potential to provide a meaningful hearing.[5]

Section B of the chapter explores five popular arguments favouring judicial review. It establishes that these arguments are instrumentalist and that their instrumentalist nature exposes them to powerful objections. Section C argues that individuals have a right to raise their grievances in front of judicial (or quasi-judicial) bodies, and that these bodies also ought to have the power to make authoritative judgments. This 'right to a hearing' or 'right to raise a grievance' ought to be respected independently of the instrumental contributions that judicial review makes (or may make) to other values of democratic or liberal societies. Section D explores whether and to what extent the right to a hearing can be adequately protected in systems which grants courts a privileged, but not a supreme, role in shaping constitutional rights, e.g., in systems characterized by weak judicial review. As the right to a hearing hinges on the robustness of the adjudicative process, what

---

[5] This conclusion was elaborated in greater detail in Alon Harel and Adam Shinar, 'Between Judicial and Legislative Supremacy: A Cautious Defense of Constrained Judicial Review' 10 *International Journal of Constitutional Law* 950 (2010).

counts is preserving a robust adjudicative process and not necessarily preserving the supreme powers of courts or judges.

B. The Instrumentalist Justifications for Judicial Review

This section establishes that the prominent theories purporting to justify judicial review are instrumentalist, and that these theories fail for this reason. Judicial review, as understood here, consists of the following two components. (1) Courts have the power to make binding decisions concerning the constitutional validity of statutes that apply to individual cases brought before them, and these decisions ought to be respected by all other branches of government. (2) No branch of government has the power to immunize its operation from judicial scrutiny. This analysis implies that courts are not 'equal partners' in the enterprise of constitutional interpretation, but instead that they have a privileged role in constitutional interpretation.[6]

Under instrumentalist theories, judicial review is justified to the extent that it is likely to bring about *contingent* desirable consequences. While there are important differences among the five theories examined in this section, they all share important structural similarities. Under each one of these theories, the constitutional theorist differentiates sharply between two stages of analysis. At the first stage, the theorist addresses the question of what the point of the constitution is and, consequently, how it should be interpreted. Once the 'point' of the constitution is settled, the theorist turns to identify the institutions best capable of realizing the 'point' of the constitution. Instrumentalist theories of judicial review perceive this second step, namely identifying the institutions in charge of interpreting the constitution, as subservient to the findings in the first stage. The institution in charge of interpreting

---

[6] This claim however does not directly justify judicial supremacy. Judicial supremacy as opposed to judicial review includes a third component, namely the claim that courts do not merely resolve particular disputes involving the litigants directly before it. They also authoritatively interpret constitutional meaning. Judicial supremacy requires deference by other government officials to the constitutional dictates of the courts not only with respect to the particular case but also with respect to their interpretation of the constitutional norms. For a definition of judicial supremacy, see Keith Whittington, *Political Foundations of Judicial Supremacy: The Presidency, the Supreme Court, and Constitutional Leadership in U.S. History* (Princeton: Princeton University Press, 2007).

the constitution is simply the institution most likely to interpret the constitution 'rightly' or 'correctly', or the institution whose decisions are the most conducive to the constitutional goals or values as defined at the first stage of analysis. Interpreting the constitution can therefore be described as a task in search of an agent capable of performing it, the agent being an instrument whose suitability depends solely on the quality and the costs of its performance.

To establish the dominance of instrumentalist theories, let me briefly survey five influential theories purporting to justify judicial review: rights-based theories, democracy-enhancement theories, the settlement theory of judicial review, the dualist democracy argument, and institutionalist instrumentalism. Each one of these theories characterizes the constitutional goals differently. Yet, once the constitutional goals are identified, each one of the theories justifies judicial review on the grounds that it is the best institutional means of realizing the constitutional goal.

Rights-based theories maintain that judicial review is justified in order to guarantee an efficacious protection of rights.[7] Many theorists believe that judges are superior to other officials in their ability (or willingness) to identify the scope of rights and assign them the proper weight. Some theorists believe that the superiority of judges is attributable to their expertise; judges, under this view, form a class of experts on rights.[8] Others believe that judicial review can be justified on the basis of the nature of the judicial process, and the relative detachment and independence of judges from political constraints.[9] Judicial review is justified to the extent that it is likely to contribute to the protection of rights—either directly, by correcting legislative decisions that violate individual rights, or indirectly, by inhibiting the legislature from making decisions that would violate individual rights.[10] This view is

---

[7] Alon Harel, 'Rights-Based Judicial Review: A Democratic Justification', 22 *Law & Phil.* 247 (2003).

[8] Charles Black, *A New Birth of Freedom: Human Rights, Named and Unnamed* (New York: G. P. Putnam, 1997).

[9] Owen Fiss, 'The Supreme Court 1978 Term Foreword: The Forms of Justice', 93 *Harv. L. Rev.* 1 (1978); Owen Fiss, 'Two Models of Adjudication', in Robert Goodwin and William Schambra (eds.), *How Does the Constitution Secure Rights?* (Washington, DC: American Enterprise Institute for Public Policy Research, 1985); Michael Perry, *The Constitution, the Courts and Human Rights: An Inquiry into the Legitimacy of Constitutional Policymaking by the Judiciary* (New Haven: Yale University Press, 1982); Lawrence Sager, *Justice in Plainclothes: A Theory of American Constitutional Practice* (New Haven: Yale University Press, 2004).

[10] Henry Abraham, *The Judicial Process* (7th edn., New York: Oxford University Press, 1998).

perhaps the most popular and well entrenched in American legal thought.[11]

Democracy-enhancing theories argue that the constitution is designed to protect the representative nature of government. The most influential advocate of this view—John Hart Ely—maintains that the 'pursuit of participational goals of broadened access to the processes and bounty of representative government' ought to replace 'the more traditional and academically popular insistence upon the provision of a series of particular substantive goods or values deemed fundamental'.[12] The constitution, in Ely's view, is essentially a procedural document, and the goals of the constitution and those of the institutional structures designed to protect it should favour a 'participation-oriented representation reinforcing approach to judicial review'.[13] This has important implications concerning judicial review. Judicial review is justified to the extent that it serves the purpose of enhancing participation.[14]

Annabelle Lever develops a different version of this argument. She denies that courts are designed to protect the traditional political institutions from being eroded by anti-democratic laws. Instead, she believes that courts are as democratic as legislatures. In her view, there are different forms of representation and elections are only one form of representation. Courts are democratic institutions in that they are accountable to the public, constrained by reputational mechanisms,

---

[11] It has most famously been argued by Alexander Hamilton. See *The Federalist*, no. 78, (ed.) Henry B. Dawson (New York: Scribner's, 1891), 544–5. Jeremy Waldron also expressed the view that the concern most commonly expressed is that legislative procedures... [are] endemically and constitutionally in danger of encroaching upon the rights of individuals or minorities. See Waldron, *Law and Disagreement*, 11 (n 2).

[12] John Ely, *Democracy and Distrust: A Theory of Judicial Review* (Cambridge, Mass.: Harvard University Press, 1980), 74.

[13] Ely, *Democracy and Distrust*, 87 (n 12).

[14] Despite major differences, it is easy to detect the structural similarity between traditional rights-based theories and Ely's participational theory. Under both theories courts are assigned review powers because of the alleged superior quality of their decisions with respect to a certain sphere of decisions. While rights theorists believe that judicial review is justified because courts are better than legislatures at protecting rights, Ely believes that it is justified because courts are better than legislatures at protecting democratic representation and enhancing popular participation. Indeed, this similarity was noticed by Ronald Dworkin, who believes that Ely was wrong only in 'limiting this account to constitutional rights that can be understood as enhancements of constitutional procedure rather than as more substantive rights'. See Ronald Dworkin, *Freedom's Law: The Moral Reading of the American Constitution* (Cambridge, Mass.: Harvard University Press, 1980), 373 n 5.

and represent in various ways voices that are not sufficiently represented in the regular political process.[15]

Settlement theories of judicial review maintain that judicial supremacy is justified on the grounds that it is conducive to settlement, coordination, and stability.[16] Alexander and Schauer—the most influential contemporary advocates of settlement theories—suggest that the authoritative settlement of disagreements is sometimes desirable, even when the settlement is suboptimal. In their view:

[O]ne of the chief functions of law in general, and constitutional law in particular, is to provide a degree of coordinated settlement for settlement's sake of what is to be done. In a world of moral and political disagreement law can often provide a settlement of these disagreements, a settlement neither final nor conclusive, but nevertheless authoritative and thus providing for those in first-order disagreement a second-order resolution of that disagreement that will make it possible for a decision to be made, actions to be coordinated, and life to go on.[17]

Alexander and Schauer believe that courts in general and the Supreme Court in particular are better capable of maintaining stability and achieving settlement than other institutions, e.g., the legislature.[18]

The '*dualist democracy*' position advocated by Bruce Ackerman distinguishes between two different types of decisions: decisions made by the American people and decisions made by their governments.[19] The American Constitution is designed to protect the first type of

---

[15] See Annabelle Lever, 'Democracy and Judicial Review: Are they Really Incompatible' 7 *Perspectives on Politics* 805 (2009).

[16] Larry Alexander and Fredrick Schauer, 'On Extrajudicial Constitutional Interpretation', 110 *Harv. L. Rev.* 1359 (1997); Larry Alexander and Fredrick Schauer, 'Defending Judicial Supremacy: A Reply', 17 *Const. Comment.* 455 (2000). This argument was first made by Daniel Webster, Cong. Deb. 6, 78 (1830). More recently, the argument has been raised and rejected by Alexander Bickel, who maintains that: 'The ends of uniformity and of vindication of federal authority' can be served without recourse to any power in the federal judiciary to lay down the meaning of the Constitution. See Bickel, *The Least Dangerous Branch*, 12 (n 1).

[17] See Alexander and Schauer, *Defending Judicial Supremacy*, 467 (n 16).

[18] In purporting to establish the Supreme Court's special virtues in realizing these goals, Alexander and Schauer rely on the relative insulation of the Court from political winds, on the 'established and constraining procedures through which constitutional issues are brought before the court,' on the small number of members of the Supreme Court, the life term they serve, and the fact that the court cannot pick its own agenda. Alexander and Schauer, *Defending Judicial Supremacy*, 477 (n 16).

[19] Bruce Ackerman, *We the People*, i: *Foundations* (Cambridge, Mass.: Harvard University Press, 1991).

decisions—decisions of 'We the People' from being eroded by the second type—decisions of 'We the Politicians'. The rare periods in which supreme law is formed by the American people are labelled by Ackerman as periods of 'constitutional politics'. In contrast, in periods of 'normal politics', decisions made by the government occur daily, are made primarily by politicians, and are undeserving of the status of higher law. The courts are assigned the task of preserving this dual structure. In Ackerman's view '*Quite simply*, the Justices are the only ones around with the training and the inclination to look back to past moments of popular sovereignty and to check the pretensions of our elected politicians when they endanger the great achievements of the past.'[20]

Institutionalist instrumentalism aims at providing a more coherent and scientific instrumentalist theory. Institutionalists raise many concerns with respect to the four instrumentalist theories described herein, in particular with respect to the question of whether judicial review is indeed instrumental in realizing the constitutional goals set by constitutional theorists.[21] Yet institutionalists such as Einer Elhauge, Neil Komesar, and Adrian Vermeule share with other instrumentalists the belief that constitutional design is ultimately an instrument used to achieve desirable social goals. More specifically, what ought to determine the scope of judicial powers to review legislation is an institutional choice based on 'the relative strengths and weaknesses of the reviewer (the adjudicative process) and of the reviewed (the political process)'.[22]

Adrian Vermeule describes institutionalism as a form of rule consequentialism. In his view 'judges should interpret legal texts in accordance with rules whose observance produces the best consequences overall'.[23] Rule consequentialism requires the theorist to look not at any particular decision that courts or legislatures are likely to generate, but at the broader and more foundational institutional characteristics of courts and legislatures. In Vermuele's view, the relevant variables for determining the powers of judicial institutions are highly complex, and include 'the agency costs and the costs of uncertainty, systemic effects

---

[20]   Bruce Ackerman, 'The Living Constitution', 120 *Harv. L. Rev.* 1737, 1806–7 (2007).
[21]   Einer Elhauge, 'Does Interest Group Theory Justify More Intrusive Judicial Review?', 101 *Yale LJ* 31–110 (1991).
[22]   Neil Komesar, *Imperfect Alternatives: Choosing Institutions in Law, Economics and Public Policy* (Chicago: Chicago University Press, 1994).
[23]   Vermeule, *Judging under Uncertainty*, 5 (n 3).

(especially a form of moral hazard), the optimal rate of constitutional updating, and the transition costs of switching from one regime to another'.[24]

All of these theories are instrumentalist; they are all based on a conjunction of two claims. (1) The constitution is designed to realize certain (contingent) goals (e.g., to protect rights, to enhance democracy, to guarantee stability and coherence, to protect constitutional politics or, more generally, to bring about the best consequences overall). (2) Judicial review is desirable only to the extent that it succeeds in realizing the constitutional goals.

I believe that this instrumentalist structure is responsible for the failure of these theories. Instrumentalist theories are misguided for three reasons. First, I am sceptical as to whether instrumentalists can in fact make reliable assertions concerning the likely performance of courts versus legislatures or other institutions.[25] Second, even if instrumentalist advocates of judicial review establish that courts are better in protecting constitutional rights or other constitutional values, it hardly follows that courts ought to be granted review powers. Participatory concerns are very likely to override or even annul the relevance of the concerns for a better decision-making process. Third, instrumentalist arguments in general and institutionalist arguments in particular are subject to the insincerity or inauthenticity objection. They fail to capture what the debate is really about and they fail to understand the roots of the appeal of constitutionalism in general and judicial review in particular.

The first flaw of instrumentalist theories provides the basis for a standard objection on the part of opponents of judicial review. Many constitutional theorists point out the weaknesses in establishing that judicial review is conducive to the realization of constitutional goals. Critics of rights-based justifications point out that judges are not necessarily or even typically the best protectors of rights.[26] As Vermeule argues 'Courts may not understand what justice requires, or may not be good at producing justice even when they understand it.'[27] Historical evidence does not support the conjecture that courts are

---

[24] Vermeule, *Judging under Uncertainty*, 5 (n 3).
[25] This scepticism is also shared by Annabelle Lever. See Lever, 'Democracy and Judicial Review' (n 15).
[26] Komesar, *Imperfect Alternatives*, 256–61 (n 22); Vermeule, *Judging under Uncertainty*, 243 (n 3).
[27] Vermeule, *Judging under Uncertainty*, 243 (n 3).

better protectors of rights, even in the context of classical rights such as freedom of speech.[28] Similar objections have been raised with respect to Ely's defence of judicial review. Neil Komesar challenged Ely's conviction that courts are indeed necessary both for 'clearing the channels for political change' and to 'facilitate the representation of minorities'.[29] In his view, Ely's analysis fails because it does not engage in *comparative* institutional analysis; it fails to compare the quality of decision-making of different institutional alternatives.[30] While Ely detects the imperfections of the legislature in making procedural decisions, he is mistaken in inferring from these imperfections that courts should be assigned powers to make these decisions. Such a conclusion requires comparing the virtues and vices of courts and legislatures, while taking into account the complex interdependencies between these institutions. As Komesar establishes, such a comparison does not necessarily favour courts over legislatures. Other theorists have questioned whether courts in general, and the Supreme Court in particular, are the institutions most capable of maintaining stability and reaching settlement.[31] One of the critics of Alexander and Schauer asks: 'Would legislative supremacy produce more or less stability than judicial supremacy? Inertia or structural status quo bias is built into legislative institutions by voting rules, bicameralism, and other features. Is this stronger or weaker than the status quo built into judicial institutions?'[32]

---

[28] David Rabban, *Free Speech in Its Forgotten Years* (Cambridge: Cambridge University Press, 1997); Wojciech Sadurski, 'Judicial Review and the Protection of Constitutional Rights', 22 *Oxford J. Leg. Studies* 275 (2002); Vermeule, *Judging under Uncertainty*, 231 (n 3). Using historical experience is dubious, however. Historical arguments fail to capture the complex interdependencies between different institutions. Thus, even if one can establish that courts have systematically been worse than legislatures in protecting rights, it does not follow that eliminating judicial review is conducive to the protection of rights since judicial review may have contributed to the superior quality of the legislature's decision-making by deterring legislatures from infringing individual rights. See Abraham, *The Judicial Process*, 371 (n 10). Similarly even if one can establish that courts have systematically been better than legislatures, it does not follow that judicial review is conducive to the protection of rights because it is possible that a legislature operating in a world without judicial review is more reflective and deliberative than a legislature in a world without judicial review. See James Thayer, 'The Origin and Scope of the American Doctrine of Constitutional law', 7 *Harv. L. Rev.* 129 (1893). These possibilities only serve to illustrate the complexity of the considerations required for establishing rights-based arguments for or against judicial review.

[29] Komesar, *Imperfect Alternatives*, 203 (n 22).

[30] Komesar, *Imperfect Alternatives*, 199 (n 22).

[31] Keith Whittington, 'Extrajudicial Constitutional Interpretation: "Three Objections and Responses"', 80 *North Carolina L. Rev.* 773, 794–6 (2002).

[32] Vermeule, *Judging under Uncertainty*, 249 (n 3).

Another critic even asserts that 'Court opinions can unsettle as well as settle the legal and constitutional environment.'[33] Finally, no evidence has been provided by Ackerman to establish his conjecture that judges are more faithful to constitutional politics than legislatures.

More generally, reliable predictions concerning the performance of the courts can be made only with respect to certain historical or social circumstances. The optimal institutional design therefore depends on the particular contingencies of the relevant society. The ambition of constitutional theorists to design foundational institutional mechanisms independently of these contingencies indicates that non-instrumental considerations lurk behind the overly rationalist instrumentalist effort to promote constitutional values. The instrumentalist explanations fail to identify what is really important about judicial review.

A second reason for the failure of many (although not all) instrumentalist theories is based on what I described in the introduction to Part III as a caveat to the epistemic justification. It seems that the alleged superior performance of courts or their epistemic advantages may not be sufficient to justify judicial review, as depriving individuals of their power to make normative judgments *on the grounds that they are incapable of doing so* on their own offends their dignity. Otherwise, the mere fact that moral philosophers (or the philosopher kings governing Kallipolis) may be even better than both legislators *and* judges in protecting rights would justify granting philosophers review powers over legislation. While this concern does not apply to all instrumentalist theories, it clearly applies to those who are based on epistemic considerations.

Third and most importantly, instrumentalist accounts misconstrue the essence of the debate concerning judicial review and fail to identify the spirit underlying this debate. The controversy concerning constitutionalism cannot be about the expertise of judges versus legislatures or the quality of the performance of these institutions; it is to a large extent a debate about the political morality and legitimacy of constitutional decision-making. The debate concerning judicial review is conducted by political philosophers, constitutional lawyers, and citizens. While some of the arguments raised by the participants are instrumentalist, the spirit of the debate and the range of participants indicate that the debate concerning judicial review and its optimal

---

[33] Whittington, 'Extrajudicial Constitutional Interpretation', 800 (n 31).

scope cannot reasonably be construed as a debate concerning the likely consequences of different systems of constitutional design. I believe that by purporting to provide an instrumental rationale for judicial review, its advocates fail to capture what really underlies the passions of the participants of this debate.

C. Judicial Review and the Right to a Hearing

1. Introduction

Section B demonstrated the inadequacy of instrumentalist justifications for judicial review. This section defends a non-instrumentalist justification for judicial review. What is distinctive about courts is not the special wisdom of judicial decisions or other desirable *contingent* consequences that follow from judicial decisions, but the procedures and the mode of deliberation that characterize courts. These procedures are intrinsically valuable independently of the quality of decisions rendered by courts because these procedures are, in themselves, a realization of the right to a hearing.

The argument proceeds in two parts. Section C2 discusses the right to a hearing, and establishes its importance. It argues that individuals have a right to a hearing consisting of an opportunity to challenge what is considered (by the purported right-holder) justifiably or unjustifiably to be a violation of a right. Section C3 establishes that the right to a hearing is embedded in the procedures of the legal process, and that judicial review or quasi-judicial review is the only manner in which the right to a hearing can (as a conceptual matter) be protected. Judicial review is not a means for protecting the right to a hearing; it is, in reality, its institutional embodiment.

2. The Right to a Hearing

The proposed justification rests upon the view that judicial review is designed to facilitate the voicing of grievances by protecting the right to a hearing. The right to a hearing consists of three components: the opportunity to voice a grievance, the opportunity to be provided with a justification for a decision that impinges (or may impinge) upon one's rights, and the duty to reconsider the initial decision giving rise to the grievance. The right to a hearing is valued independently of the merit of the decision likely to result at the end of this process.

When and why do individuals have a right to a hearing? The right to a hearing, I argue, depends on the right-holder's claim concerning the existence of an all-things-considered right that is subject to a challenge. The right to a hearing therefore presupposes a moral controversy concerning the existence of a prior right. There are two types of controversies that give rise to a right to a hearing. The first is a controversy concerning the justifiability of an infringement of a right X. In such a case, the right-holder challenges the justifiability of the infringement on the basis of the shared assumption that there is a (prima facie) right, and that there was an infringement of that right. Here, the right to a hearing is designed to provide the right-holder with an opportunity to establish that, contrary to the conjectures of the person who (arguably) bears the duty to honour X, the infringement of X violates a right and is therefore unjustified. The second type of controversy occurs when there is a genuine dispute concerning the very existence of a prior right X. In this case, the right-holder challenges the claim that no right is being infringed. Here, the right to a hearing is designed to provide the right-holder with an opportunity to establish the existence of such a right. In both cases, I argue, the right to a hearing is not contingent upon the soundness of the grievance of the right-holder. Even if the alleged right-holder is wrong in her grievance, she is entitled to a hearing. Let us investigate and examine each one of these cases.

The first type of controversy occurs when the right-holder challenges the justifiability of an infringement of a right. A right is justifiably infringed when it is overridden by conflicting interests or rights.[34] If, in the course of walking to a lunch appointment, I have to stop to save a child and consequently I miss my appointment, the right of the person who expects to meet me is being (justifiably) infringed.

Infringements of rights can give rise to two distinct complaints on the part of the right-holder. One complaint is based simply on the claim that the infringement is an unjustified infringement rather than a justified infringement, i.e., that it is a violation. The second complaint, however, is procedural in nature. When one infringes another's rights,

---

[34] Judith Jarvis Thomson, 'Some Ruminations on Rights', 19 *Ariz. L. Rev.* 45 (1977); Alon Harel, 'Theories of Rights', in Martin Golding and William Edmundson (eds.), *The Blackwell Guide to the Philosophy of Law and Legal Theory* (Malden, Mass.: Blackwell Publishing Ltd, 2005), 191. For doubts concerning the soundness of the distinction, see John Oberdiek, 'Lost in Moral Space: On the Infringing/Violating Distinction and its Place in the Theory of Rights', 23 *Law & Phil.* 325 (2004).

one typically encounters a complaint based not on the conviction that the infringement is unjustified, but on the grounds that an infringement, even when justified, must be done only if the right-holder is provided with an opportunity to raise a grievance and to challenge the infringement. The complaints elicited by a disappointed promisee may illustrate the force of such a grievance. The disappointed promisee may protest: 'you have no right to break your promise *without consulting me first.*' This rhetorical use of 'right' invokes the commonplace intuition that when someone's rights are at stake, that person is entitled to voice her grievance, demand an explanation, or challenge the infringement. Such a right cannot be accounted for by the conviction that honouring it guarantees the efficacious protection of the promisee's rights. Even under circumstances in which the promisee's rights would be better protected if no such hearing were to take place, the promisee should be provided with an opportunity to challenge the promisor's decision.

Infringements of rights trigger a duty to provide a hearing. In fact, some theorists of rights have argued that the right to a hearing provides a litmus test to differentiate cases involving justified infringements of prima facie rights, from cases in which no prima facie right exists in the first place. In pointing this out, Phillip Montague has argued that:

If Jones has a right to do A and is prevented from acting, then he is owed an apology at least. But if Jones has only a prima facie right to do A, so that preventing him from acting is permissible, then whoever prevented him from acting has no obligation to apologize. *He almost certainly owes Jones an explanation, however.* And this obligation to explain strikes me as sufficient to distinguish situations in which prima facie rights are infringed from situations in which no rights—not even prima facie rights—are at stake.[35]

The right to a hearing in cases of a dispute concerning the justifiability of an infringement is contingent upon the existence of a prima facie right that is being infringed (either justifiably or unjustifiably). There is thus an important link between individual rights and the right to a hearing. The existence of a prima facie right gives the right-holder a stake in that right and power over it, even when the right is justifiably overridden. The right to a hearing is grounded in the fact that people

---

[35] Phillip Montague, 'The Nature of Rights: Some Logical Considerations', 19 *Nous* 365, 368 (1985) (emphasis added). See also Phillip Montague, 'When Rights are Presumably Infringed', 53 *Phil. Stud.* 347 (1988).

occupy a special position with respect to their rights. Rights demarcate a boundary that has to be respected, a region in which the right-holder is a master. One's special relation to the right, i.e., one's dominion, does not vanish even when the right is justifiably overridden. When the infringement of the right is at stake, the question of whether it might be justifiable to infringe that right is not tantamount to the question of whether one should have dominion over the matter. A determination that the right has been justifiably infringed does not nullify the privileged position of the right-holder. Instead, his privileged position is made concrete by granting the right-holder a right to a hearing. Thus, infringing the right unilaterally is wrong even when the infringement itself is justified because the right-holder is not treated as someone who has a say in the matter.

What does the right to a hearing triggered by an infringement of a prior right consist of? There are three components of the right to a hearing: an opportunity for the victim of infringement to voice her grievance (to be heard), the provision of an explanation to the victim of the infringement that addresses her grievance, and a principled willingness to honour the right if it transpires that the infringement is unjustified.

To establish the importance of these components, consider the following example. Assume that A promises to meet B for lunch, but unexpected circumstances, e.g., a memorial, disrupts A's plans. The promisor believes that these circumstances override the obligation to go to the lunch. It seems that the promisee under these circumstances deserves a 'hearing' (to the extent that it is practically possible), consisting of three components. First, the promisor must provide the promisee with an opportunity to challenge her decision to breach. Second, she must be willing to engage in meaningful moral deliberation, addressing the grievance in light of the particular circumstances. Finally, the promisor must be willing to reconsider the decision to breach.

The first component, namely the duty of the promisor to provide the promisee with an opportunity to challenge her decision, is self-explanatory. The second and third components require further clarification. To understand the significance of the willingness to engage in meaningful moral deliberation, imagine the following: the promisor informs the promisee that sometime in the past, after thorough deliberation, she adopted a rule that in cases of conflicts between lunches and memorials, she always ought to attend the memorials. When challenged by the promisee, the promisor recites the arguments used in past deliberations without demonstrating that those arguments justify infringing this promise in the specific circumstances at hand, and without taking the present promisee into consideration in any way. Such behaviour violates the promisor's duty to engage in meaningful moral deliberation. The duty to a hearing requires deliberation concerning the justifiability of the decision in light of the specific circumstances. This is not because the original deliberation leading to forming the rule was necessarily flawed or even likely to be flawed. Perhaps the early deliberation leading to forming the rule was flawless, and perhaps such an abstract, detached rule-like deliberation is even more likely to generate sound decisions than deliberation addressed to evaluating the justifiability of the infringement in the present circumstances. The obligation to provide a hearing is not an instrumental obligation designed to improve the quality of decision-making and, consequently, its force does not depend on whether the hearing is more likely to generate a better decision. The obligation to engage in moral deliberation is owed to the purported right-holder as a matter of justice. The promisee is entitled to question and challenge the decision because it is her rights that are being infringed.

Does this view entail that rules can never be used in addressing a rights-based grievance? If so, does not this proposal undermine the very ability to use rules-based deliberation, and thereby impose unrealistic burdens on decision-making? To address this objection another clarification is necessary. The concrete examination required by the promisor or any other duty-holder does not preclude the use of rules. The use of rules is sometimes necessary to identify the scope and weight of rights of individuals. Yet even in order to establish that rules of the type 'memorials always override lunches' ought to guide the promisor, a concrete examination is necessary. A concrete examination of the appropriateness of applying a rule in this case is always required. Sometimes the appropriate scope and depth of the concrete examination is minimal and, consequently, it imposes few burdens on the decision-maker. At other times, the scope and depth required of the decision-maker is extensive.

Lastly, note the significance of the third component; namely, the willingness to reconsider the initial decision based on the conviction that the right can be justifiably infringed. To note its significance, imagine a promisor who is willing to engage in a moral deliberation but announces (or, even worse, decides without announcing) that her decision is final. It is evident that such a promisor breaches the duty to provide a hearing even if she is willing to provide an opportunity for the promisee to raise his grievance and even if she is providing an explanation. A genuine hearing requires an 'open heart', i.e., a principled willingness to reconsider one's decision in light of the moral deliberation. This is not because the willingness to reconsider the decision necessarily generates a better decision on the part of the promisor. Reconsideration is required even when it does not increase the likelihood that the 'right' decision is rendered.

So far we have examined the right to a hearing in the first type of controversy about rights, namely controversies concerning whether a given *infringement* of a right is justified. Let us turn our attention to a second type of controversy, namely, the case in which there is a genuine dispute concerning the existence of a (prima facie) right in the first place. To establish the existence of a right to a hearing in such a case, let me first establish the intuitive force of the claim by providing an example. I will explore here also what principled justifications one can provide for the existence of a right to a hearing under such circumstances.

Consider the following case. John promises his friend Susan that in the absence of special reasons making it especially inconvenient for him, he will take her to the airport. The next day, a few hours before the agreed-upon time, John has a mild sore throat and he informs Susan that he cannot take her. Given the conditional nature of his promise, John argues that Susan has no right (not even a prima facie right) to be taken to the airport.

Unlike in the previous case, the dispute between Susan and John is not over whether the promise is justifiably overridden by unexpected circumstances (a memorial), but whether the conditions giving rise to the right were fulfilled to start with. John maintains that a mild sore throat is 'a special reason making it particularly inconvenient for him' to take Susan to the airport and, consequently he believes that Susan has no right whatsoever to be taken by him to the airport. Susan disagrees. She believes that a mild sore throat is not 'a special reason making it particularly inconvenient' for John to take her to the airport and consequently that she has a right to be taken by John to the airport.

It seems that irrespective of whether John or Susan is right, John has a duty to engage in a hearing that requires him to deliberate jointly with Susan. Failure to do so is a moral failure on the part of John irrespective of whether John is justified in his belief that the conditions of the promise were not satisfied in this case. Furthermore, John's duty to provide a 'hearing' does not seem to depend on whether a hearing is indeed conducive to the making of the 'right' or 'correct' decision. The duty to provide a hearing does not turn on instrumental considerations.

The right to a hearing in such a case has a similar structure to the right to a hearing triggered by a case where the dispute is about the justifiability of the infringement. It consists of the same three components. First, John must provide Susan with an opportunity to challenge his decision to stay at home; i.e., to establish that she has a right that he take her to the airport. Second, John must be willing to engage in meaningful moral deliberation, addressing Susan's grievance in light of the particular circumstances. It would thus be wrong on the part of John to use a general rule, e.g., a rule that states that 'any physical inconvenience is a special reason to infringe such a promise,' without examining the soundness of the rule in light of the particular circumstances. Finally, John must be willing to reconsider the decision in light of the arguments provided in the course of the moral deliberation and act accordingly. Principled and genuine willingness on the part of John to act in accordance with the deliberation is necessary for honouring the right to a hearing.

This example may have provided some intuitive force to the claim that the right to a hearing applies not only in cases of a controversy concerning the justifiability of the infringement of an existing right but also in cases in which there is a genuine and reasonable dispute concerning the very existence of a right. Yet, arguably, it is more difficult to account for the normative foundation of a right to air a grievance when the very right providing the foundation for the grievance might not exist. How can such a right to a hearing be vindicated when, unlike in the case of infringement, it cannot rest on the uncontroversial existence of a prior prima facie right?

I am not going to fully explore the foundations of the right to a hearing as I believe that the intuitive force of the example is sufficient to establish the claim that a right to a hearing exists. Let me however speculate that if there is a right to a hearing in such a case, it must be grounded in the special status of right-holders. Arguably, right-holders ought to have the opportunity of establishing their conviction that they are indeed owed a particular right. Depriving them of such an opportunity (even in cases in which they unjustifiably maintain that they have a right) is unfair because such a deprivation fails to respect them as potential right-holders. Under this argument, precisely as a prima facie right that is justifiably infringed leaves its fingerprint (or moral residue) in the form of a right to a hearing, so too a dispute concerning the existence of a right leaves a fingerprint in the form of a right to a hearing even when, after further inquiry, one can conclude that the 'right' giving rise to the dispute never existed in the first place. This view can provide an alternative way of understanding what the control of right-holders consists of. Under this view, the control of right-holders (or purported right-holders) grants right-holders an opportunity to participate in rights-based reasoning or deliberation.

The right to a hearing can be conceptualized in terms of deliberative duties. By raising a grievance, a purported right-holder can impose a deliberative duty on the alleged duty-holder. Such a deliberative duty is not grounded in epistemic considerations and it is not designed to improve decision-making. Instead, it is designed to facilitate joint deliberation by both the purported right-holder and the alleged duty-holder. When I claim a right, I thereby trigger a duty on the part of the alleged duty-holder to deliberate and also a duty to let me establish the soundness of my grievance.

Arguably, it seems that the right to a hearing cannot apply in *every* case of a moral dispute concerning rights. After all, some grievances could be so absurd or petty that it is unfair that such claims would ever trigger duties. Under this objection it seems that my claim is too demanding, as individuals can trigger the right to a hearing for no reason whatsoever, simply by asserting that they have a right. A person who crazily believes that each time I have breakfast I violate her rights would be entitled to a hearing. The right to a hearing—if it is to retain any plausibility—must be granted more selectively, e.g., the right must be granted only to those who raise reasonable or plausible claims of rights.

I disagree and maintain that the right to a hearing ought to be granted in any case of a dispute. Admittedly the scope and depth of a satisfactory hearing could differ from one case to another. In the case of crazy demands, a simple shrug of the shoulders could constitute a satisfactory hearing. The scope and depth of the hearing differs in accordance with the nature of the grievance and its reasonableness.

It might be argued that both cases discussed here (the lunch example and the airport example) are irrelevant to the case at hand. Unlike a promisor, the state is in a position of authority legitimized by the democratic process. It might be claimed that locutions such as 'you have no right' belong to the interpersonal realm, that the intuitiveness of the right to a hearing is confined to such contexts, and that the supposed right to a hearing does not extend to authoritative relationships. This view would hold that just as an army commander is not required to reconsider her commands in light of every grievance, neither is the state. The state cannot be required to provide a hearing, and the denial of a hearing does not compromise the state's legitimate authority.

This is not the way political theorists view the relations between the state and its citizens. Legal and political theorists share the view that the state has a broad duty to provide a hearing. As Laurence Tribe says:

Both the right to be heard from, and the right to be told why, are analytically distinct from the right to secure a different outcome; these rights to interchange expresses the elementary idea that to be a person, rather than a thing, is at least to be consulted about what is done with one.[36]

The contours of this position favouring judicial review can now be discerned more clearly. There are two types of cases that, under my view, justify judicial review of legislation. First, when a person has a right and that right is (justifiably or unjustifiably) infringed by the legislature, that person is owed a right to a hearing. Second, when there is a dispute over whether a person has a right and the legislature passes a statute that arguably violates the disputed right, the individual is owed a right to a hearing.[37] In both cases, the right to a hearing consists of a duty on the part of the state to provide the right-holder an opportunity to challenge the infringement, willingness on the part of the state to engage in moral deliberation and provide an explanation, and a willingness to reconsider the presumed violation in light of the deliberation. Furthermore, the moral deliberation required of the state cannot consist of an abstract or general deliberation—the kind of deliberation that characterizes the legislative process. It must consist of a particularized or individualized deliberation that accounts for the particular grievance in light of the particular circumstances.

---

[36] Laurence Tribe, *American Constitutional Law* (1st edn., Mineola, NY: Foundation Press, 1978), 53.

[37] The distinction between these two types of cases is familiar to constitutional lawyers. For instance Canadian constitutional law distinguishes sharply between two stages of constitutional scrutiny analogous to the ones discussed here. For the Canadian discussion, see, e.g., Peter Hogg, *Constitutional Law of Canada* (2nd edn., Toronto: Carswell, 1985), 808.

The right to a hearing is not designed to improve decision-making. I am not even committed to the view that granting a right to a hearing is more likely to generate superior decisions. The force of the right-to-a-hearing conception of judicial review does not depend on establishing that judicial review is more congenial to the protection of rights than alternative systems, or that granting the right to a hearing better protects democracy, stability, the dual-democracy structure, or even that it serves to maximize the hearing given to grievances. This is precisely what makes this position immune to the objections raised against instrumentalist views. The only virtue of judicial review is the fact that it constitutes the hearing owed to citizens as a matter of right.

Before turning to examine the role of courts in facilitating a hearing, let us investigate further this last statement. As stated here, the soundness of the right-to-a-hearing conception of judicial review does not depend on establishing that a hearing is more congenial to the protection of any substantive value than alternative systems. But the right-to-a-hearing conception of judicial review is not entirely insensitive to the quality of judicial decision-making. The right-to-a-hearing conception dictates that individual grievances are seriously considered and evaluated, and that the institutions designed to investigate these grievances are engaged in good faith and serious moral deliberation. While the right-to-a-hearing conception of judicial review rejects the instrumentalist view that judicial review is justified only if and to the extent it 'maximizes' the likelihood of rendering 'right' or 'correct' decisions, or best promotes constitutional goals, this conception still maintains that courts ought to engage in serious good-faith deliberation in order to honour that right. It is unlikely that such serious good-faith deliberation fails to protect rights in an adequate manner.

3. The Right to a Hearing and the Judicial Process

So far we have established that individuals have a right to a hearing. Such a right comes into play when (other) rights are infringed (justifiably or unjustifiably), or when the very existence of (other) rights is disputed (justifiably or unjustifiably). It is time to explore the exact relationship between a right to a hearing and judicial review. In what ways, if any, can a right to a hearing provide a justification for judicial review? Can we not entrench procedures of 'legislative review' or non-judicial review that will be superior or, at least, adequate in protecting the right to a hearing?

This possibility can be regarded as a challenge to the fundamental distinction drawn in section B between instrumentalist and non-instrumentalist justifications for judicial review. Under this objection, the attempt to replace instrumentalist justifications for judicial review founded on extrinsic goals (such as protecting rights or participation, or maintaining stability and coherence) with non-instrumentalist justifications (based on the right to a hearing) fails because there is nothing intrinsically judicial in the procedures designed to protect a right to a hearing. Put differently, under this objection the institutional scheme designed to protect the right to a hearing could itself be conceptualized as instrumentalist: judges ought to be assigned with the task of reviewing legislation because they are instrumental to the protection of the right to a hearing.

Such an instrumentalist approach to the right to a hearing would maintain that the constitution is designed to protect or promote hearings and that the institution which ought to be assigned with the task of reviewing statutes should be an institution that facilitates or maximizes respect for the right to a hearing. Arguably, even if such an institution happens in our system to be a court, it does not *necessarily* have to be a court. Thus, judicial review is always subject to the instrumentalist challenge that it is not the best institutional mechanism to facilitate a hearing. If this is true, there is no fundamental structural difference between the instrumentalist justifications described and criticized in section B (maintaining that judicial review is designed to protect substantive rights, democracy, or stability) and the right-to-a-hearing justification for judicial review (maintaining that judicial review is designed to protect the right to a hearing, or maximize the prospects of hearing grievances).

To establish the claim that the right to a hearing provides a non-instrumentalist justification for judicial review, I need to establish that judicial procedures are not merely an instrument to providing a hearing. In fact these procedures *constitute* a hearing. There is a special affinity between judicial deliberation and the right to a hearing, such that judicial deliberation is tantamount to protecting the right to a hearing. To defend this claim, I will show that (a) courts are specially designed to conduct a hearing, and (b) to the extent that other institutions can conduct a hearing, it is only because they operate in a judicial manner and thereby functionally become courts. Operating in a judicial manner is (as a matter of conceptual truth) a form of honouring the right to a hearing. If these observations are correct, the right-to-a-hearing theory of judicial review differs fundamentally from other theories of judicial review, as its soundness does not require any empirical conjectures.

The first task, i.e., establishing that courts are especially suited to facilitate a hearing, requires looking at the procedures that characterize courts. It seems uncontroversial (to the extent that anything can be uncontroversial) that courts are designed to investigate individual grievances. This is not a feature that is unique to constitutional litigation. It characterizes both criminal and civil litigation, and it is widely regarded as a characteristic feature of the judicial process as such.[38] The judicial way of assessing individual grievances comprises three components. First, the judicial process provides an opportunity for an individual to form a grievance and challenge a decision. Second, it imposes a duty on the part of the state (or other entities) to provide a reasoned justification for the decision giving rise to the challenge. Lastly, the judicial process involves, ideally at least, a genuine reconsideration of the decision giving rise to a challenge, which may ultimately lead to overriding the initial decision giving rise to the grievance. If the judicial review of legislation can be shown to be normatively grounded in these procedural features, it follows that courts are particularly appropriate to perform such a review.

To establish this claim, consider the nature of a failure on the part of courts to protect the right to a hearing. Such a failure is different from a failure on the part of the court to render a right or a just decision. The latter failure indicates only the obvious, namely that courts like all institutions are fallible; but it does not challenge their status as courts. In contrast, the former failure, namely a failure to protect the right to a hearing, is a failure on the part of courts to do what courts are specially designed to do; it is a failure to act judicially. In short, it is a failure to function like a court. It seems evident therefore that courts are especially suited to protect the right to a hearing.

The second task requires establishing that to the extent that other institutions conduct a hearing they operate in a judicial manner. The right-to-a-hearing justification for judicial review does not require review by courts or judges. It merely requires guaranteeing that grievances be examined *in certain ways* and *by using certain procedures* and *modes*

---

[38] See, e.g., Bickel, *The Least Dangerous Branch*, 173 (n 1); Donald Horowitz, 'The Judiciary: Umpire or Empire?', 6 *Law & Hum. Behav.* 129, 131 (1982); Richard Fallon, 'Reflections on the Hart and Wechsler Paradigm', 47 *Vand. L. Rev.* 953, 958 (1994).

of reasoning, but it tells us nothing of the identity of the institutions in charge of performing this task. Thus, in principle, the right to a hearing can be protected by any institution, including perhaps the legislature.

This may seem strange, but I would argue for this seemingly implausible claim. What is crucial about courts is the mode of reasoning characterizing them. Whichever institution performs the hearing, it would inevitably use procedures that are indistinguishable from those used by courts; it will in other words operate like a court and effectively become a court.

I showed earlier in this section that courts are designed to investigate individual grievances, and that such an investigation is crucial for protecting the right to a hearing. This suitability of courts, however, is not accidental; it is an essential characteristic of the judicial process. Courts provide individuals an opportunity to raise their grievances and challenge what the individuals perceive (justifiably or unjustifiably) as a violation of their rights. Courts also engage in reasoned deliberation and provide an explanation for the alleged violation. Finally, courts reconsider the presumed violation in light of the deliberation. Institutions that operate in this way thereby inevitably become institutions that operate in a judicial manner. The more effective institutions are in facilitating a hearing, the more these institutions resemble courts. The right-to-a-hearing justification for judicial review accounts not only for the need to establish *some* institution designed to honour this right but also establishes the claim that *the* institution conducting a hearing necessarily operates in a court-like manner and effectively becomes a court. After all, 'if it walks like a duck, quacks like a duck, looks like a duck, it must be a duck.' Similarly, if it provides an opportunity to raise grievances, examines these grievances, and reconsiders the decision giving rise to the grievance, it is nothing but a court irrespective of what its title is.

What has been shown so far is that judicial review is nothing but a hearing and to the extent that individuals have a right to a hearing, they effectively also have a right to judicial review. This however is not sufficient to establish the justifiability of judicial supremacy. Judicial supremacy, as opposed to judicial review, maintains that courts do not merely resolve particular disputes involving the litigants directly before them, but also authoritatively interpret constitutional meaning. Judicial supremacy therefore requires deference by other government officials to the constitutional dictates of the courts not only with respect to the particular case but also with respect to future cases.

It seems that the right to a hearing cannot justify judicial supremacy. At most, it can justify courts (or any other institutions designed to protect the right to a hearing) in making particular and concrete decisions that apply to the grievance at hand. The right to a hearing dictates that the persons whose rights may be at stake should have an opportunity to raise their grievances, that they will be provided with an explanation that addresses their grievances, and that the alleged violation in their cases will be reconsidered in light of the hearing. But why should such a decision carry further normative force? Why should it set a precedent for other cases or carry any normative weight?

Strictly speaking, the right to a hearing can only justify courts in reconsidering concerns raised by a person whose rights may have been infringed and who wishes to challenge the alleged infringement. One can label a system that satisfies these conditions a system of 'case specific review'. The ancient Roman system is an example of such a system. Under the Roman system, the tribunes had the power to veto—that is, to forbid the act of any magistrate that bore unjustly upon any citizen—but not to invalidate the law on the basis of which the act was performed.[39] However, it is easy to see the deficiencies of such a system. There are compelling reasons why decisions rendered in courts should have normative ramifications that extend beyond the case at hand. Glancing at the huge amount of literature concerning precedents provides us with a variety of such arguments. Considerations of certainty, predictability, coordination, etc. provide independent reasons for granting courts' decisions a broader and more extensive normative application. Compelling considerations support the conjecture that judicial decisions have normative repercussions that extend beyond the particular grievances considered by courts. The normative forces

---

[39] H. F. Jolowicz and Nicholas Barry, *Historical Introduction to the Study of Roman Law* (3rd edn., Cambridge: Cambridge University Press, 1972). To some extent this system is the one prevailing in the USA. Most constitutional challenges in the USA are 'as applied' challenges. See *Gonzales v Carhart* 550 US 1, 38 (2007). When a court issues an as-applied remedy, it rules that a given statute cannot be applied in a given set of circumstances. This ruling is only binding on the parties before the court. In contrast when the court issues a 'facial' remedy, it declares that the statute itself (or part thereof) is unconstitutional with respect to all litigants. The practical difference between the two remedies is clear from the perspective of future litigants. If a law is struck down as-applied to a given set of circumstances, a future litigant has to argue that they too are under the same or similar circumstances, and a court will have to accept this argument and declare the law unconstitutional with respect to the new litigant. On the other hand, if a law is struck down facially, this is unnecessary, and all political and legal actors, particularly litigants, may ignore the unconstitutional law or part thereof.

that such decisions carry may be controversial. But it is evident that particular judicial decisions ought to have some normative force that extends beyond the particular cases at hand.

To sum up, the right to a hearing can justify judicial review. The right to a hearing requires the establishment of institutions that are capable of following certain procedures and conducting certain forms of reasoning designed to protect the right to a hearing. The institutions that are designed to protect the right to a hearing are only courts or court-like institutions—institutions that operate in a judicial manner. The right to a hearing does not directly explain the precedential force of these decisions. Yet, *given* that courts have (or should have) the powers necessary to protect the right to a hearing, their decisions ought to have ramifications that extend beyond the particular cases considered by them. It is time now to expand the analysis beyond the boundaries of courts. Section D examines to what extent the right to a hearing can be protected in systems of limited, weak, or constrained judicial review.

D. Constrained Judicial Review

1. Introduction

Section C established that what is distinctive about courts is the adjudicative process; not the label 'courts' or 'judges'. The adjudicative process is tantamount to a hearing, and as individuals have a right to a hearing, they in effect have a right to an adjudicative process. This section shows how institutions which are not courts can in effect contribute to the protection of the right to a hearing.

The motivation for such an enterprise rests upon the fact that many constitutional theorists challenge the constitutional supremacy of courts, and adopt an intermediate position which grants courts a privileged but not a supreme, role in shaping constitutional rights. It is important to explore whether such intermediate constitutional schemes can protect the right to a hearing despite the weakening of the powers of the courts. As the right to a hearing is contingent upon the robustness of the adjudicative process, what counts is preserving a robust adjudicative process and not necessarily the powers of courts or judges. Adam Shinar and I labelled theories that adopt an intermediate position granting courts privileged but not a supreme role in constitutional interpretation: 'theories of constrained judicial review'.[40]

There are two observations which Shinar and I established. First, proponents of constrained judicial review invest much effort in establishing that granting supreme powers to courts to evaluate the constitutionality of statues is not instrumentally conducive to realizing or promoting constitutional values. Instead they advocate a more balanced approach granting both courts and legislatures a role in constitutional interpretation. Yet if the rationale underlying judicial review is grounded in the right to a hearing, this finding is simply irrelevant. Even if the advocates of constrained judicial review succeed in establishing such claims, it does not follow that courts ought not to have supreme constitutional powers, as courts may still serve an important purpose, namely to protect the right to a hearing. Second, Shinar and I argue that weakening the powers of the courts as suggested by proponents of constrained judicial review is not necessarily fatal to the right to a hearing as other institutions can also perform a quasi-adjudicative procedure, i.e., participate in facilitating a hearing and contribute to its robustness.

It follows from this analysis that the real privileges underlying the powers of the courts are not the courts' privileges, but the privileges of petitioners to be heard. The individual grievance and the attempts to address the grievance are the focal centre of the adjudicative process. Courts are simply the entities that traditionally voice the petitioners' grievances. However, other institutions can perform a similar function. Section D2 characterizes what constrained judicial review is and investigates the contemporary theories advocating it. Section D3 establishes how constrained judicial review can effectively protect the right to a hearing.

2. Theories of Constrained Judicial Review

Constrained judicial review differs both from legislative supremacy and from judicial supremacy. On the one hand, theories of constrained judicial review reject legislative supremacy, as these theories affirm that courts have a privileged status in interpreting the constitution. At the same time, these theories also reject judicial supremacy, as they

---

[40] Harel and Shinar, 'Between Judicial and Legislative Supremacy' (n 5). This section summarizes the main argument of this article.

maintain that judicial privileges should be constrained and greater constitutional responsibilities ought to be given to the legislature or even the executive.

For many years, there has been basically one idea undergirding the practice of judicial review—American style judicial review, (now) known as strong judicial review. Under that view, the judiciary is the 'ultimate expositor' of constitutional meaning, having the final say over constitutional interpretation. Over the years, the institution of judicial review has come under attack by many scholars on various grounds. Alongside defenders of strong judicial review—or judicial supremacy— I identify below three strands in current constitutional theory scholarship advocating different forms of judicial constitutional privileges that are less robust than judicial supremacy. The three different strands seek to de-privilege courts by rescinding their role as the sole and supreme expositors of the constitutional text: popular constitutionalism, departmentalism, and weak judicial review.

Popular constitutionalism is primarily a US effort on the part of influential theorists including Mark Tushnet and Larry Kramer to challenge the supremacy of the US Court. Tushnet's 1999 book, *Taking the Constitution away from the Courts*,[41] launched the opening salvo of modern popular constitutionalism by calling for the elimination of judicial review altogether. Tushnet criticizes judicial review mainly on the grounds that, empirically speaking, the legislature is just as capable (if not more so) of identifying and promoting constitutional values when it engages in constitutional interpretation, as are the courts. Further, on average, judicial decisions do not deviate considerably from the dominant political opinions, making judicial review a lot of 'noise around zero'.[42] Larry Kramer offers a different version of popular constitutionalism. Unlike Tushnet, Kramer does not seek to eliminate judicial review altogether, although he too wants to discard judicial supremacy. According to Kramer, 'No one of the branches was meant to be superior to any other, unless it were the legislature, and when it came to constitutional law, all were meant to be subordinated to the people.'[43] To the extent that judicial review is perceived as legitimate, it is only perceived so when it is understood as 'another

---

[41]   Tushnet, *Taking the Constitution away from the Courts* (n 2); Kramer, *The People Themselves* (n 2).

[42]   Tushnet, *Taking the Constitution away from the Courts*, 153 (n 2).

[43]   Kramer, *The People Themselves*, 58 (n 2).

instance of the right of every citizen to refuse to recognize the validity of unconstitutional laws—a "political-legal" duty and responsibility rather than a strictly legal one.'[44] Judicial (or, for that matter, any other institutional) supremacy is seen by him as a product of America's political and legal elites struggling to gain monopoly power over the interpretation of the constitution.[45]

Departmentalism places authority over constitutional interpretation not with 'the people' directly, but with the different governmental departments. According to the most influential version of departmentalism, advanced by President Lincoln[46] in response to the *Dred Scott* decision, and later by Attorney General Edwin Meese,[47] each branch of the government has 'final interpretive authority over all constitutional questions decided within the branch, irrespective of which branch those constitutional questions concern'.[48] Thus, each issue that comes before Congress, the President, or the courts requires their independent determination of its constitutionality, regardless of what the other branch has said. The rationale underlying this conception of departmentalism is that each branch is coequal to the others, and all are equally subordinate to the constitution. As such, each branch is bound by the constitution (or its own vision of the constitution), but not by another branch's interpretation of the constitution.

Last, like popular constitutionalism and departmentalism, *weak judicial review* also de-privileges courts by rejecting judicial supremacy and strong judicial review. Unlike the former, however, systems of weak judicial review offer actual institutional arrangements that attempt to accomplish this goal.[49] Weak judicial review can therefore be regarded as a doctrinal manifestation, or an elaboration, of the values that undergird either departmentalism or popular constitutionalism. Under weak judicial review, the courts' interpretations merit great respect and have great weight, but their decisions can at times be

---

[44] Kramer, *The People Themselves*, 39 (n 2).

[45] Kramer, *The People Themselves*, 247 (n 2); Ran Hirschl, *Constitutional Theocracy* (Cambridge, Mass.: Harvard University Press, 2010).

[46] Abraham Lincoln, Sixth Debate with Stephen A. Douglas, at Quincy, Illinois (13 October 1858), in *The Collected Works of Abraham Lincoln*, ed. Roy P. Basler (New Brunswick, NJ: Rutgers University Press, 1953), iii. 245, 255.

[47] Edwin Meese III, 'The Law of the Constitution', 61 *Tul. L. Rev.* 979, 983–6 (1987).

[48] Larry Alexander and Larry Solum, 'Popular? Constitutionalism?', 118 *Harv. L. Rev.* 1595, 1613 (2005).

[49] Stephen Gardbaum, 'The New Commonwealth Model of Constitutionalism', 49 *Am. J. Comp. L.* 707 (2001).

overridden or rejected by legislatures. Thus, weak judicial review seeks what can be regarded as a middle path between judicial supremacy and legislative supremacy.[50]

Most of the discussion of constrained judicial review is based on instrumentalist concerns. Most abstractly, proponents of constrained judicial review point out that constitutional decisions are founded on different types of considerations that require different types of expertise. Consequently, they believe that institutions with different perspectives and expertise ought to be involved in such decisions, guaranteeing that the constitutional output is based on a comprehensive evaluation of all of these considerations. Courts, legislatures, and other agents have different expertise and a different outlook on constitutional questions. Courts have special institutional competence in relation to matters of principle and fundamental values.[51] Legislators may be less principled but, at the same time, are more attuned to considerations of policy, public opinion, and political pressures.[52] The combined input of all these institutions is likely to bring about a better balance between the different considerations.

Yet, under the view developed in section C, these observations may be relevant but they are inconclusive, as the powers of the courts are not grounded in the fact that courts (and judges) are good decision-makers, or faithful interpreters of the constitution; instead, courts are privileged simply because they voice the grievances of individuals and facilitate deliberation concerning these grievances. The question to be examined in section D3 is whether constrained judicial review can in reality give such a voice to individual grievances.

3. A Hearing outside Courts

This section establishes that constrained judicial review can in principle effectively protect the right to a hearing. To do so we ought to examine separately the different components of the right to a hearing,

---

[50] Stephen Gardbaum, 'Reassessing the New Model of Commonwealth Constitutionalism', 8 Int'l. J. Const. L. 167, 171 (2010).

[51] Kent Roach, The Supreme Court on Trial: Judicial Activism or Democratic Dialogue (Toronto: Irwin Law, 2001), 286.

[52] Benjamin I. Page and Robert Y. Shapiro, 'Effects of Public Opinion on Policy', 77 Am. Pol. Sci. Rev. 175 (1983); Daniel A. Farber and Philip P. Frickey, Law and Public Choice: A Critical Introduction (Chicago: The University of Chicago Press, 1991).

and identify which if any of the different components of the right can be adequately protected by a system of constrained judicial review.

The right to a hearing consists of three distinct elements: first, the state ought to provide an opportunity for a person to challenge its decision; second, it ought to be willing to engage in meaningful deliberation, addressing the grievance in light of the particular circumstances; finally, it must be willing to reconsider the decision, to change it if the deliberation triggered by the individual grievance exposes that the decision is wrong. Such reconsideration ought to rely on the prior deliberation triggered by the individual grievance.

The component that is most vulnerable under systems of constrained judicial review is the third component, namely the willingness to reconsider the decision made by the polity. Proponents of constrained judicial review typically believe that individuals ought to be able to voice their grievances in courts, and that courts ought to investigate these grievances and address them. Thus, unlike systems of legislative supremacy, under most systems of constrained judicial review it is the case that (a) real or imaginary victims of rights violations are entitled to raise their grievances in the courts, and (b) courts are required to provide a reasoned decision in addressing the grievance.

The primary difference between strong and constrained judicial review lies in the third condition, namely the duty of reconsideration on the part of the polity. Strong judicial review imposes a robust and demanding duty of reconsideration performed by courts. The reconsideration performed by courts is not only triggered by the grievance, but is intimately tied up with the particularities of the individual grievance. In contrast, constrained judicial review often limits or constrains the powers of the courts, and assigns the ultimate decision to institutions whose commitment to reasoned deliberation is weaker than that of the court. Let me establish this observation.

Under popular constitutionalism, the ability and the willingness to reconsider a decision in light of the grievance is much weaker than the ability and willingness to reconsider it under strong judicial review. As popular constitutionalism transfers the ultimate power from courts to the people, it is almost inevitable that the grievance giving rise to reconsideration is less prominent and vivid in the deliberations of the people. After all 'the people' did not have an opportunity to hear the grievance and benefit from the judicial deliberation. They are also not trained or accustomed to the type of deliberation characteristic of courts or of the adjudicative process. Similar concerns apply to departmentalism. The relevance and the power of the grievance is diluted, as the entities in charge of interpreting the constitution (other branches of the government) are more remote from the grievance, and less familiar than the court with the petitioner raising the grievance and the circumstances under which it was raised. Lastly, while advocates of weak judicial review are fully aware of the importance of the first two components of the right to a hearing, they are less demanding with respect to the third component. For example, under the British Human Rights Act, the petitioner can raise a grievance and she is entitled to a full account of whether her rights have been violated (a declaration of incompatibility). But the reconsideration is left to the legislature and its good will, and in principle the legislature is not obliged to rely in its decision on the particularities of the case. The Canadian system grants a greater role to the grievance in the adjudicative process than the British one. But despite the greater reverence given to the judicial process, the courts' decision is still subject to the possibility of a legislative override. Presumably in both the British and the Canadian cases Parliament is expected to reconsider the statute given the court's decision and such reconsideration ought to be sensitive to the grievance giving rise to that decision; yet the reconsideration performed by legislative or executive bodies is more remote from the particular grievance and less attuned to its particularities than the decision of the court.

Weakening the powers of courts in the ways suggested by proponents of constrained judicial review is particularly detrimental to the third component of the right to a hearing. What differentiates strong judicial review from constrained judicial review is the fact that under strong judicial review the adjudicative body is exclusively assigned the task of reconsideration, while under constrained judicial review the decision is subject to reconsideration by non-adjudicative entities— entities that are not necessarily fully and completely attentive to the particular grievance or to the adjudicative deliberative process triggered by the grievance.

Yet, Shinar and I argue that constrained judicial review does not undermine the possibility of meaningful reconsideration. The more the bodies in charge of reconsideration take into account the input of the court, the more their decision reflects concern for the individual grievance and the circumstances triggering it. The question whether such a system is satisfactory depends upon the ability of an individual petitioner to draw attention to her circumstances and to the ways in which the law impacts her rights and is also contingent upon whether it triggers a normative investigation of her case by the polity. Thus, constrained judicial review can be protective of the right to a hearing if the non-judicial bodies act as if they were judicial, i.e., they are willing to attend to individual grievances and their particularities, i.e., resemble in their reasoning adjudicative bodies and take seriously the deliberations of the adjudicative bodies.

We can therefore reconceptualize the rationale underlying constrained judicial review. The existence of courts and the privileges granted to courts under constrained judicial review help in facilitating the hearing of grievances and draw attention to the particularities of such grievances. Courts also serve to induce non-adjudicative bodies to be attentive to the grievances, but, under constrained judicial review, part of the burden of hearing the grievance will be borne not by courts but by other institutions. The more these bodies are attentive to individual grievances, the more constrained judicial review protects the right to a hearing. Ultimately, whether non-adjudicative bodies attend to the grievance and its particularities and whether the reconsideration of the grievance performed by such bodies is satisfactory depends on the rules governing the system as well as the surrounding political culture.

It is commonly assumed that constrained judicial review enriches the political debate, or improves the quality of decision-making by providing an opportunity for courts to insert their own input to the political discourse. The focus of attention of these theories is the quality of decision-making. I reject this view. The ultimate justification for judicial review is grounded not in the courts, nor in their institutional interactions with the other political branches, but in their addressing the individual grievances of petitioners. This is as true about theories of constrained judicial review as it is about theories of strong judicial review. What is crucial is that the bodies in charge of reconsidering the decision giving rise to the grievance (courts, legislatures, or other bodies) take the grievance seriously, and facilitate a hearing, or take seriously the hearings conducted by courts even if they are not obliged to accept their judgments. Such seriousness is unlikely to follow automatically from the institutional design of constrained judicial review. Rather, it must be grounded in an appropriate legal and political culture.

E. Conclusion

This chapter has developed both a negative and a positive argument concerning judicial review. Section B established the negative argument. It establishes that the traditional justifications for judicial review face grave difficulties and that these difficulties are attributable to their instrumental nature. Section C developed a new rationale for judicial review. In searching for a non-instrumental justification, this chapter has established that judicial review ought to be understood as the institutional embodiment of the right to a hearing. It follows from this observation that the value of judicial review is grounded in the adjudicative process and not in the institutions of courts or the professional background of judges.

This chapter adds to the arsenal of arguments favouring judicial review a non-instrumentalist argument that, given its non-instrumentalist nature, is immune to many of the objections raised against judicial review. Advocates of judicial review can therefore rest assured that the case for judicial review is not contingent upon speculative empirical conjectures. Judicial review is valuable not (only) because it improves the quality of decision-making, but because it compels government to be attentive to the grievances of its citizens.

7

Conclusion

This book has argued that some political and legal institutions or procedures are not merely contingent means to valuable ends such as improving the quality of decision-making, enhancing the effectiveness of the protection of rights, bringing about greater accountability in promoting the public interest and providing public goods, establishing a just society, etc. Instead sometimes such institutions and procedures matter as such; they are necessary for the realization of certain values and consequently they are indispensable.

I do not wish to deny that instrumental arguments resting on contingent psychological and sociological facts may be valuable and ought to guide us in establishing and structuring legal and political institutions and procedures. Yet as I illustrated in Chapter 1 sometimes instrumentalist arguments distort what these institutions or procedures are about, and, in particular they fail to account for what arouses our passion and interest in these institutions and procedures in the first place. One of the by-products of such arguments is the existence of an unbridgeable gap between political theory (aiming at rationalizing political institutions and legal procedures) and civic practice and discourse (resting on unarticulated and under-theorized beliefs and sensibilities). In contrast my attempt has been not merely to justify certain institutions and procedures but also to provide (as much as possible) justifications that echo the sentiments and passions of those who support, sustain, and even challenge the political and legal institutional order. This observation does not imply that instrumentalist arguments are always inferior to non-instrumentalist ones. As said in Chapter 1 the book ought to be judged on the basis of the soundness of the arguments not on the basis of its success in establishing the soundness of a certain mode of justification or methodology, as this latter task has not been the intention of this book.

The political or legal theorist could question the primacy given in this book to justifications that are respectful or sensitive to the passions of citizens and popular sensibilities. Arguably what ultimately is important is the soundness of the justifications and not the degree to which they echo existing sentiments or converge with the implicit rationales sustaining popular support for the institutions and procedures. The theorist could further point out that the mere fact that citizens cherish their political institutions does not guarantee that those are indeed justified, and certainly does not guarantee that those institutions are justified for the reason citizens believe they are. For many years individuals were confident of the integrity and rationality of economic institutions and the 2008 crisis gives rise to the suspicion that this trust was deeply misguided. Could not citizens be misguided as to the value of their own political or legal institutions or as to the reasons and rationales justifying these institutions?

These are serious concerns and one ought to bear them in mind. Yet, at times there is a special value in developing justifications that echo popular sentiments. This is because some institutions and procedures may gain normative meaning from the ways they are understood, from the significance attributed to them and the values associated with them. In other words, such institutions and procedures are valuable because and to the extent that they are inextricably linked with certain values of the political community. The link between the institutions and the values is a by-product of our understandings and perceptions and, consequently without identifying these public perceptions we may fail to detect an important normative dimension embodied in these institutions and procedures.

Such a link between institutional and procedural practices on the one hand and values on the other hand is a prevailing feature of our political and legal culture. Parliaments in our culture signify commitments to majoritarian sentiments; courts on the other hand signify commitments to individualism. The support or opposition to such institutions is indicative of one's normative framework. This book rests on the conviction that other institutional and procedural features of our public life are forms in which public values are realized. Hence, at times these institutions and procedures cannot be dispensed with without thereby undermining or eroding the values associated with them.

This analysis implies also some limitations and qualifications. There are three cautionary words which ought to be remembered in developing this perspective.

First, given that the justifications provided in this book rely on the significance and meaning attributed by citizens, judges, and politicians to political institutions and procedures, the arguments are not universal ones; they are grounded in the ways our institutions have developed in western liberal traditions and, in particular the ways in which they are understood by citizens. The meanings attributed to the institutions are ultimately our creation and they could have been developed differently. Hence, an objection based on the claim that 'things could have been otherwise' is beside the point as none of the claims made here are intended to apply universally.

Second, such justifications do not preclude the need of political theorists to expose the illusions underlying the trust in basic political institutions. At times we attribute to political institutions virtues that they do not have. At other times the illusions that need to be exposed are not about the institutions as such but the ways in which existing institutions operate and the degree to which liberal ideals converge with the realities of these institutions.

Last and most importantly, to justify political and legal institutions it is neither necessary nor sufficient to establish that the justification accurately captures popular sensibilities. It is not necessary because it is possible at times that the traditional justifications in terms of the contingent desirable consequences of political institutions and procedures are sound (and those as I have argued deviate from public perceptions). Perhaps (as mentioned in Chapter 3) public institutions are more accountable (as their advocates argue) to the public interest than private individuals and, consequently privatization is wrong on instrumental grounds. It is also possible that despite my arguments in Chapter 6 courts are as a matter of fact more protective of rights or of democracy or freedom than legislatures. In such a case the instrumental justifications for judicial review have merit.

Further, the mere fact that a justification accurately captures popular sensibilities is not sufficient. Perhaps the popular sensibilities ultimately fail because there is no way to rationalize the institutions and procedures in terms that are respectful of the passions of those who uphold them. Perhaps citizens are deeply misguided, and consequently such an attempt is doomed to fail.

The former suspicion, namely the suspicion that the institutions may be successfully rationalized in terms that are not attentive to public sensibilities is not destructive to my enterprise. Although for reasons discussed earlier, explanations that rely on contingent consequences of political institutions and procedures raise some difficulties, I do not wish to deny that institutions can at times be contingently conducive (or detrimental) to justice and that this fact can justify establishing such institutions (or dismantling them). The latter suspicion is more destructive. To overcome it I have established again and again in this book that institutions and procedures are not merely contingent means to what is valuable. In fact their existence is often necessary to facilitate, sustain, or reinforce value. Let me briefly summarize what has been shown.

Chapter 2 established that rights are not mere replica of the values underlying them. The relation between rights and values is reciprocal; rights are justified in terms of the values underlying them but they are also necessary for the realization of these values. Certain values, e.g., autonomy can therefore be successfully realized only by identifying and protecting activities such as speech or religion in which individuals exercise autonomy. One of the implications of this view is that the narrowly defined rights (catalogues of rights) are not an accidental (or pragmatic) feature of rights; they are essential for sustaining a culture that facilitates their exercise. This observation addresses successfully the challenge of the 'rationalist paradigm' aiming to replace rights with values.

Chapter 3 established that public institutions are not mere contingent means to guarantee accountability of agents. Instead some goods are intrinsically public goods—goods whose value is contingent upon the identity of the agent providing them. In particular it was shown that some decisions and acts must be performed by public officials, namely by agents who operate in accordance with the dictates of fidelity of deference. This is not because public officials are more accountable or make better decisions but because only public officials can act in the name of the state and acting in the name of the state is necessary for the provision of certain goods (intrinsically public goods).

Chapter 4 established that in cases of emergency agents ought to reason in a rule-free way. The agents who make decisions in exceptional circumstances ought not to be guided by general rules or principles. Instead, they ought to make particular judgments, not guided by norms. This is because the use of rules or principles in exceptional cases presupposes the commensurability of human lives: some human lives may have to be sacrificed for the sake of protecting others. But, as human life in the Kantian tradition has value but not a price, no such exchange value can be fixed, and, consequently the use of rule-based reasoning is impermissible.

Chapter 5 established why constitutional directives matter as such (rather than merely as means for protecting rights or promoting justice). It is only binding constitutional directives which constitute publicly recognized limitations on the powers of the legislature. In the absence of such directives, the legislature's decision not to violate rights does not depend upon its publicly recognized duties; instead, it is publicly understood to be contingent on the legislature's judgments (or inclinations). It was also shown that public recognition of rights-based duties (by means of constitutional entrenchment) is essential for the protection of freedom (understood as non-domination). These conclusions, I argued, apply also to global and international law norms and they may explain therefore the popularity of globalism.

Lastly, Chapter 6 defended judicial review on the grounds that judicial review is an embodiment of the right to a hearing. Judicial review is not grounded in contingent institutional features; instead it is grounded in the importance of the right to raise a grievance, the right that the grievance be addressed, and the right that a decision giving rise to a grievance be reconsidered on the basis of such a deliberative process. This account establishes that what ultimately judicial review is about is not courts or judges but the adjudicative process as such.

In all of these cases exposing the underlying rationale for an institution or for a procedure transforms also the very understanding of what the relevant institution or procedure is. To illustrate, once it is understood that public officials are essentially agents who defer to the sovereign, it follows that to be a public official requires engaging in an integrative practice, as only such a practice facilitates deference. Once the nature of constitutional directives is understood, a better understanding of what counts as a constitution follows. What becomes clear for instance is that the fundamental characteristic of constitutions is their binding nature rather than (only) the effectiveness of mechanisms of enforcement such as judicial review. Last by uncovering the rationale underlying judicial review, it becomes clear that what the term 'judicial' stands for is not judges or courts but a distinctive process of deliberation—the process consisting of raising grievances, addressing these grievances and deciding on the basis of this deliberation.

The primary ambition of this book has been to track what lurks beneath the surface, namely to identify, articulate, and most importantly voice the sensibilities and the passions which underlie political and legal controversies concerning rights, privatization, public goods, dignity, constitutional directives, judicial review, etc. In doing so one inevitably changes the meanings of these institutions, redescribes and reconceptualizes these institutions and procedures. In engaging in this enterprise I was guided by the attempt to look at these institutions from within through the perspective of those who support and cherish them. I argued that at least sometimes law matters not only because of its contingent contributions to justice or to the protection of rights but rather that it matters *as such*.

Index

Introductory Note

References such as '126–8' indicate a discussion of a topic across a range of pages (not necessarily continuous). Because the book is about 'rights', the 'state' and 'constitutionalism', the use of these terms (and a few certain others) as an index entries has been minimized. References can be found under the corresponding detailed topics.

18544220R00140

Printed in Great Britain
by Amazon